HOW THE
Brain Learns

SECOND EDITION

*Who dares to teach
must never cease to learn.*

– John Cotton Dana

David A. Sousa

HOW THE
Brain Learns

A Classroom Teacher's Guide

SECOND EDITION

CORWIN PRESS, INC.
A Sage Publications Company
Thousand Oaks, California

For information address:

Corwin Press, Inc.
A Sage Publications Company
2455 Teller Road
Thousand Oaks, California 91320
E-mail: order@corwinpress.com

Sage Publications Ltd.
6 Bonhill Street
London EC2A 4PU
United Kingdom

Sage Publications India Pvt. Ltd.
M-32 Market
Greater Kailash I
New Delhi 110 048 India

Printed in the United States of America

Library of Congress Cataloging-in-Publication Data

Sousa, David A.
    How the brain learns: A classroom teacher's guide / David A. Sousa. — 2nd ed.
        p.   cm.
    Includes bibliographical references and index.
    ISBN 0-7619-7764-3 (hardcover: alk. paper)
    ISBN 0-7619-7765-1 (paperback: alk. paper)
    1. Learning, Psychology of.   2. Learning—Physiological aspects.   3. Brain.
    I. Title.
    LB1057 .S69   2000
    370.15′23—dc21   00-010236

This book is printed on acid-free paper.

        03   04   05   06   07   7   6   5   4

Production Editor: S. Marlene Head
Editorial Assistant: Kristen L. Gibson
Cover Designer: Tracy E. Miller

Contents

PREFACE TO THE SECOND EDITION ix

ABOUT THE AUTHOR xi

INTRODUCTION 1
What Teachers Learned in the Past 1
The New Research 2
Implications for Teaching 3
Some Cautions and Predictions 3
Why This Book Can Help Improve Teaching and Learning 4
Try It Yourself—Do Action Research 6

CHAPTER 1 - Basic Brain Facts and Brain Development 15
Some Exterior Parts of the Brain 16
Some Interior Parts of the Brain 17
Neuron Development in Children 23
The Brain as a Novelty Seeker 27
Environmental Factors Enhancing the Brain's Search for Novelty 27
The Brain and the Mind 29

CHAPTER 2 - How the Brain Processes Information 36
The Information Processing Model 37
The Senses 40
Sensory Register 40
Short-Term Memory 41
Long-Term Storage 49
Self-Concept 51

CHAPTER 3 - Memory, Retention, and Learning 78
How Memory Forms 79
Stages and Types of Memory 81
Learning and Retention 84
Factors Affecting Retention of Learning 85
Implications for Teaching 89
Learning Motor Skills 96
Does Practice Make Perfect? 97

How Daily Biological Rhythms Affect Teaching and Learning   101
Intelligence and Retrieval   104

CHAPTER 4 - The Power of Transfer   **136**
What Is Transfer?   136
Types of Transfer   138
Factors Affecting Transfer   141
Teaching for Transfer   146

CHAPTER 5 - Brain Specialization and Learning   **166**
Hemisphere Specialization   167
Spoken Language Specialization   177

CHAPTER 6 - The Brain and the Arts   **214**
The Arts Are Basic to the Human Experience   214
Why Teach the Arts?   216
The Sciences Need the Arts   216
Impact of the Arts on Student Learning   219
Music   221
The Visual Arts   228
Movement   229

CHAPTER 7 - Thinking Skills and Learning   **245**
The Thinking Brain   246
Can Thinking Be Taught?   248
The Dimensions of Human Thinking   249
Revisiting Bloom's Taxonomy of the Cognitive Domain   251

CHAPTER 8 - Putting It All Together: Planning for Today and Tomorrow   **275**
Considerations for Daily Planning   276
Maintaining Skills for the Future   281
Conclusion   283

GLOSSARY   **287**

BIBLIOGRAPHY   **292**

INDEX   **303**

LIST OF PRACTITIONER'S CORNERS

Introduction

    What Do You Already Know?   8

    How Brain Compatible Is My Teaching/School/District?   9

    Using Action Research   10

Chapter 1

    Fist for a Brain   30

    Review of Brain Area Functions   31

    Using Novelty in Lessons   32

Chapter 2

    Walking Through the Brain   55

    Redesigning the Information Processing Model   56

    Sensory Preferences and Learning Style   57

    Determining Your Sensory Preferences   58

    Developing a Classroom Climate Conducive to Learning   61

    Using Humor to Enhance Climate and Promote Retention   63

    Increasing Processing Time Through Motivation   66

    Creating Meaning in New Learning   69

    Using Closure to Enhance Sense and Meaning   70

    Testing Whether Information Is in Long-Term Storage   71

    Using Synergy to Enhance Learning   73

    NeuroBingo   75

Chapter 3

    Avoid Teaching Two Very Similar Motor Skills   116

    Using Rehearsal to Enhance Retention   117

    Using the Primacy-Recency Effect in the Classroom   120

    Strategies for Block Scheduling   122

    Using Practice Effectively   124

    Relearning Through Recall   125

    Impact of Circadian Rhythms on Schools and Classrooms   126

    Using Wait Time to Increase Student Participation   128

    Using Chunking to Enhance Retention   129

    Using Mnemonics to Help Retention   131

Chapter 4

    Strategies for Connecting to Past Learnings   150

    Avoid Teaching Concepts That Are Very Similar   151

    Identifying Critical Attributes for Accurate Transfer   153

Teaching for Transfer: Bridging   157

Teaching for Transfer: Hugging   159

Using Metaphors to Enhance Transfer   161

Using Journal Writing to Promote Transfer and Retention   163

Chapter 5

Testing Your Hemispheric Preference   187

Teaching to the Whole Brain: General Guidelines   190

Strategies for Teaching to the Whole Brain   192

Concept Mapping—General Guidelines   196

Acquiring a Second Language   201

Considerations for Teaching Reading   205

Reading Guidelines for All Teachers   208

Chapter 6

Including the Arts in All Lessons   233

Using Music in the Classroom   234

Using Imagery   237

Visualized Notetaking   238

Strategies for Using Movement   240

Chapter 7

Understanding Bloom's Taxonomy   264

Take a Concept/Situation Up the Taxonomy!   266

Some Tips on Using Bloom's Taxonomy   267

Bloom's Taxonomy: Increasing Complexity   268

Understanding the Difference Between Complexity and Difficulty   269

Questions to Stimulate Higher-Order Thinking   272

Chapter 8

Reflections on Lesson Design   284

PREFACE TO THE SECOND EDITION

In the six years since the first edition of this book was published, neuroscientists have made remarkable advances in their understanding of the human brain. More sophisticated scanning techniques are able to track brain activity faster and more accurately than ever before. Although many studies were originally focused on brain disorders, the number of studies conducted with normal participants is increasing substantially. The normal-centered studies are of particular interest to educators because of the potential application to their practice.

For this second edition, I have had to make some changes in the text as a result of new knowledge about the brain. Specifically, I have

◆   Updated the Information Processing Model to reflect new terminology regarding the memory systems
◆   Added the exciting research about how the brain learns motor skills
◆   Added a chapter on the implications of the arts in learning
◆   Where appropriate, included primary sources for those who wish to review the actual research

I am particularly pleased that more educators are becoming familiar with brain research and recognizing that this is not "just another bandwagon." Like in any profession, we must use caution when deciding whether new knowledge can improve our practice. But if the last ten years are any indication, the future holds the promise of a deeper understanding of the learning process. Armed with that knowledge, teachers face the exciting prospect of being dramatically more successful with their students.

David A. Sousa

ABOUT THE AUTHOR

David A. Sousa, Ed.D., is an international educational consultant. He has conducted workshops on brain research and science education in hundreds of school districts and at several colleges and universities. He has made presentations at national conventions of educational organizations and has served as a consultant to regional and local school districts across the United States, Canada, and Europe.

Dr. Sousa has a bachelor's degree in chemistry from Massachusetts State College at Bridgewater, a Master of Arts in Teaching degree in science from Harvard University, and a doctorate from Rutgers University. His teaching experience covers all levels. He has taught junior and senior high school science, served as a K–12 director of science, and was Supervisor of Instruction for the West Orange, New Jersey, schools. He then became superintendent of the New Providence, New Jersey, public schools. He has been an adjunct professor of education at Seton Hall University, and a visiting lecturer at Rutgers University. He was president of the National Staff Development Council in 1992.

Dr. Sousa has edited science books and published numerous articles in leading educational journals on staff development, science education, and brain research. He is listed in *Who's Who in the East* and *Who's Who in American Education* and has received awards from professional associations and school districts for his commitment to research, staff development, and science education.

He has been interviewed on the NBC *Today* show and National Public Radio about his work with schools using brain research. He makes his home in Florida.

CORWIN
PRESS

INTRODUCTION

You start out as a single cell derived from the coupling of a sperm and egg; this divides into two, then four, then eight, and so on, and at a certain stage there emerges a single cell which will have as all its progeny the human brain. The mere existence of that cell should be one of the great astonishments of the earth.

– Lewis Thomas,
The Medusa and the Snail

The human brain is an amazing structure—a universe of infinite possibilities and mystery. It constantly shapes and reshapes itself as a result of experience, yet it can take off on its own without input from the outside world. How does it form a human mind, capture experience, or stop time in memory? Although it does not generate enough energy to light a simple bulb, its capabilities make it the most powerful force on Earth.

For thousands of years, humans have been delving into this mysterious universe and trying to determine how it accomplishes its amazing feats. How the brain learns has been of particular interest to all kinds of teachers. As we enter the 21st century, there is new hope that our understanding of this remarkable process called teaching and learning will improve dramatically.

What Teachers Learned in the Past

Educators have been trying to understand the workings of this remarkable brain so that the teaching-learning process could be more effective. For many teachers, their training on how the brain learns has focused essentially on the behaviorist model which tries to explain what is happening *inside* the brain (following a stimulus) by observing *outside* behavior (the response). After sufficient observation, the behaviorists made informed guesses about brain processes. Some of these guesses have stood the test of time; others have been overtaken by neuroscience. I suspect, though, that in many schools of education today, the behaviorist model is still the primary—if not only—model presented to prospective teachers.

For all their good work, the behaviorists—and even the cognitive psychologists who came later—had two very significant limitations. First, they couldn't see inside the brain while its owner was still alive and using it, and second, they had to deal with free will—that is, a person's behavior was not always an accurate reflection of what was happening in the brain. Although there is still a lot for teachers to learn from behavioral and cognitive psychology, there is even more to discover in the exciting area of biology, including the research in neuroscience.

The New Research

In 1989, the U.S. scientific community declared the 1990s "the decade of the brain," and what a decade it was! Much has been written in recent years about the research that has looked at the workings of the human brain. The more we learn about the brain, the more remarkable it seems. Increasingly sophisticated medical instruments are producing new charts of the brain at work. *Computerized tomography* (CT, formerly called CAT) scanners use focused X-rays to produce detailed cross sections of brain structure. They can detect strokes, cancer, and malformations but cannot reveal brain functions. In fact, a CT scan cannot distinguish a live brain from a dead one.

Positron-emission tomography (PET) detects radioactively tagged sugar injected into the patient to track where blood flows in the brain, an indicator for brain activity. When a person sings a song, eats an apple, or recalls a memory, different areas of the brain are activated and recorded by the PET scanner and translated into images. By giving moment-to-moment pictures of the brain during these events, PET scans provide an inside look at how and where the brain activity occurs.

Magnetic resonance imaging (MRI) uses radio waves to disturb the alignment of the body's atoms in a magnetic field. The atoms then emit radio signals that differ according to the tissue present. The resulting signals are recorded and formed by a computer. It can record changes in the brain that occur only 50 milliseconds apart and can take a picture of the entire brain once every second.

Functional MRI (fMRI) also reveals brain activity by measuring blood flow. These scanners can produce multiple images per second. Because it takes the brain about one-half second to respond to a stimulus, this rapid scanning technique can show the changes in activity in different parts of the brain as it responds to different stimuli and assumes certain tasks. A series of fMRI images can create computer-generated movies of the brain performing various activities, such as reading, talking, and seeing. Moreover, the fMRI measures blood flow from outside the patient, so it avoids the drawback of injecting a radioactive substance. By using PET, MRI, and fMRI scans, researchers can determine which parts of the brain are involved in specific tasks and which parts are dormant.[1] An even more sophisticated version of the classic *electroencephalogram* (EEG) has been developed. Called *magnetoencephalography* (MEG), this noninvasive technology can yield 4,000 magnetic brain measurements per second.

Researchers have also discovered a whole family of brain chemicals called *neurotransmitters* and are investigating their association with various brain functions. To determine which parts of the brain control various functions, neurosurgeons use tiny electrodes to stimulate individual nerve cells and record their reactions. Besides the information collected by these techniques, the growing body of case studies of individuals recovering from various types of brain damage is giving us new evidence about and insights into how the brain develops, changes, learns, and remembers.

Implications for Teaching

As we examine the clues that this research is yielding about learning, we recognize its importance to the teaching profession. Every day teachers enter their classrooms with lesson plans, experience, and the hope that what they are about to present will be understood, remembered, and useful to their students. The extent that this hope is realized depends largely on the knowledge base that these teachers use in designing those plans and, perhaps more important, on the instructional techniques they select during the lessons. Teachers try to change the human brain every day. The more they know about how it learns, the more successful they can be. As Francis Bacon said four centuries ago, "Knowledge is power."

> *Teachers try to change the human brain every day. The more they know about how it learns, the more successful they can be. Knowledge is power.*

Although it has been nearly 20 years since researchers began making major discoveries about how the brain learns, many practicing and prospective classroom teachers are only marginally aware of them. In the past few years, however, more educators have become interested in brain research and its potential applications to educational practice. Signs of this increased awareness are everywhere. Staff development programs are devoting more time to this area, more books about the brain are available, brain-compatible teaching units are sprouting up, and the journals of most major educational organizations have devoted special issues to the topic.[2] I believe this focus on recent brain research can improve the quality of our profession's performance and its success in helping others learn.

Some Cautions and Predictions

Research studies are revealing the remarkable way the human brain continually reorganizes itself on the basis of input. This process, called *neuroplasticity*, continues throughout our life but is exceptionally rapid in the early years. Thus, the experiences the young brain has in the home and at school help shape the neural circuits that will determine how and what that brain learns.

As research continues to provide a deeper understanding of the workings of the human brain, educators need to be cautious about how they apply these findings to practice. There are critics who believe that brain research should not be used at this time in schools and classrooms. Some critics say it will be years before this has any application to educational practice. Others fear that unsubstantiated claims are being made, and that educators are not sufficiently trained to tell scientific fact from hype. The concerns are understandable but should not prevent educators from learning what they need to know to decide whether a research study has applications to their practice.

There are researchers who strongly disagree with the critics and decry educators' lack of attention to neuroscience. Michael Merzenich, a neurobiologist at the University of California, San Francisco, believes that the increased understanding of how the brain learns will lead to neuroscience-based education. He predicts that in 10 to 15 years every school will be able to deliver help based on each student's brain plasticity.[3] Harry Chugani, a pediatric neurologist at Wayne State University in Detroit, argues that "we're not paying attention to the biological principles of education," and that the new discoveries about the brain require a fundamental change in the nation's educational curricula.[4]

There is, of course, no panacea that will make teaching and learning a perfect process—and that includes brain research. It is a long leap from making a research finding in a laboratory to the changing of schools and practice because of that finding. These are exciting times for educators, but we must ensure that we don't let the excitement cloud our common sense.

Why This Book Can Help Improve Teaching and Learning

What I have tried to do here is report on research (from neuroscience as well as the behavioral and cognitive sciences) that seems to be sufficiently reliable that it can inform educational practice. This is hardly a novel idea. Madeline Hunter in the late 1960s introduced the notion of teachers using what we are learning about learning and modifying traditional classroom procedures and instructional techniques accordingly. Her program at the UCLA School of Education came to be called "Instructional Theory Into Practice," or ITIP. Readers familiar with that model will recognize some of Dr. Hunter's work here, especially in the areas of transfer and practice. I had the privilege of working periodically with her for nine years, and I firmly believe that she was the major force that awakened educators to the importance of continually updating their knowledge base and focusing on research-based strategies.

This book will help answer questions such as:

When do students remember best in a learning episode?

How can I help students understand and remember more of what I teach?

Why is focus so important, and why is it so difficult to get?

How can I teach motor skills effectively?

How can humor and music help the teaching-learning process?

How can I get students to find meaning in what they are learning?

Why is transfer such a powerful principle of learning, and how can it destroy a lesson without my realizing it?

What classroom strategies are more likely to appeal to the brain of today's student?

This book will be useful to **classroom teachers** because it presents a research-based rationale for why and when certain instructional strategies should be considered. It focuses on the brain as the organ of thinking and learning and takes the approach that the more teachers know about how the brain learns, the more instructional options become available. Increasing the options that teachers have during the dynamic process of instruction also increases the likelihood that successful learning will occur.

The book should also help **staff developers** who continually need to update their own knowledge base and include research and research-based strategies and support systems as part of their repertoire. Chapter 8 offers some suggestions to help staff developers implement and maintain the knowledge and strategies suggested here.

> *This book can help teachers, staff developers, principals, college instructors, and parents.*

Principals should find here a substantial source of topics for discussion at faculty meetings, which should include, after all, instructional as well as informational items. In doing so, they support the attitude that professional growth is an ongoing school responsibility and not an occasional event. More important, being familiar with these topics enhances the principal's credibility as the school's instructional leader and promotes the notion that the school is a learning organization for *all* its occupants.

My hope is that **college and university instructors** will also find merit in the research and applications presented here, as both suggestions to improve their own teaching as well as information to be passed on to prospective teachers.

Some of the information in this book will be useful to **parents**, who are, after all, the child's first teachers.

Indeed, the ideas in this book provide the research support for a variety of initiatives, such as cooperative learning groups, integrated thematic units, and the interdisciplinary approach to curriculum. Those who are familiar with constructivism will recognize many similarities in the ideas presented here. The research is yielding more evidence that knowledge is not only transmitted from the teacher to the learners but is transformed in the learner's mind as a result of cultural and social mediation. Much of this occurs through elaborative rehearsal and transfer and is discussed in several chapters.

Some **Practitioner's Corners** include activities that check for understanding of the major concepts and research presented in the chapter. Others offer my interpretation of how this research might translate into effective classroom strategies that improve the teaching-learning process. Readers are invited to critically review my suggestions and rationale to determine if they have any value for their work.

Main thoughts are highlighted in boxes throughout the book. At the end of each chapter, you will find a page called **Key Points to Ponder**, an organizing tool to help you remember important ideas, strategies, and resources you may wish to consider later.

At the end of each chapter, the **Notes** contain additional information, references, and resources that may be of interest to readers.

Where appropriate, I have explained some of the chemical and biological processes occurring within the brain. However, I have intentionally omitted complex chemical formulas and reactions, and have avoided side issues that would distract from the main purpose of this book. My intent is to present just enough science to help the average reader understand the research and the rationale for any suggestions I offer.

Try It Yourself—Do Action Research

Benefits of Action Research. One of the best ways to assess the value of the strategies suggested in this book is to try them out in your own classroom or in any other location where you are teaching. Conducting this action research allows you to gather data to determine the effectiveness of new strategies and affirm those you already use, to acclaim and enhance the use of research in our profession, and to further your own professional development.

Other benefits of action research are that it provides teachers with consistent feedback for self-evaluation, it introduces alternative forms of student assessment, and its results may lead to important changes in curriculum. Action research can be the

> *Using action research provides valuable data, affirms best practices, and enhances the integrity of the profession.*

work of just one teacher, but its value grows immensely when it is the consistent effort of a teacher team, department, school staff, or even an entire district. Incorporating action research as a regular part of the K–12 academic scene not only provides useful data but also enhances the integrity of the profession and gains much-needed respect from the broad community that schools serve.

Teachers are often hesitant to engage in action research, concerned that it may take too much time or that it represents another accountability measure in an already test-saturated environment. Yet, with all the programs and strategies emerging today in the name of reform, we need data to help determine their validity. The valuable results of cognitive neuroscience will continue to be ignored in schools unless there is reliable evidence to support their use. Action research is a cost-effective means of assessing the effectiveness of brain-compatible strategies that are likely to result in greater student learning.

The Outcomes of Action Research. The classroom is a laboratory in which the teaching and learning processes meet and interact. Action research can provide continual feedback on the success of that interaction. The teacher is always in control of the type of data collected, the pace of assessment, and the analysis of the results. This process encourages teachers to reflect on their practices, to refine their skills as a practitioner, and to direct their own professional development. This is a new view of the profession, with the teacher as the main agent of change.

Building administrators have a special obligation to encourage action research among their teachers. With so much responsibility being placed on schools and teachers, action research can quickly assess the effectiveness of instructional strategies. By supporting such a program, principals demonstrate by action that they are truly instructional leaders and not just building managers.

See the Practitioner's Corner at the end of this chapter on page 10 for suggestions on using action research in the classroom.

Finally, this edition of the book reflects what I have gathered about the brain and learning at the time of publication. Because this is an area of intense research and scrutiny, educators need to constantly read about new discoveries and adjust their understandings accordingly. As we discover more about how the brain learns, we can devise strategies that can make the teaching-learning process more efficient, effective, and enjoyable.

PRACTITIONER'S CORNER

What Do You Already Know?

The value of this book can be measured in part by how it enhances your understanding of the brain and the way it learns. Take the following true-false test to assess your current knowledge of the brain. Decide whether the statements are generally true or false and circle T or F. Explanations for the answers are identified throughout the book in special boxes.

1.　T　F　The structures responsible for deciding what gets stored in long-term memory are located in the brain's rational system.

2.　T　F　Learners who can perform a new learning task well are likely to retain it.

3.　T　F　Reviewing material just before a test is a good practice to determine how much has been retained.

4.　T　F　Increased time on task increases retention of new learning.

5.　T　F　Two very similar concepts or motor skills should be taught at the same time.

6.　T　F　The rate at which a learner retrieves information from memory is closely related to intelligence.

7.　T　F　The amount of information a learner can deal with at one time is genetically linked.

8.　T　F　It is usually not possible to increase the amount of information that the working (temporary) memory can deal with at one time.

9.　T　F　Most of the time, the transfer of information from long-term storage is under the conscious control of the learner.

10.　T　F　People must be taught how to do higher-order thinking.

PRACTITIONER'S CORNER

How Brain Compatible Is My Teaching/School/District?

Directions: On a scale of 1 (lowest) to 5 (highest), circle the number that indicates the degree to which your teaching/school/district does the following. Connect the circles to see a profile.

1. I/We adapt the curriculum to recognize the windows of opportunity students have during their cognitive growth.   1----2----3----4----5

2. I/We are trained to provoke strong, positive emotions in students during the learning process.   1----2----3----4----5

3. I/We are trained to help students adjust their self-concept to be more successful in different learning situations.   1----2----3----4----5

4. I/We provide an enriched and varied learning environment.   1----2----3----4----5

   using Novelty in lessons p. 32

5. I/We search constantly for opportunities to integrate curriculum concepts between and among subject areas.   1----2----3----4----5

6. Students have frequent opportunities during class to talk about what they are learning, while they are learning.   1----2----3----4----5

7. I/We do not use lecture as the main mode of instruction.   1----2----3----4----5

8. One of the main criteria I/we use to decide on classroom activities and curriculum is relevancy to students.   1----2----3----4----5

9. I/We understand the power of chunking and use it in the design of curriculum and in daily instruction.   1----2----3----4----5

10. I/We understand the primacy-recency effect and use it regularly in the classroom to enhance retention of learning.   1----2----3----4----5

PRACTITIONER'S CORNER

Using Action Research

Basic Guidelines

Action research helps teachers assess systematically the effectiveness of their own educational practices using the techniques of research.[5] Because data collection is essential to this process, teachers need to identify the elements of the research question that can be measured.

- **Select the Research Question**. Because you need to collect data, choose a research question that involves elements which can be easily measured quantitatively or qualitatively. Some examples:

1. How does the chunking of material affect the learner's retention? This can be measured by a short oral or written quiz.
2. How does teaching material at the beginning or middle of a lesson affect learner retention? This can be measured by quizzes.
3. How does changing the length of wait time affect student participation? This can be measured by comparing the length of the wait time to the number of subsequent student responses.
4. Does using humor or music increase student focus? Can be measured by number of students who are on/off task with or without humor or music.

- **Collect the Data**. Remember that you need baseline data before you try the research strategy to provide a comparison. Plan carefully the methods you will use to measure and collect the data. Try not to use paper-and-pencil tests exclusively. You will collect pretrial and posttrial data.

    Pretrial. Select a control group, which is usually the same group of students that will be used with the research strategy. Collect test data without using the research strategy.

    Posttrial. Use the strategy (e.g., chunking, prime-time-1, wait time, humor) and then collect the appropriate data.

– Continued –

Using Action Research—Continued

- **Analyze the Data**. Use simple analytical techniques, such as comparing the average group test scores before and after using the research strategy. What changes did you notice in the two sets of data? Did the research strategy produce the desired result? If not, why not? Was there an unexpected consequence (positive or negative) of using the strategy?

- **Share the Data**. Sharing the data with colleagues is an important component of the action research process. Too often, teachers work in isolation, with few or no opportunities to interact continuously with colleagues to design and discuss their lessons.

- **Implement the Change**. If the research strategy produced the desired results, decide how you will make it part of your teaching repertoire. If you did not get the desired results, decide whether you need to change some aspect of the strategy or perhaps use a different measure.

- **Try New Practices**. Repeat the above steps with other strategies so that action research becomes part of your ongoing professional development.

The Teacher Work Sample

Another action research method allows teachers to use individual or groups of students from their classes to evaluate teaching methods. The work samples tie specific learner outcomes to a professional teaching standard and usually provide short-term data.

Teacher Work Sample Process

- ▸ Choose a lesson or unit.
- ▸ State learner outcome(s).
- ▸ Tie learner outcome(s) to teaching standard.
- ▸ State strategies/methods for lesson.
- ▸ Pretest.
- ▸ Teach the lesson.
- ▸ Posttest.

– Continued –

Using Action Research—Continued

- ▸ Analyze learner gains.
- ▸ Reflect on effectiveness of teaching tool.
- ▸ Evaluate learner outcomes.
- ▸ Reflect on changes in written format.
- ▸ Share data and outcomes with colleagues.

These teacher work samples are particularly helpful in assisting novice and veteran teachers in assessing their skills, refining their craft, and improving their classroom presentations. It also serves to measure the training outcomes of professional development initiatives and to validate new teaching practices.

INTRODUCTION–NOTES

1. For an excellent explanation of brain mapping techniques, see Carter (1998).

2. See, for example, the issues of *School Administrator*, January 1998; NASSP *Bulletin*, May 1998; and *Educational Leadership*, November 1998.

3. Other exciting predictions about the brain are in Begley (2000), pp. 63–65.

4. Quoted and cited in Kotulak (1996), p. 36.

5. Much of the information in this Practitioner's Corner comes from an action research component developed at Cardinal Stritch University in Milwaukee, WI. I am indebted to Dr. Joan L. Whitman, Program Chair in Graduate Education, for her valuable contribution.

CHAPTER 1

BASIC BRAIN FACTS AND
BRAIN DEVELOPMENT

*With our new knowledge of the brain, we are just
dimly beginning to realize that we can now
understand humans, including ourselves, as never
before, and that this is the greatest advance of the
century, and quite possibly the most significant in all
human history.*

— Leslie A. Hart,
Human Brain and Human Learning

Chapter Highlights: This chapter introduces some of the basic
structures of the human brain and their functions. It briefly
describes neuron operations and distinguishes between the brain and
the mind. It also discusses the growth of the young brain and some
of the environmental factors that influence its development into
adolescence.

The adult human brain is a wet, fragile mass that weighs a little over three pounds. It is about
the size of a small grapefruit, is shaped like a walnut, and can fit in the palm of your hand.
Cradled in the skull and surrounded by protective membranes, it is poised at the top of the
spinal column. The brain works ceaselessly, even when we are asleep. Although it represents only
about 2 percent of our body weight, it consumes nearly 20 percent of our calories! The more we
think, the more calories we burn. Perhaps this can be a new diet fad, and we could modify
Descartes' famous quotation from "I think, therefore I am" to "I think, therefore I'm thin"!

Through the centuries, surveyors of the brain have examined every cerebral feature,
sprinkling the landscape with Latin and Greek names to describe what they saw. They analyzed
structures and functions and sought concepts to explain their observations. One early concept

15

divided the brain by location—forebrain, midbrain, and hindbrain. Another, proposed by Paul MacLean in the 1960s, described the triune brain according to stages of evolution: reptilian, paleo-mammalian, and mammalian.

For our purposes, we will take a look at major parts of the outside of the brain (Figure 1.1), including the frontal, temporal, occipital, and parietal lobes, the motor cortex, and the cerebellum. We will then look at the inside of the brain and divide it into three parts on the basis of their general functions: the brain stem, limbic system, and cerebrum (Figure 1.2). We will also examine the structure of the brain's nerve cells, called *neurons*.

Some Exterior Parts of the Brain

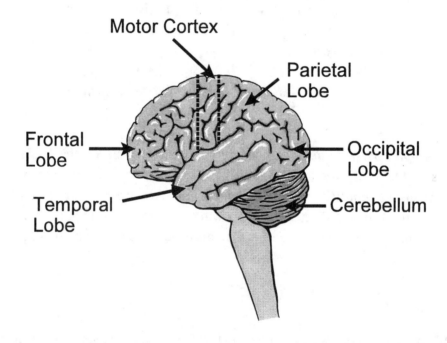

Figure 1.1 *This diagram shows the four major lobes of the brain as well as the motor cortex and the cerebellum.*

Although the minor wrinkles are unique in each brain, several major wrinkles and folds are common to all brains. These folds form a set of four lobes in each hemisphere. Each lobe tends to specialize for certain functions.

At the front are the *frontal lobes*, which deal with planning and thinking (more on the frontal lobes later). Above the ears rest the *temporal lobes*, which deal with sound, speech (although this is usually on the left side only), and some parts of long-term memory. At the back is the *occipital lobe*, which is used almost exclusively for visual processing. Near the top is the *parietal lobe*, which deals mainly with orientation, calculation, and certain types of recognition.

Between the parietal and frontal lobes is a band across the top of the brain from ear to ear called the *motor cortex*. This strip controls body movement and, as we will learn later, works with the cerebellum to coordinate the learning of motor skills.

Some Interior Parts of the Brain

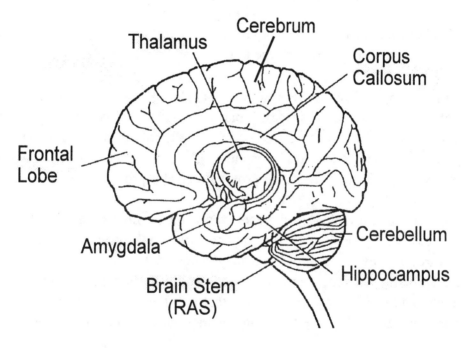

Figure 1.2 *A cross section of the human brain.*

Brain Stem

The first part is the brain stem, the oldest and deepest area of the brain, that evolved 500 million years ago. It is often referred to as the reptilian brain because it resembles the entire brain of a reptile. Of the 12 body nerves that go to the brain, 11 end in the brain stem (the olfactory nerve—for smell—goes directly to the limbic system, an evolutionary artifact). Here is where vital body functions, such as heartbeat, respiration, body temperature, and digestion, are monitored and controlled. The brain stem also houses the reticular activating system (RAS), responsible for the brain's alertness and about which more will be explained in the next chapter.

The Limbic System

Nestled above the brain stem lies the limbic system, sometimes called the old mammalian brain. Most of the structures in the limbic system are duplicated in each hemisphere of the brain. These structures carry out a number of different functions including the generation of emotions. Its placement between the cerebrum and the brain stem permits the interplay of emotion and reason.

Three parts of the limbic system are important to learning and memory. They are:

The Thalamus. All incoming sensory information (except smell) goes first to the thalamus. From here it is directed to other parts of the brain for additional processing.

The Hippocampus. Located near the base of the limbic area is the hippocampus (the Greek word for "seahorse," because of its shape). It plays a major role in consolidating learning and in converting information from working memory via electrical signals to the long-term storage regions, a process that may take days to months. It constantly checks information relayed to working memory and compares it to stored experiences. This process is essential for the creation of meaning.

Its role was first revealed by patients whose hippocampus was damaged or removed because of disease. These patients could remember everything that happened before the operation, but not afterward. If they were introduced to you today, you would be a stranger to them tomorrow. Because they can remember information for only a few minutes, they can read the same article repeatedly and believe on each occasion that it is the first time they have read it. Brain scans have confirmed the role of the hippocampus in permanent memory storage.

The Amygdala. Attached to the end of the hippocampus is the amygdala (Greek for "almond"). This almond-shaped structure is part of the limbic system and plays an important role in emotions, especially fear. Electrical stimulation of the amygdala can incite rage. Its surgical removal can turn a raging psychotic into a docile individual. Stimulation does not always produce rage; it can also cause fear or pleasure.

Because of its proximity to the hippocampus and its activity on PET scans, researchers believe that the amygdala encodes an emotional message, if one is present, whenever a memory is tagged for long-term storage. It is not known at this time whether the emotional memories themselves are actually stored in the amygdala. One possibility is that the emotional component of a memory is stored in the amygdala while other cognitive components (names, dates, etc.) are stored elsewhere.[1] The emotional component is recalled whenever the memory is recalled. This explains why people recalling an emotional memory will often experience those emotions again.

Teachers, of course, hope that their students will permanently remember what was taught. Therefore, it is intriguing to realize that the two structures in the brain mainly responsible for long-term remembering are located in the *emotional* system. Understanding the connection between emotions and cognitive learning and memory will be discussed in later chapters.

Test Question No. 1: The structures responsible for deciding what gets stored in long-term memory are located in the brain's rational system.

Answer: False. These structures are located in the emotional (limbic) system.

Cerebrum

A soft jellylike mass, the cerebrum is the largest of the four areas, representing over 80 percent of the brain by weight. Its surface is pale gray, wrinkled, and marked by furrows called fissures. One large fissure runs from front to back and divides the cerebrum into two halves, called the *cerebral hemispheres.* For some still unexplained reason, the nerves from the left side of the body cross over to the right hemisphere, and those from the right side of the body cross to the left hemisphere. The two hemispheres are connected by a thick cable of over 250 million nerve fibers called the *corpus callosum.* The hemispheres use this bridge to communicate with each other and coordinate activities.

The hemispheres are covered by a thin but tough laminated *cortex* (meaning "tree bark"), rich in cells, that is about 1/10th of an inch thick and, because of its folds, has a surface area of about 2.5 square feet. The cortex is composed of six layers of cells meshed in about 10,000 miles of connecting fibers per cubic inch! Here, in a layer just the thickness of three human hairs, is where most of the action takes place. Thinking, memory, speech, and muscular movement are controlled by areas in the cerebrum.

Frontal Lobe. The front of the cerebrum is known as the *frontal lobe* or *frontal cortex.* Lying just behind the forehead, it is the executive control center of the brain, monitoring higher-order thinking, directing problem solving, and regulating the excesses of the emotional system. The frontal lobe also contains our self-will area—what some might call our personality. Trauma to the frontal lobe can cause dramatic—and sometimes permanent—behavior and personality

> **Because the rational system matures slowly in adolescents, they are more likely to submit to their emotions.**

changes. Because most of the working memory is located here, it is the area where focus occurs.[2] The frontal lobe matures slowly. MRI studies of post-adolescents reveal that the frontal lobe continues to mature into early adulthood. Thus, the emotional regulation capability of the frontal lobe is not fully operational during adolescence.[3] This is one reason why adolescents are more likely than adults to submit to their emotions and resort to high-risk behavior.

Cerebellum

The cerebellum (Latin for "little brain") is located just below the rear part of the cerebrum. It is the area that coordinates every movement. Because the cerebellum monitors impulses from nerve endings in the muscles, it is important in the learning, performance, and timing of complex motor tasks. It modifies and coordinates commands to swing a golf club, smooth a dancer's footsteps, and allow a hand to bring a cup to the lips without spilling its contents. The cerebellum may also store the memory of rote movements, such as touch-typing and tying a shoelace. A person whose cerebellum is damaged cannot coordinate movement, catch a ball, or complete a handshake.

There is new evidence that the cerebellum also has a role in cognitive processing by coordinating and fine-tuning our thoughts, emotions, senses, and memories.[4]

Brain Cells

The brain is composed of a trillion cells of at least two known types, nerve cells and glial cells. The nerve cells are called *neurons* and represent about one-tenth of the total—roughly 100 billion. Most of the cells are *glial* (Greek for "glue") cells that hold the neurons together and act as filters to keep harmful substances out of the neurons. Very recent studies seem to indicate that some glial cells, called *astrocytes*, may have a role in regulating the rate of neuron signaling.[5]

The neurons are the functioning core for the brain and the entire nervous system. Neurons come in different sizes, but the body of each brain neuron is about 1/100th the size of the period at the end of this sentence. Unlike other cells, the neuron (see Figure 1.3) has tens of thousands of branches emerging from its core, called *dendrites* (from the Greek word for "tree"). The dendrites receive electrical impulses from other neurons and transmit them along a long fiber, called the *axon* (Greek for "axis"). There is normally only one axon per neuron. A layer called the *myelin sheath* surrounds each axon. The sheath insulates the axon from the other cells and increases the speed of impulse transmission. This impulse travels along the neurons through an electrochemical process and can move through the entire length of a 6-foot adult in 2/10ths of a second. A neuron can transmit between 250 and 2,500 impulses per second. Neurons have no direct contact with each other. Between each dendrite and axon is a small gap of about a millionth of an inch called a *synapse* (from the Greek, meaning "to join together"). A typical neuron collects signals from others through the dendrites, which are covered at the synapse with thousands of tiny bumps, called *spines*. The neuron sends out spikes of electrical activity (impulses) through the axon to the synapse where the activity releases chemicals stored in sacs (called *synaptic vesicles*) at the end of the axon.

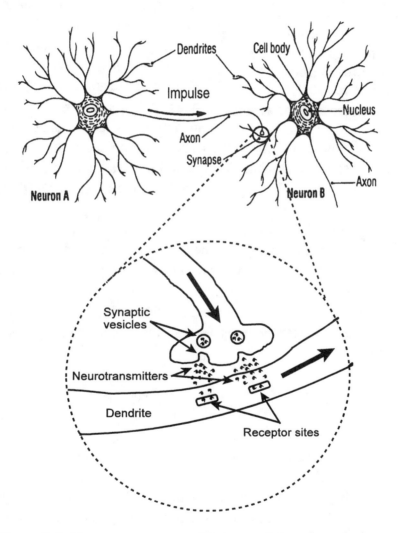

Figure 1.3 Neurons, or nerve cells, transmit impulses along an axon and across the synapse to the dendrites of the neighboring cell.

These chemicals, called *neurotransmitters*, either excite or inhibit the neighboring neuron. Nearly 100 different neurotransmitters have been discovered so far. (Some of the common neurotransmitters are acetylcholine, epinephrine, serotonin, and dopamine.) Learning occurs by changing the synapses so that the influence of one neuron on another also changes.

There also seems to be a direct connection between the physical world of the brain and the work of the brain's owner. Recent studies of neurons in people of different occupations (e.g., professional musicians) show that the more complex the skills demanded of the occupation, the more dendrites were found on the neurons. This increase in dendrites allows for more connections between neurons resulting in more sites in which to store learnings.

There are about 100 billion neurons in the adult human brain—about 16 times as many neurons as people on this planet and about the number of stars in the Milky Way. Each neuron can have up to 10 thousand dendrite branches. This means that it is possible to have up to one quadrillion (that's a one followed by 15 zeros) synaptic connections in one brain. This inconceivably large number allows the brain to process the data coming continuously from the senses; to store decades of memories, faces, and places; to learn languages; and to combine information in a way that no other individual on this planet has ever thought of before. This is a remarkable achievement for just three pounds of soft tissue!

> **Believe it or not, the number of potential synaptic connections in just one human brain is about 1,000,000,000,000,000.**

Conventional wisdom has been that neurons were the only body cells that never regenerate. However, researchers discovered recently that the adult human brain does generate neurons in at least one site—the hippocampus. This discovery raises the question of whether neurons regenerate in other parts of the brain and, if so, if it might be possible to stimulate them to repair and heal damaged brains, especially for the growing number of people with Alzheimer's disease.[6] Research into Alzheimer's disease is exploring ways to stop the deadly mechanisms that trigger the destruction of neurons.[7]

Brain Fuel

Brain cells consume oxygen and glucose (a form of sugar) for fuel. The more challenging the brain's task, the more fuel it consumes. Therefore, it is important to have adequate amounts of these fuels present in the brain for optimum functioning. Low amounts of oxygen and glucose in the blood can produce lethargy and sleepiness. Eating a moderate portion of food containing glucose (fruits are an excellent source) can boost the performance and accuracy of working memory, attention, and motor function.[8]

Water, also essential for healthy brain activity, is required to move neuron signals through the brain. Low concentrations of water diminish the rate and efficiency of these signals. Moreover, water keeps the lungs sufficiently moist to allow for the efficient transfer of oxygen into the bloodstream.

> *Many students (and their teachers) do not eat a breakfast with sufficient glucose nor drink enough water during the day for healthy brain function.*

Many students (and their teachers, too) do not eat a breakfast that contains sufficient glucose, nor do they drink enough water during the day to maintain healthy brain function. Schools should have breakfast programs and educate students on the need to have sufficient blood levels of glucose during the day. Schools should also provide frequent opportunities for students and staff to drink plenty of water. The current recommended amount is one eight-ounce glass of water a day for each 25 pounds of body weight.

Neuron Development in Children

Neuron development starts in the embryo shortly after conception and proceeds at an astonishing rate. In the first four months of gestation, about 200 billion neurons are formed, but about half will die off during the fifth month because they fail to connect with any areas of the growing embryo. This purposeful destruction of neurons (called *apoptosis*) is genetically programmed to ensure that only those neurons that have made connections are preserved, and to prevent the brain from being overcrowded with unconnected cells.[9] Any drugs or alcohol that the mother takes during this time can interfere with the growing brain cells, increasing the risk of fetal addiction and mental defects.

The neurons of a newborn are immature; many of their axons lack the protective myelin layer and there are few connections between them. Thus, most regions of the cerebral cortex are quiet. Understandably, the most active areas are the brainstem (body functions) and the cerebellum (movement).

The neurons in a child's brain make many more connections than those in adults. A newborn's brain makes connections at an incredible pace as the child absorbs its environment. Information is entering the brain through "windows" that open and close at various times. The richer the environment, the greater the number of interconnections that are made; consequently, learning can take place faster and with greater meaning.

As the child approaches puberty, the pace slackens and two other processes begin: Connections the brain finds useful become permanent; those not useful are eliminated (apoptosis) as the brain selectively strengthens and prunes connections based on experience. This process continues throughout our lives, but it appears to be most intense between the ages of 3 and 12.

Thus, at an early age, experiences are already shaping the brain and designing the unique neural architecture that will influence how it handles future experiences in school, work, and other places.

Windows of Opportunity

Windows of opportunity represent important periods in which the brain responds to certain types of input to create or consolidate neural networks. Figure 1.4 shows just a few windows. Some windows are critical. For example, if even a perfect brain doesn't receive visual stimuli by the age of two, the person will be forever blind, and if it doesn't hear words by the age of ten, the person will never learn a language. When these critical windows close, the brain cells assigned to those tasks lose their ability to perform them.[10]

Other windows are more plastic, but still significant. It is important to remember that learning can occur in each of the areas for the rest of our lives, even after a window closes. However, the skill level probably will not be as high.

Let's examine a few of these windows to understand their importance.

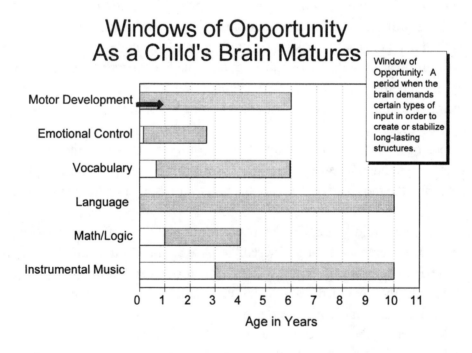

Figure 1.4 *The chart shows some of the sensitive periods for learning.*

24

Motor Development. This window opens during fetal development. Those who have borne children remember all too well the movement of the fetus during the third trimester as motor connections and systems are consolidating. The child's ability to learn motor skills appears to be most pronounced in the first six years. Such seemingly simple tasks as crawling and walking require complicated associations of neural networks, including integrating information from the balance sensors in the inner ear and output signals to the leg

> *What is learned while a window of opportunity is opened will most likely be learned masterfully.*

and arm muscles. Of course, a person can learn motor skills after the window closes. However, what is learned while it is open will most likely be learned masterfully. For example, most concert virtuosos, Olympian athletes, and professional players of individual sports (e.g., tennis and golf) began practicing their skills before the age of six.

Emotional Control. The window for developing emotional control seems to be from two to thirty months. During that time, the limbic (emotional) system and the cortex's rational system are evaluating each other's ability to get its owner what it wants. If tantrums almost always get the child satisfaction when the window is open, then that is likely the method the child will use when the window closes. This constant emotional-rational battle is one

> *The struggle between the emotional and rational systems is a major contributor to the "terrible twos."*

of the major contributors to the "terrible twos." Certainly, one can learn to control emotions after that age. But what the child learned during that window period will be difficult to change, and it will strongly influence what is learned after the window closes.

In an astonishing example of how nurturing can influence nature, there is considerable evidence confirming that how parents respond to their children emotionally during this time frame can encourage or stifle genetic tendencies. Biology is not destiny, so gene expression is not necessarily inevitable. To produce their effects, genes must be turned on.[11] For example, shyness is a trait that seems to be partially hereditary.[12] If parents are overprotective of their bashful young daughter, the toddler is likely to remain shy. On the other hand, if they encourage her to interact with other toddlers, she may overcome it. Thus, genetic bents toward intelligence, sociability, or schizophrenia and aggression can ignite or moderate the genetic contribution based on parental response and other environmental influences.[13]

Vocabulary. Because the brain is genetically programmed for language, babies start uttering sounds and babble phrases as early as the age of two months. The language areas of the brain become really active at eighteen to twenty months. A baby can learn ten or more words per day, yielding a vocabulary of about 900 words at age three, increasing to 2,500 to 3,000 words by the age of five.[14]

Here's testimony to the power of talk: Researchers have shown that babies whose mothers talked to them more had significantly larger vocabularies. Further, talking can also raise a child's IQ.[15]

Language Acquisition. The newborn's brain is not the *tabula rasa* (blank slate) we once thought. Certain areas are specialized and prewired for certain stimuli, including spoken language. The window for acquiring spoken language opens soon after birth and closes around the age of ten or eleven. Beyond that age, learning any language becomes far more difficult. Children found in feral environments often make up their own language. There is also evidence that the human ability to acquire grammar may have a specific window of opportunity in the early years.[16] Knowing this, it seems illogical that many schools still *start* foreign language instruction in high school rather than in the primary grades. Chapter 5 deals in greater detail with how the brain acquires spoken language.

Mathematics and Logic. How and when the young brain understands numbers is uncertain, but there is mounting evidence that infants have a rudimentary number sense which is wired into certain brain sites at birth. The purpose of these sites is to categorize the world in terms of the "number of things" in a collection. We drive along a road and see horses in a field. While we are noticing that they are brown and black, we cannot help but see that there are four of them. Over time, humans have extended these number sites to develop the schemes of mathematics.[17]

Using PET scans and MRI, researchers have located the exact areas in the brain where mathematics takes place—mostly in the left parietal lobe (see Figure 1.1).[18] It is uncertain exactly when these areas begin functioning, but one study showed that toddlers as young as five months have a number sense and reasoning ability that could be called baby arithmetic.[19]

Instrumental Music. There appears to be a window for creating music that opens around the age of two or three. Mozart was playing the harpsichord and composing at age four. In a famous study, Gordon Shaw and Frances Rauscher showed that children ages three to four who received piano lessons and group-singing lessons scored significantly higher in spatial-temporal tasks than a group who did not get the music training. Further, the increase was long-term, that is, it lasted more than a day.[20] Brain imaging reveals that creating vocal or instrumental music excites the same regions of the left frontal lobe responsible for mathematics and logic. See Chapter 6 for more on the effects of music on the brain and learning.

Summary. Research on how the young brain develops suggests that an enriched home and preschool environment during the early years can help children build neural connections and make full use of their mental abilities. Because of the importance of early years, I believe school districts should communicate with the parents of newborns and offer their services and resources to help parents succeed as the first teachers of their children. Such programs are already in place on a statewide basis in Michigan, Missouri,[21] and Kentucky, and similar programs sponsored by local school districts are springing up elsewhere. But we need to work faster toward achieving this important goal.

> *School districts should communicate with the parents of newborns and offer their services and resources to help parents succeed as the first teachers of their children.*

The Brain as a Novelty Seeker

Part of our success as a species can be attributed to the brain's persistent interest in novelty, that is, changes occurring in the environment. The brain is constantly scanning its environment for stimuli. When an unexpected stimulus arises—such as a loud noise from an empty room—a rush of adrenalin closes down all unnecessary activity and focuses the brain's attention so it can spring into action. Conversely, an environment that contains mainly predictable or repeated stimuli (like some classrooms?) lowers the brain's interest in the outside world and tempts it to turn within for novel sensations.

Environmental Factors Enhancing the Brain's Search for Novelty

We often hear teachers remark that students are more different today in the way they learn than ever before. They seem to have shorter attention spans and bore easily. Why is that? Is there something happening in the environment of learners that alters the way they approach the learning process?

The Environment of the Past

From the moment of birth (some say earlier), the brain is collecting information and learning from its environment. The home environment of a child several decades ago was usually quiet—some might say boring compared to today. Parents and children did a lot of talking and reading. The occasional radio program was an exciting event. For these children, school was a much more interesting place because it had television, films, field trips, and guest speakers—experiences not usually found at home. Because there were few other distractions, school was an important influence in a child's life and the primary source of information.

The Environment of Today

In recent years, children have been growing up in a very different environment. The rapidly changing multimedia-based culture and the stresses from an ever-increasing pace of living are changing what the developing brain learns from the world. Children have become accustomed to these rapid sensory and emotional changes, and respond by engaging in all types of activities of short duration at home and in the malls. By acclimating itself to these changes, the brain responds more than ever to the unique and different—what is called *novelty*. Adult skeptics need but watch MTV for just a few minutes to discover that the images change every few seconds and play heavily on emotions. Compare, for example, the TV format of Don Herbert's *Mr. Wizard* in the 1950s to the current *Bill Nye, the Science Guy*.

School is but one of many factors influencing today's children. They are wrestling with the need to be different while under pressure to conform. They have to develop and deal with relationships, identify peer groups, and respond to religious influences. Add to this mix the changes in family patterns and lifestyles, as well as the effects of diet, drugs, and sleep deprivation, and we can realize how very different the environment of today's child is from that of just 15 years ago.

Have Schools Changed With the Environment?

Schools and teaching, however, haven't changed much. The computers found in many schools provide few of the options that students get with their more powerful computers at home. In high schools, lecturing continues to be the main method of instruction, and the overhead projector is often the most advanced technology used. Students remark that school is a dull, nonengaging environment that is much less interesting than what is available outside school. They have a difficult time focusing for extended periods and are easily

> **Now that we have a more scientifically based understanding about today's novel brain, we must rethink what we do in schools and classrooms.**

distracted. Because they see little novelty and relevancy in what they are learning, they keep asking the eternal question, "Why do we need to know this?"

Educators can either decry the changing brain and culture or recognize that we must adjust schools to accommodate these changes. Now that we have a more scientifically based understanding about today's novel brain and how it learns, we must rethink what we do in classrooms and schools.

There is a dark side to this increased novelty-seeking behavior. Some adolescents who perceive little novelty in their environment may turn to mind-altering drugs, such as ecstasy and amphetamines for stimulation. This drug dependence can further enhance the brain's demand for novelty to the point that it becomes unbalanced and resorts to extremes-oriented behavior.[22]

The Brain and the Mind

I do not equate the brain and the mind. In my view, they are separate entities. The brain is the physical organ composed of atoms and molecules that inhabits the skull. The mind is much more than that; it transcends the head and operates throughout the body. Of course, they are linked and intertwined. Every few years, nearly every atom in the brain (and the rest of the body as well) is replaced. Yet one's persona, memories, hopes, and dreams remain unchanged and survive this complete makeover of the physical self.

The qualities of the mind include its ability to be aware of itself (consciousness), to understand its place on the planet and in time, and to use language for abstract representations. The mind puts meaning and purpose into our lives and gives us a worldview. It has no boundaries and permeates every cell of our body. While this book will deal primarily with *brain* function and learning, I cannot ignore the realization that the mind can do many more things that no one can explain ... at least, not yet.[23]

PRACTITIONER'S CORNER

Fist for a Brain

This activity shows how you can use your fists to represent the human brain. Metaphors are excellent learning and remembering tools. When you are comfortable with the activity, share it with your students. They are often very interested in knowing how their brain is constructed and how it works. This is a good example of novelty.

1. Extend both arms with palms open and facing down and lock your thumbs.

2. Curl your fingers to make two fists.

3. Turn your fists inward until the knuckles touch.

4. While the fists are touching, pull both toward your chest until you are looking down on your knuckles. This is the approximate size of your brain! Not as big as you thought? Remember, it's not the size of the brain that matters; it's the number of connections between the neurons. Those connections form when stimuli result in learning. The thumbs are the front and are crossed to remind us that the left side of the brain controls the right side of the body, and the right side of the brain controls the left side of the body. The knuckles and outside part of the hands represent the **cerebrum** or thinking part of the brain.

5. Spread your palms apart while keeping the knuckles touching. Look at the tips of your fingers, which represent the **limbic** or emotional system. Note how this system is buried deep within the brain, and how the fingers are mirror-imaged. This reminds us that most of the structures of the limbic system are duplicated in each hemisphere.

6. The wrists are the **brainstem** where vital body functions (such as body temperature, heart beat, blood pressure) are controlled. Rotating your hands shows how the brain can move on top of the spinal column, which is represented by your forearms.

PRACTITIONER'S CORNER

Review of Brain Area Functions

Here is an opportunity to assess your understanding of the major brain areas. Write in the table below your own key words and phrases to describe the functions of each of the seven brain areas. Then draw an arrow to each brain area on the diagram below and label it. What do **you** believe is the difference between the mind and the brain? Consider sharing this information with your students.

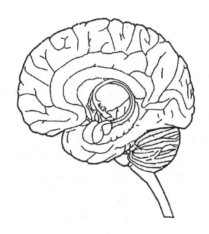

Cerebrum:	
Frontal Lobe:	
Thalamus:	
Hippocampus:	
Amygdala:	
Cerebellum:	
Brain Stem:	

PRACTITIONER'S CORNER

Using Novelty in Lessons

Using novelty does *not* mean that the teacher needs to be a stand-up comic nor the classroom a three-ring circus. It simply means using a varied teaching approach that involves more student activity. Here are a few suggestions for incorporating novelty in your lessons.

- **Humor.** There are many positive benefits that come from using humor in the classroom at *all* grade levels. See the **Practitioner's Corner** in Chapter 2 (p. 50) which suggests guidelines and beneficial reasons for using humor.

- **Movement.** When we sit for more than twenty minutes, our blood pools in our seat and in our feet. By getting up and moving, we recirculate that blood. Within a minute, there is about 15 percent more blood in our brain. We do think better on our feet than on our seat! Students sit too much in classrooms, especially in secondary schools. Look for ways to get students up and moving, especially when they are verbally rehearsing what they have learned.

- **Multi-Sensory Instruction.** Today's students are acclimated to a multi-sensory environment. They are more likely to give attention if there are interesting, colorful visuals and if they can walk around and talk about their learning.

- **Quiz Games.** Have students develop a quiz game or other similar activity to test each other on their knowledge of the concepts taught. This is a common strategy in elementary classrooms, but underutilized in secondary schools. Besides being fun, it has the added value of making students rehearse and understand the concepts in order to create the quiz questions and answers.

- **Music.** Although the research is inconclusive, there are some benefits of playing music in the classroom at certain times during the learning episode. See the **Practitioner's Corner** in Chapter 6 (p. 221) on the use of music.

Chapter 1—Basic Brain Facts and Brain Development

Key Points to Ponder

Jot down on this page key points, ideas, strategies, and resources you want to consider later. This sheet is your personal journal summary and will help to jog your memory.

_____

_____

_____

_____

_____

_____

_____

_____

_____

_____

CHAPTER 1–NOTES

1. Squire and Kandel (1999), pp. 170–171.

2. Smith and Jonides (1999).

3. Sowell, Thompson, Holmes, Jernigan, and Toga (1999).

4. Leonard (1999).

5. Research into the role of glial cells was reported by Maiken Nedergaard at the 29th annual meeting of the Society for Neuroscience, Miami Beach, FL, October 1999.

6. Kempermann and Gage (1999).

7. Alzheimer's disease develops when the brain's disposal system fails to remove a sticky by-product of neuron maintenance called beta-amyloid. The increasing number of beta-amyloid molecules fold into large clusters called *plaques*, which damage and kill neurons. Genetic predisposition and environmental factors trigger the disease.

8. Korol and Gold (1998); Scholey, Moss, Neave, and Wesnes (1999).

9. Sometimes apoptosis gets out of control and connections that might otherwise have imparted certain intuitive skills—such as photographic memory—may be pruned as well. Defective apoptosis may also explain both the amazing abilities and deficits of idiot savants, and the impaired intelligence associated with Down's syndrome.

10. Diamond and Hopson (1998), pp. 57–63.

11. To further clarify this notion, here's an example. The cells on the tip of your nose contain the same genetic code as those in your stomach lining. But the gene that codes for producing stomach acid is activated in your stomach, yet idled on your nose.

12. Much of the new research on genetic traits and markers is the result of the Human Genome Project, which in June, 2000 completed a general map of the entire human genetic code—a sequence of about 3 billion molecules forming the 80,000 or so genes on our 23 pairs of chromosomes. Identifying a gene's location and structure can lead to genetic therapies to cure terrible diseases. To follow the progress of this exciting and significant research, check out the Project's website at: www.ornl.gov/TechResources/Human_Genome/home.html.

13. Reiss, Neiderheiser, Hetherington, and Plomin (2000).

14. Diamond and Hopson (1998), p. 154.

15. Kotulak (1996), pp. 33–34.

16. Diamond and Hopson (1998), p. 172.

17. See Butterworth (1999) for the research and a full explanation of these number sites.

18. Dehaene (1997).

19. Wynn (1995).

20. Rauscher et al. (1997). Most cognitive neuroscientists use a twenty-four hour period as the standard to measure a long-term memory effect. That is because information or skills in the temporary memories usually fade away in seconds or minutes. See Chapter 2 for a discussion of different types of memories.

21. The impact of the long-standing Missouri program (Parents as Teachers) has been particularly successful in improving student success in kindergarten. Information on the program is available at its website: www.patnc.org.

22. Laviola, Adriani, Terranova, and Gerra (1999).

23. Those interested in pursuing the brain-mind connection should read Damasio (1999).

CHAPTER 2

HOW THE BRAIN
PROCESSES INFORMATION

*There are probably more differences in human brains
than in any other animal partly because the human
brain does most of its developing in the outside
world.*

– Robert Ornstein and Richard Thompson,
The Amazing Brain

Chapter Highlights: This chapter presents a modern dynamic model
of how the brain deals with information from the senses. It covers
the behavior of the two temporary memories, the criteria for long-
term storage, and the impact of the self-concept on learning.

Although the brain remains largely a mystery beyond its own understanding, we are slowly
uncovering more about its baffling processes. Using scanning technologies, researchers can
display in vivid color the differences in brain cell metabolism that occur in response to
different types of brain work. A computer constructs a color-coded map indicating what different
areas are doing during such activities as learning new words, analyzing tones, doing mathematical
calculations, or responding to images. One thing is clear: The brain calls selected areas into play
depending on what the individual is doing at the moment. This knowledge encourages us to
construct models that explain data and behavior, but models are useful only when they contain
some predictability about specific operations. In choosing a model, it is necessary to select those
specific operations that can be meaningfully depicted and represented in a way that is consistent
with more recent research findings.

The Information Processing Model

Several models exist to explain brain behavior. In designing a model for this book, I needed one that would accurately represent the complex research of neuroscientists in such a way as to be understood by educational practitioners. I recognize that a model is just one person's view of reality, and I readily admit that this particular information processing model comes closest to *my* view of how the brain learns. It differs from other models in that it escapes the limits of the computer metaphor and recognizes that learning, storing, and remembering are dynamic and interactive processes. Beyond that, the model incorporates much of the recent findings of research and is sufficiently flexible to adjust to new findings as they are revealed. I have already made several changes in this model since I began working with it nearly 15 years ago. A few changes are a result of new information learned since the first edition of this book was published. My hope is that classroom teachers will be encouraged to reflect on their methodology and decide if there are new insights here that could affect their instruction and improve learning.

Origins of the Model

The precursor of this model was developed by Robert Stahl (1985) of Arizona State University in the early 1980s. Stahl's more complex model synthesized the research in the 1960s and 1970s on cognitive processing and learning. His goal was to convince teacher educators that they should use this model to help prospective teachers understand how and why learning occurs. He also used the model to develop an elaborate and fascinating learning taxonomy designed to promote higher-order thinking skills.

Usefulness of the Model

The model discussed here (Figure 2.1) is a significantly modified version of Stahl's original. It has been updated and streamlined so that it can be used by the widest range of teacher educators and practitioners. It uses common objects to represent various stages in the process. Even this revised model does not pretend to include all the ways that researchers believe the human brain deals with information, thought, and behavior. It limits its scope to the major cerebral operations that deal with the collecting, evaluating, storing, and retrieving of information—the parts most useful to educators.

The model starts with information from our environment and shows how the senses reject or accept it for further processing. It then explains the two temporary memories, how they operate, and the factors that determine if a learning is likely to be stored. Finally, it shows the

Information Processing Model

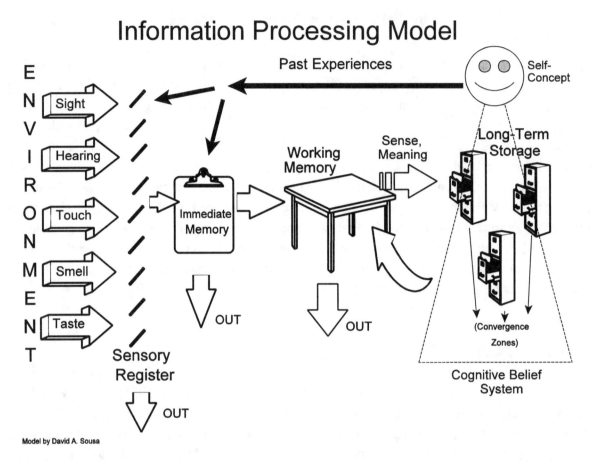

Model by David A. Sousa

Figure 2.1 *The Information Processing Model shows how the brain deals with information from the environment. (Adaptation and enhancement of original model by Robert Stahl.)*

inescapable impact that experiences and self-concept have on future learning. The model is simple, but the processes are extraordinarily complex. Knowing how the human brain seems to process information and learn can help teachers plan lessons that students are more likely to understand and remember.

Limitations of the Model

Although the explanation of the model will follow items going through the processing system, it is important to note that this linear approach is used solely for simplicity and

> **The brain changes its own properties as a result of experience.**

clarity. Much of the recent evidence on memory supports a model of parallel processing. That is, many items are processed quickly and simultaneously (within limits), taking different paths through and out of the system. Memories are dynamic and dispersed, and the brain has the capacity to change its own properties as the result of experience.

Even though the model may seem to represent learning and remembering as a mechanistic process, it must be remembered that we are describing a *biological process*. Nonetheless, I have avoided a detailed discussion of the biochemical changes that occur within and between neurons. That would not contribute to the understanding necessary to convert the fruits of research and this model into successful classroom practice, which is, after all, our goal.

Inadequacy of the Computer Model

The rapid proliferation of computers has encouraged the use of the computer model to explain brain functions. This is indeed tempting. Using the analogy of input, processing, and output seems so natural, but there are serious problems with such a model. Certainly, the smallest hand-held calculator can out-tally the human brain in solving complex mathematical operations. Larger computers can play chess, translate one language into another, and correct massive manuscripts for most spelling and grammatical errors in just seconds. The brain performs more slowly because of the time it takes for a nerve impulse to travel along the axon, synaptic delays, and because the capacity of its

> *As you read these words, neurons in your brain are interacting with each other in patterns that correspond to your new learning.*

working memory is limited. But computers cannot exercise judgment with the ease of the human brain. Even the most sophisticated computers are closed linear systems limited to binary code, the 0s and 1s in linear sequences that are the language of computer operations.

The human brain has no such limitations. It is an open, parallel-processing system continually interacting with the physical and social worlds outside. It analyzes, integrates, and synthesizes information and abstracts generalities from it. Each neuron is alive and altered by its experiences and its environment. As you read these words, neurons are interacting with each other, reforming and dissolving storage sites, and establishing different electrical patterns that correspond to your new learning.

Moreover, emotions play an important role in human processing and creativity. And the ideas generated by the human brain often come from images, not from logical propositions. For these and many other reasons, the computer model is, in my opinion, inadequate and misleading.

The Model and Constructivism

At first glance, the model may seem to perpetuate the traditional approach to teaching and learning—that students repeat newly learned information in quizzes, tests, and reports. On the contrary, the new research is revealing that students are more likely to gain greater understanding of and derive greater pleasure from learning when allowed to *transform* the learning into creative thoughts and products. This model emphasizes the power of transfer during learning and the importance of moving students through higher levels of complexity of thought. This will be explained further in Chapter 4.

The Senses

Our brain takes in more information from our environment in a single day than the largest computer does in a year. That information is detected by our five senses.[1] All sensory stimuli enter the brain as a stream of electrical impulses that result from neurons firing in sequence along the specific sensory pathways. Thus, the brain does not see light waves or hear sound waves. Rather, certain specialized modules of neurons process the electrical impulses created by the light and sound waves into what the brain *perceives* as vision and sound.

The senses do not all contribute equally to our learning. Over the course of our lives, sight, hearing, and touch (including kinesthetic experiences) contribute the most to new learning. Our senses constantly collect tens of thousands of bits of information from the environment every second, even while we sleep. That number may seem very high, but think about it. The nerve endings all over your skin are detecting the clothes you are wearing. Your ears are hearing sounds around you, the rods and cones in your eyes are picking up this print as they move across the page, you may still be tasting recent food or drink, and your nose may be detecting an odor. Put these bits of data together and it is easy to see how they can add up. Of course, the stimuli must be strong enough for the senses to record them.

Sensory Register

Imagine if the brain had to give its full attention to all those bits of data at once; we would blow the cerebral equivalent of a fuse! Fortunately, the brain has evolved a system for screening all these data to determine their importance to the individual. This system involves the *thalamus* (located in the limbic system) and a portion of the brain stem known as the *reticular activation system* (RAS). This system, which I call the *sensory register*, is drawn in the model as the side view of venetian blind slats (see the slashes in Figure 2.1); the reason will become clear later.

All incoming sensory information (except smell) is sent first to the thalamus, which briefly monitors the strength and nature of the sensory impulses for survival content and, in just milliseconds (a millisecond is 1/1,000th of a second), uses the individual's past experiences to determine the data's degree of importance. Most of the data signals are unimportant, so the sensory register allows them to drop out of the processing system. Have you ever noticed how you can be in a room studying while there is construction noise outside? Eventually, it seems that you no longer hear the noise. Your sensory register is blocking these repetitive stimuli, allowing your conscious brain to focus on more important things. This process is called *perceptual* or *sensory filtering*, and, to a large degree, we are consciously unaware of it.

Short-Term Memory

As researchers gain greater insight into the brain's memory processes, they have had to devise and revise terms that describe the various stages of memory. As of this printing, the term *short-term memory* is used by cognitive neuroscientists to include all of the early steps of temporary memory that lead to stable long-term memory. Short-term memory primarily includes *immediate memory* and *working memory*.[2]

Immediate Memory

Sensory data that are not lost move from the thalamus to the sensory processing areas of the cortex and through the first of two temporary memories, now called *immediate memory*. If you took a psychology course more than a decade ago, you learned that we had two memories—one short-term (temporary) memory and one long-term (permanent) memory. The idea that we seem to have two temporary memories is recent. It is a way of explaining how the brain deals with large amounts of sensory data, and how we can continue to process these stimuli subconsciously for many seconds beyond the sensory register's time limits.

The immediate memory area is represented in the model as a clipboard, a place where we put information briefly until we make a decision on how to dispose of it. Immediate memory operates subconsciously or consciously and holds data for up to about 30 seconds.[3] The individual's experiences determine its importance. If the datum is of little or no importance within this time frame, it drops out of the system. For example, when you look up the telephone number of the local pizza parlor, you usually can remember it just long enough to make the call. After that, the number is of no further importance and drops out of immediate memory.

Examples of Immediate Memory at Work. Here are two other examples to understand how the processing occurs up to this point. Suppose you decide to wear a new pair of shoes to work today. They are snug, so when you put them on, the receptors in your skin send pain impulses to the sensory register. For a short time you feel discomfort. After a while, however, as you get involved with work, you do not notice the discomfort signals anymore. The sensory register is now blocking the impulses from reaching your consciousness. Should you move your foot in a way that causes the shoe to pinch, however, the sensory register will pass this pain stimulus along to your consciousness and you become aware of it.

Another example: You are sitting in a classroom and a police car with its siren wailing passes by. Experience recalls that a siren is an important sound. Signals from the sensory register pass the auditory stimuli over to immediate memory. If over the next few seconds the sound of the siren gets fainter, experience signals the immediate memory that the sound is of no further importance and the auditory data are blocked and dropped from the system. All this is happening subconsciously while your attention is focused on something else. If asked about the sound later, you will not remember it. You cannot recall what you have not stored.

Suppose, on the other hand, that the siren sound gets louder and suddenly stops, followed by another siren that gets louder and stops. Experience will now signal that the sounds are important because they are nearby, may affect your survival, and therefore require your attention. At this point, the now-important auditory data move rapidly into working memory for conscious processing.

Threats and Emotions Affect Memory Processing. This last example illustrates another characteristic of brain processing: There is a hierarchy of response to sensory input (Figure 2.2). Any input that is of higher priority diminishes the processing of data of lower priority. The brain's main job is to help its owner survive. Thus, data interpreted as posing a threat to the survival of the individual, such as a burning odor, a snarling dog, or someone threatening bodily injury, are processed immediately. Upon receiving the stimulus, the reticular activating system sends a rush of adrenaline throughout the brain, shutting down all unnecessary activity and directing the brain's attention to the source of the stimulus.

Emotional data also take high priority. When an individual responds emotionally to a situation, the older limbic system (stimulated by the amygdala) takes a major role and the complex cerebral processes are suspended. We have all had experiences when anger, fear of the unknown, or joy quickly overcame our rational thoughts. This override of conscious thought can be strong enough to cause temporary inability to talk ("I was dumbfounded") or move ("I froze"). This happens because the hippocampus is susceptible to stress hormones which can inhibit cognitive functioning and long-term memory.

Under certain conditions, emotions can enhance memory by causing the release of hormones that stimulate the amygdala to signal brain regions to strengthen memory. Strong emotions can shut down conscious processing during the event while enhancing our memory of it. Emotion is a powerful and misunderstood force in learning and memory. Another way of stating the situation illustrated in Figure 2.2 is that before students will turn their attention to cognitive learning (the curriculum), they must feel physically safe and emotionally secure.

> **How a person "feels" about a learning situation determines the amount of attention devoted to it.**

Daniel Goleman's 1995 book, *Emotional Intelligence*, summarized the breakthroughs in understanding the strong influence that emotions have as we grow and learn. How a person "feels" about a learning situation determines the amount of attention devoted to it. Emotions interact with reason to support or inhibit learning. To be successful learners and productive citizens, we need to know how to use our emotions intelligently.

Over the years, most teacher-training classes have told prospective teachers to focus on reason and avoid emotions in their lessons. Now, we need to enlighten educators about how emotions consistently affect attention and learning.

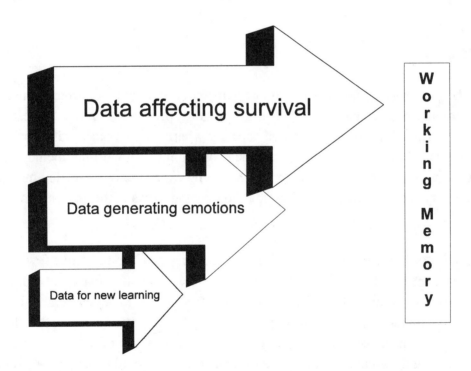

Figure 2.2 *Data that affect survival and data that generate emotions are processed ahead of data for new cognitive learning.*

> **Students must feel physically safe and emotionally secure before they can focus on the curriculum.**

Districts must ensure that schools are free of weapons and violence. Teachers can then promote emotional security in the classroom by establishing a positive climate that encourages students to take appropriate risks. Students must sense that the teacher wants to help them be right rather than catch them being wrong.

Moreover, superintendents and board members need to examine their actions, which set the emotional climate of a district. Is it a place where people want to come to work? Does the district reward or frown on appropriate risk taking?

> **We may need to teach students how to handle their emotions.**

We also have to explore what and how we teach students about their emotions. Goleman suggests we teach about controlling impulses, delaying gratification, expressing feelings, managing relationships, and reducing stress. Students should recognize that they can manage their emotions for greater productivity and can develop emotional skills for greater success in life.

Working Memory

Working memory is the second temporary memory and the place where conscious, rather than subconscious, processing occurs.[4] The information processing model represents working memory as a work table, a place of limited capacity where we can build, take apart, or rework ideas for eventual storage somewhere else. When something is in working memory, it generally captures our focus and demands our attention. Scanning experiments show that most of working memory's activity occurs in the frontal lobes, although other parts of the brain are often called into action.

Capacity of Working Memory. Working memory can handle only a few items at once. This functional capacity changes with age. Table 2.1 shows how the capacity of working memory increases as one passes through the major growth spurts in cognitive development.[5]

Preschool infants can deal with about two items of information at once. Preadolescents can handle three to seven items, with an average of five. Through adolescence, further cognitive expansion occurs and the capacity increases to a range of five to nine, with an average of seven. For most people, that number remains constant throughout life.

Let's test this notion. Get a pencil and a piece of paper. When ready, stare at the number below for seven seconds, then look away and write it down. Ready? Go.

9217053

Check the number you wrote down. Chances are you got it right. Let's try it again with the same rules. Stare at the number below for seven seconds, then look away and write it down. Ready? Go.

4915082637

Again, check the number you wrote down. Did you get all 10 of the digits in the correct sequence? Probably not. Because the digits were random, you had to treat each digit as a single item, and your working memory just ran out of functional capacity.

This limited capacity explains why we have to memorize a song or a poem in stages. We start with the first group of lines by repeating them frequently (a process called *rehearsal*). Then we memorize the next lines and repeat them with the first group, and so on. It is possible to increase the number of items within the functional capacity of working memory through a process called *chunking*. This process will be explained in the next chapter.

Table 2.1 Changes in Capacity of Working Memory With Age			
Approximate Age Range in Years	Capacity of Working Memory in Number of Chunks		
	Minimum	Maximum	Average
Younger Than 5	1	3	2
Between 5 and 14	3	7	5
14 and Older	5	9	7

Time Limits of Working Memory. Working memory is temporary and can deal with items for only a limited time. How long is that time? This intriguing question has been clinically investigated for over a century, starting with the work of Hermann Ebbinghaus (1850-1909) during the 1880s. He concluded that we can process items intently in working memory (he called it short-term memory) for up to 45 minutes before becoming fatigued. Because Ebbinghaus mainly used himself as the subject to measure retention in laboratory conditions, the results are not readily transferable to the average high school classroom.

Peter Russell (1979) shows this time span to be much shorter and age dependent. For preadolescents, it is more likely to be 5 to 10 minutes, and for adolescents and adults, 10 to 20 minutes. These are average times, and it is important to understand what the numbers mean. An adolescent (or adult) normally can process an item in working memory intently for 10 to 20 minutes before fatigue or boredom with that item occurs and the individual's focus drifts. For focus to continue, there must be some change in the way the individual is dealing with the item. For example, the person may switch from thinking about it to physically using it, or making different connections to other learnings. If something else is not done with the item, it is likely to drop from the working memory.

This is not to say that some items cannot remain in working memory for hours, or perhaps days. Sometimes, we have an item that remains unresolved—a question whose answer we seek or a troublesome family or work decision that must be made. These items can remain in working memory, continually commanding some attention and, if of sufficient importance, interfere with our accurate processing of other information.

Criteria for Long-Term Storage

Now comes the most important decision of all: Should the items in working memory move to long-term storage for future recall, or should they drop out of the system? This is an important decision because we cannot recall what we have not stored. Yet teachers teach with the hope that students will retain the learning objective for future use. So, if the learner is ever to recall this information in the future, it has to be stored.

What criteria does the working memory use to make that decision? Figure 2.2 can help us here. Information that has survival value is quickly stored. You don't want to have to learn every day that walking in front of a moving bus or touching a hot stove can injure you. Emotional experiences also have a high likelihood of being permanently stored. We tend to remember the best and worst things that happened to us.

> **Information is most likely to get stored if it makes sense and has meaning.**

But in classrooms, where the survival and emotional elements are minimal or absent, other factors come into play. It seems that the working memory connects with the learner's past experiences and asks just two questions to determine whether an item is saved or rejected. They are: "Does this make *sense*?" and "Does this have *meaning*?" Imagine the many hours that go into planning and teaching lessons, and it all comes down to these two questions! Let's review them.

"Does this make sense?" This question refers to whether the learner can understand the item on the basis of experience. Does it "fit" into what the learner knows about how the world works? When a student says, "I don't understand," it means the student is having a problem making sense of the learning.

"Does it have meaning?" This question refers to whether the item is *relevant* to the learner. For what purpose should the learner remember it? Meaning, of course, is a very personal thing and is greatly influenced by that person's experiences. The same item can have great meaning for one student and none for another. When a student asks "Why do I have to know this?" or "When will I ever use this?", it indicates the student has not, for whatever reason, accepted this learning as relevant.

Here are two examples to explain the difference between sense and meaning. Suppose I tell a 15-year-old student that the minimum age for getting a driver's license in his state is age 16, but it is 17 in a neighboring state. He can understand this information, so it satisfies the sense criterion. But the age in his own state is much more relevant to him, because this is where he will apply for his license. Chances are high that he will remember his own state's minimum age (it has both sense *and* meaning) but will forget that of the neighboring state (it has sense but lacks meaning).

Suppose you are a teacher and you read in the newspaper that the average salary for dock workers last year was $52,000, whereas the average for teachers was $38,000. Both numbers make sense to you, but the average teacher's salary has more meaning because you are in that profession.

Whenever the learner's working memory decides that an item does not make sense or have meaning, the probability of it being stored is extremely low (see Figure 2.3). If either sense or meaning is present, the probability of storage increases significantly (assuming, you remember, no survival or emotional component). If both sense *and* meaning are present, the likelihood of long-term storage is very high.

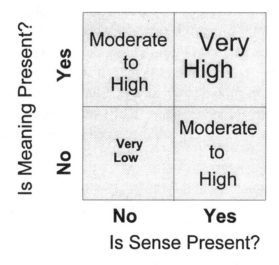

Figure 2.3 *The probability of storing information varies with the degree of sense and meaning that are present.*

Relationship of Sense to Meaning

Sense and meaning are independent of each other. Thus, it is possible to remember an item because it makes sense but has no meaning. If you have ever played *Trivial Pursuit*, you may have been surprised at some of the answers you knew. If another player asked how you knew that answer, you may have replied, "I don't know. It was just there!" This happens to all of us. During our lifetime, we pick up bits of information that made sense at the time and, although they were trivial and had no meaning, they made their way into our long-term storage.

It is also possible to remember an item that makes no sense but has meaning. My sixth-grade teacher once asked the class to memorize Lewis Carroll's nonsense poem "Jabberwocky." It begins, *Twas brillig, and the slithy toves did gyre and gimble in the wabe.* The poem made no sense to us sixth graders, but when the teacher said that she would call on each of us the next day to recite it before the class, it suddenly had meaning. Since I didn't want to make a fool of myself in front of my peers, I memorized it and recited it correctly the next day, even though I had no idea what the sense of it was.

Brain scans have shown that when new learning is readily comprehensible (sense) and can be connected to past experiences (meaning), there is substantially more cerebral activity followed by dramatically improved retention.[6]

Meaning Is More Significant

Of the two criteria, meaning has the greater impact on the probability that information will be stored. Think of all the television programs you have watched that are NOT stored, even though you spent one or two hours with the program. The show's content or story line made sense to you, but if meaning was absent, you just did not save it. It was *entertainment* and no learning resulted from it. You might have remembered a summary of the show or whether it was enjoyable or boring, but not the details. On the other hand, if the story reminded you of a personal experience, then meaning was present and you were more likely to remember some details of the program.

> **Test Question No. 2:** Learners who can perform a new learning task well are likely to retain it.
>
> **Answer:** False. We cannot presume that because a learner performs a new learning well, it will be permanently stored. Sense and/or meaning must be present in some degree for storage to occur.

Now think of this process in the classroom. Every day, students listen to things that make sense but lack meaning. They may diligently follow the teacher's instructions to perform a task repeatedly, and may even get the correct answers, but if they have not found meaning after the learning episode, there is little likelihood of long-term storage. Mathematics teachers are often frustrated by this. They see students using a certain formula to solve problems correctly one day, but they cannot remember how to do it the next day. If the process was not stored, the information is treated as brand new again!

Sometimes, when students ask why they need to know something, the teacher's response is, "Because it's going to be on the test." This response adds little meaning to a learning. Students resort to writing the learning in a notebook so that it is preserved in writing, but not in memory. We wonder the next day why they forgot the lesson.

Effect of Past Experiences. Past experiences always influence new learning. What we already know acts as a filter, helping us attend to those things that have meaning (i.e., relevancy) and discard those that don't. Meaning, therefore, has a great impact on whether information and skills will be learned and stored. If students have not found meaning by the end of a learning episode, there is little likelihood that much will be remembered.

> *Past experiences always influence new learning.*

Teachers spend about 90 percent of their planning time devising lessons so that students will *understand* the learning objective (i.e., make sense of it). But to convince a learner's brain to persist with that objective, teachers need to be more mindful of helping students establish *meaning*. We should remember that what was meaningful for us as children may not be necessarily meaningful for children today.

If we expect students to find meaning, we need to be certain that today's curriculum contains connections to *their* past experiences, not just ours. Further, the enormous size and the strict separation of secondary curriculum areas do little to help students find the time to make relevant connections between and among subjects. Helping students to make connections between subject areas by integrating the curriculum increases meaning and retention, especially when students recognize a future use for the new learning. Meaning is so powerful that most states prohibit trial lawyers from using what is dubbed the "golden rule" argument. It asks the jury, "If you were in this person's situation, what would you have done?"

Long-Term Storage

Storing occurs when the hippocampus encodes information and sends it to one or more long-term storage areas. The encoding process takes time and usually occurs during deep sleep.

While learners may *seem* to have acquired the new information or skill in a lesson, there is no guarantee that storage will be permanent after the lesson. How do we know if retention has occurred? If the student can accurately recall the learning after a specific period of time has passed, we say that the learning has been retained. Because research on retention shows that the greatest loss of newly acquired information or a skill occurs within 18 to 24 hours, the 24-hour period is a reasonable guideline for determining if information was transferred into long-term storage. If a learner cannot recall new learning after 24 hours, there is a high probability that it was not permanently stored and, thus, can never be recalled. This point has implications for how we test students for retention of previously learned material. See the **Practitioner's Corner** at the end of this chapter on how to test whether information is in long-term storage (p. 58).

Sometimes, we store only the gist of an experience, not the specifics. This may occur after watching a movie. We store a generalization about the plot but few, if any, details.

Test Question No. 3: Reviewing material just before a test is a good practice to determine how much has been retained in long-term storage.

Answer: False. Reviewing material just before a test allows students to enter the material into working memory for immediate use. Thus, the test cannot verify that what the learner recalls actually came from long-term storage.

The long-term storage areas are represented in the model (Figure 2.1) as file cabinets—places where information is kept in some type of order. Although there are three file cabinets in the diagram for simplicity, we do not know how many long-term storage sites actually are in the brain. Memories are not stored as a whole in one place. Different parts of a memory are stored in various sites which reassemble when the memory is recalled. These virtual assembly sites are sometimes referred to as *convergence zones*. Researchers such as Steven Rose (1992) believe that long-term memory is a dynamic, interactive system that activates storage areas distributed across the brain to retrieve and reconstruct memories.

Long-Term Memory and Long-Term Storage

This is a good place to explain the difference between the terms *long-term memory* and *long-term storage*. As used here, long-term memory refers to the process of storing and retrieving information. Long-term storage refers to where in the brain the memories are kept.

The Cognitive Belief System

The total of all that is in our long-term storage areas forms the basis for our view of the world around us. This information helps us to make sense out of events, to understand the laws of nature, to recognize cause and effect, and to form decisions about goodness, truth, and beauty. This total construct of how we see the world is called the *cognitive belief system.* It is shown in the information processing model as a large triangle extending beyond the long-term storage areas (file cabinets). It is drawn this way to remind us that the thoughts and understandings that arise from the long-term storage data are greater than the sum of the individual items. In other words, one marvelous quality of the human brain is its ability to combine individual items in many different ways. As we accumulate more items, the number of possible combinations grows exponentially.

Because no two of us have the same data in our long-term storage (not even identical twins raised in the same environment have identical data sets), no two of us perceive the world in exactly the same way. People can put the same experiences together in many different ways. To be sure, there are areas of agreement: Gravity, for example (few rational people would dispute its effects), or inertia, since most people have experienced the lurch forward or backward when a moving vehicle rapidly changes speed. There can be strong

> **The cognitive belief system is our view of the world around us and how it works.**

disagreement, however, about what makes an object or person beautiful, or an act justified. The persistent debates over abortion and capital punishment are testimony to the wide range of perspectives that people have over any issue. These differences reflect the ways individuals use the experiences in their long-term storage areas to interpret the world around them.

Here is a simple example of how people's experiences can cause them to interpret the same information differently. Close your eyes and form the mental image of an "old bat." Go ahead, try it! What picture comes to mind? For some baseball fans, it might be a marred wooden club that has seen too many games. A zoologist, however, might picture an aging fruit bat as it flies haltingly among the trees. Still others might recall an old hag whose complaining made their lives unpleasant. Here are at least three very different images generated by the same two words, each one formed by individuals whose experiences are different from the others.

Self-Concept

Deep within the cognitive belief system lies the *self-concept*. While the cognitive belief system portrays the way we see the world, the self-concept describes the way we view *ourselves* in that world. I might conceptualize myself as a good softball player, an above-average student, or a poor mathematician. These and a long list of other descriptions form part of a person's self-concept.

The self-concept is represented in the information processing model (Figure 2.1) as a face and is placed at the apex of the triangle to emphasize its importance. *Self-concept* is used here as a neutral term that can run the gamut from very positive to very negative (Figure 2.4). The face on the diagram has a smile, indicating a positive self-concept; but for some people, the face might have a frown because they may not see themselves as positive beings in their world. Emotions play an important role in forming a person's self-concept.

Self-Concept

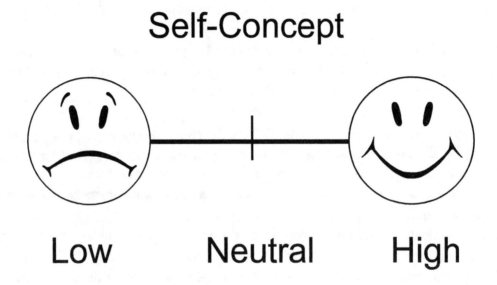

Low   Neutral   High

Figure 2.4 Self-concept describes how we see ourselves in the world. It can range from very low to very high and vary with different learning situations.

Self-Concept and Past Experiences

Our self-concept is shaped by our past experiences. Some of our experiences, such as passing a difficult test or getting recognition for a job well done, raised our self-concept. Other experiences, such as receiving a reprimand or failing to accomplish a task, lowered our self-concept. These experiences produced strong emotional reactions that the brain's amygdala encoded and stored with the cognitive event. These emotional cues are so strong that we often reexperience the original emotion each time we recall the event.

Accepting or Rejecting New Learning

Remember that the sensory register and temporary memory systems use past experiences as the guide for determining the importance of incoming stimuli to the individual. Thus, if an individual is in a new learning situation and past experience signals the sensory register that prior encounters with this information were successful, then the information is very likely to pass along to working memory. The learner now consciously recognizes that there were successes with this information and focuses on it for further processing. But if past experiences produced failure, then the sensory register is likely to block the incoming data, just as venetian blinds are closed to block light. The learner resists being part of the unwanted learning experience and resorts to some other cerebral activity, internal or external, to avoid the situation. In effect, the learner's self-concept has closed off the receptivity to the new information. As mentioned earlier in discussing the hierarchy of data processing, when a concept struggles with an emotion, the emotion almost always wins. Of course, it is possible for the rational system (frontal lobe) to override emotions, but that usually takes time and conscious effort.

> **People will participate in learning activities that have yielded success for them and avoid those that have produced failure.**

Let us use an example to explain this important phenomenon. Someone who was a very successful student in mathematics remembers how that success boosted self-concept. As a result, the individual now feels confident when faced with basic mathematical problems. On the other hand, for someone who was a poor mathematics student, lack of success would lower self-concept. Consequently, such an individual will avoid dealing with mathematical problems whenever possible. People will participate in learning activities that have yielded success for them and avoid those that have produced failure.

Dealing With Self-Concept

Students who experience self-concept shutdown in the classroom often give signs of their withdrawal—folding their arms, losing themselves in other work, or causing distraction. Too often, teachers deal with this withdrawal by reteaching the material, usually slower and louder. But they are attacking the problem from the front end of the information processing system, and this is rarely successful. It is the equivalent of putting a brighter light outside the closed venetian blinds, hoping the light will penetrate. If the blinds are fully closed and effective, no light will get through, regardless of how bright it may be.

The better intervention is to deal with the learner's emotions and convince the learner to allow the perceptual register to open the blinds and pass the information along. But since the self-concept controls the blinds, the learner must believe that participating in the learning situation will produce new successes rather than repeat past failures. When teachers provide these successes, they encourage students to open the sensory register and, ultimately, to participate and achieve in the once-avoided learning process. In short, the self-concept is an important participant in controlling the feedback loop and in determining how the individual will respond to almost any new learning situation. Recognizing this connection gives teachers new insight on how to deal with reluctant learners.

This completes our trip through the information processing model. Remember that the brain is a parallel processor and deals with many items simultaneously. Even though it rejects much data, it always stores some. The next chapter will examine the nature of memory and the factors that determine and help in the retention of learning.

PRACTITIONER'S CORNER

Walking Through the Brain

Directions: In this activity, students/participants will assume the roles of the different parts of the information processing model.

1. Each participant gets one of the following assignments:

> 3–4 persons for the **sensory register**
> 1 person for the **immediate memory**
> 1 person for the **working memory**
> 3–4 persons for the **long-term storage**
> rest of the group represents **incoming information**

2. In an open area of the classroom, the participants should arrange themselves in a pattern that approximates the information processing model shown earlier in Figure 2.1.

3. All participants, except those representing **incoming information**, briefly explain their role and function in the model.

4. The participants representing incoming information then move through the model one at a time, explaining what is happening at each stage.

5. **Variations**: Replay the activity demonstrating how information can be accepted or rejected by the sensory register, immediate memory, and working memory. One of the participants representing **long-term storage** can also represent the feedback loop of past experiences.

6. After demonstrating several different possibilities, discuss how this activity may have enhanced your understanding of the model. Note the positive effect that kinesthetic activities can have on learning new material.

PRACTITIONER'S CORNER

Redesigning the Information Processing Model

This activity gives the students/participants the opportunity to redesign the information processing model explained in this chapter.

Directions: Use the area below to redesign the information processing model using **different** metaphors (e.g., a sports game, taking a vacation, cooking recipe), for each of the major parts of the model. Be prepared to explain the metaphors and why you chose them.

PRACTITIONER'S CORNER

Sensory Preferences and Learning Style

Although we use all five senses to collect information from our environment, they do not contribute equally to our knowledge base. Most people do not use sight, hearing, and touch equally during learning. Just as most people develop a left- or right-handed preference, they also develop preferences for certain senses as they gather information from their environment. Some people have a preference for learning by sight, for example. They are called *visual* learners. Others who use hearing as the preferred sense are known as *auditory* learners. Still others who prefer touch or whole-body involvement in their learning are called *kinesthetic* learners. Sensory (also called *modality)* preferences are an important component of an individual's learning style. Teachers need to

- **Understand** that students with different sensory preferences will behave differently during learning.

- **Recognize** that they tend to teach the way they learn. A teacher who is a strong auditory learner will prefer this modality when teaching. Students who also are strong auditory learners will feel comfortable with this teacher's methods, but visual learners can have difficulty in maintaining focus. They will doodle or look at other materials to satisfy their visual craving.

- **Note,** similarly, that students with auditory preferences want to talk about their learning and can become frustrated with teachers who use primarily visual strategies. Strong kinesthetic learners require movement while learning or they become restless —tapping their pencils, squirming in their seats, or walking around the room.

- **Avoid** misinterpreting these variations in learning style behavior as inattention or as intentional misbehavior. The variations may, in fact, represent the natural responses of learners with different and strong preferences.

- **Understand** that a teacher's own learning style and sensory preferences can affect learning and teaching. Teachers should design lessons that include activities to address all sensory preference and learning styles.

PRACTITIONER'S CORNER

Determining Your Sensory Preferences

This checklist indicates your sensory preference(s). It is designed for adults and is one of many that are available. You should not rely on just one checklist for self-assessment. Remember that sensory preferences are usually evident only during prolonged and complex learning tasks.

Directions: For each item, circle "**A**" if you **agree** that the statement describes you most of the time. Circle "**D**" if you **disagree** that the statement describes you most of the time. Move quickly through the questions. Your first response is usually the more accurate one.

1. I prefer reading a story rather than listening to someone tell it. A (D)

2. I would rather watch television than listen to the radio. (A) D

3. I remember names better than faces. A (D)

4. I like classrooms with lots of posters and pictures around the room. (A) D

5. The appearance of my handwriting is important to me. (A) D

6. I think more often in pictures. A D

7. I am distracted by visual disorder or movement. (A) D

8. I have difficulty remembering directions that were told to me. (A) D

9. I would rather watch athletic events than participate in them. A (D)

10. I tend to organize my thoughts by writing them down. (A) D

11. My facial expression is a good indicator of my emotions. (A) D

12. I tend to remember names better than faces. A (D)

13. I would enjoy taking part in dramatic events like plays.   A   D

14. I tend to subvocalize and think in sounds.   A   D

15. I am easily distracted by sounds.   A   D

16. I easily forget what I read unless I talk about it.   A   D

17. I would rather listen to the radio than watch television.   A   D

18. My handwriting is not very good.   A   D

19. When faced with a problem, I tend to talk it through.   A   D

20. I express my emotions verbally.   A   D

21. I would rather be in a group discussion than read about a topic.   A   D

22. I prefer talking on the phone rather than writing a letter to someone.   A   D

23. I would rather participate in athletic events than watch them.   A   D

24. I prefer going to museums where I can touch the exhibits.   A   D

25. My handwriting deteriorates when the space becomes smaller.   A   D

26. My mental pictures are usually accompanied by movement.   A   D

27. I like being outdoors and doing things like biking, camping, swimming, hiking, etc.   A   D

28. I remember best what was done rather what was seen or talked about.   A   D

29. When faced with a problem, I often select the solution involving the greatest activity.   A   D

30. I like to make models or other hand-crafted items.   A   D

31. I would rather do experiments than read about them.   Ⓐ D

32. My body language is a good indicator of my emotions.   Ⓐ D

33. I have difficulty remembering verbal directions if I have not done the   Ⓐ D
    activity before.

Interpreting Your Score

Total the number of "A" responses in items 1–11:   _____
This is your visual score.

Total the number of "A" responses in items 12–22:   _____
This is your auditory score.

Total the number of "A" responses in items 23–33:   _____
This is your tactile/kinesthetic score.

If you scored a lot higher in any one area: This sense is *very probably* your preference during a protracted and complex learning situation.

If you scored a lot lower in any one area: This sense is *not likely* to be your preference in a learning situation.

If you have similar scores in all three areas: You can learn things in almost any way they are presented.

Reflections

A. What was your preferred sense? Were you surprised?

B. How does this preference show up in your daily life?

C. How does this preference show up in your teaching?

PRACTITIONER'S CORNER

Developing a Classroom Climate
Conducive to Learning

Learning occurs more easily in environments free from threat or intimidation. Whenever a student detects a threat, thoughtful processing gives way to emotion or survival reactions. Experienced teachers have seen this in the classroom. Under pressure to give a quick response, the student begins to stumble, stabs at answers, gets frustrated or angry, and may even resort to violence.

There are ways to deal with questions and answers that reduce the fear of giving a wrong answer. The teacher could:

● Supply the question to which the wrong answer belongs: "You would be right if I had asked ..."

● Give the student a prompt that leads to the correct answer.

● Ask another student to help.

Threats to students loom continuously in the classroom. The teacher's capacity to humiliate, embarrass, reject, and punish all constitute perceived threats. Many students even see grading more as a punitive than as a rewarding process. Students perceive threats in varying degrees, but the presence of a threat in *any* significant degree impedes learning. One's thinking and learning functions operate fully only when one feels secure.

Teachers can make their classrooms better learning environments by avoiding threats (even subtle intimidation) and by establishing democratic climates in which students are treated fairly and feel free to express their opinions during discussions. In these environments students:

● Develop trust in the teacher

● Exhibit more positive behaviors

– Continued –

Developing a Classroom Climate Conducive to Learning—Continued

- Are less likely to be disruptive

- Show greater support for school policy

- Sense that thinking is encouraged and nurtured

For Further Discussion

- What kinds of emotions in school could interfere with cognitive processing (i.e., have a negative effect on learning)?

  _____

  _____

- What strategies and structures can schools and teachers use to limit the threat and negative effects of these emotions?

  _____

  _____

- What factors in schools can foster emotions in students that promote learning (i.e., have a positive effect)?

  _____

  _____

- What strategies have you used to encourage the positive emotions that promote learning?

  _____

  _____

PRACTITIONER'S CORNER

Using Humor to Enhance Climate and Promote Retention

Humor has many benefits when used frequently and appropriately in the classroom and other school settings.

Physiological Benefits

- **More Oxygen**. The brain needs oxygen and glucose for fuel. When we laugh, we get more oxygen in the bloodstream, so the brain is better fueled.

- **Endorphin Surge**. Laughter causes the release of *endorphins* in the blood. Endorphins are the body's natural painkillers, and they also give the person a feeling of euphoria. In other words, the person enjoys the moment in body as well as in mind.

Psychological, Sociological, and Educational Benefits

- **Gets Attention**. The first thing a teacher has to do when starting a lesson is to get the students' attention or focus. Because the normal human brain loves to laugh, starting with a humorous tale (such as a joke, pun, or story) gets the learner's attention.

- **Creates a Positive Climate**. When people laugh together, they bond and a community spirit emerges—all positive forces for an climate conducive to learning.

- **Increases Retention**. We know that emotions enhance retention, so the positive feelings that result from laughter increase the probability that students will remember what they learned.

– Continued –

Using Humor to Enhance Climate and Promote Retention—Continued

- **Improves Everyone's Mental Health**. Schools and all their occupants are under more stress than ever. Taking time to laugh can relieve that stress and give the staff and students better mental attitude with which to accomplish their tasks. Let's take our work seriously and ourselves lightly.

- **Is an Effective Discipline Tool**. Good-natured humor (not teasing or sarcasm) can be an effective way of reminding students of the rules without raising tension in the classroom. Teachers who use appropriate humor are more likeable and students have a more positive feeling toward them. Discipline problems, therefore, are less likely to occur.

Using Humor as Part of Lessons. Humor should not be limited to an opening joke or story. Because of its value as an attention-getter and retention strategy, look for ways to use humor within the context of the learning objective. Droz and Ellis (1996) give many helpful suggestions on how to get students to use humor in lessons on writing, mathematics, science, and history.

Administrators and Humor. Administrators also need to remember the value of humor in their relationships with staff, students, and parents. As leaders, they set the example; in meetings and other settings, they can show that humor and laughter are acceptable in schools and classrooms.

Some Barriers to Humor in Classrooms

- **"I'm Not Funny."** Some teachers want to use humor in the classroom but don't perceive themselves as jokesters. They'll say: "I'm just not funny" or "I can't tell a joke." But the teacher doesn't have to be funny, just the material—and there's plenty of it. Books on humor are available in local stores, and don't forget that students themselves often provide humor by their responses in class and answers on tests. Be certain that you use this material appropriately, avoiding teasing or sarcasm.

- **"Students Won't Enjoy It."** Secondary teachers, particularly, believe that students won't find humor in corny jokes or that they are too sophisticated to laugh. But everyone likes to laugh (or groan) at humor. I suggest starting

– Continued –

Using Humor to Enhance Climate and Promote Retention—Continued

each class period with humor for three weeks, then stopping. I'm certain that students will say, "Hey, where's the joke?"—evidence that they *were* listening.

- **"It Takes Too Much Time."** This is a common concern. Secondary teachers often feel so pressured to cover material that they are reluctant to give time to what may seem like a frivolous activity. On the other hand, humor is an *efficient* as well as effective way to gain students' attention and improve retention of learning. It really is a useful investment of time.

Avoid Sarcasm. All of the wonderful benefits mentioned above are the result of using wholesome humor that everyone can enjoy, and not sarcasm, which is inevitably destructive to someone. Even some well-intentioned teachers say, "Oh, I know my students very well, so they can take sarcasm." More than ever, today's students are coming to school looking for emotional support. Sarcasm is one of the factors that can undermine that support and turn students against their peers and the school. Besides, there are plenty of sources of good humor without sarcasm.

PRACTITIONER'S CORNER

Increasing Processing Time Through Motivation

Working memory is a temporary memory, so items have a limited time for processing. But the longer an item is processed (or rehearsed), the greater the probability that sense and meaning may be found, and therefore, that retention will occur. One way to increase processing time is through motivation, which is essentially an emotional response. Recent research has validated long-standing beliefs that motivation is a key to the amount of attention devoted to a learning situation. Marian Diamond and Janet Hopson (1998), Raymond Wlodkowski and Judith Jaynes (1990), and Madeline Hunter (1982) recognize the importance of motivation and suggest a few ideas for teachers to consider:

- **Generate Interest.** If the learner is interested in the item, then the processing time can be extended significantly because the learner is dealing with the item in different ways and making new connections with past learnings that once were also of interest. The working memory is seeking ways to use this new learning to enhance the usefulness of the past learning. We all know students who won't give us five minutes of their undivided attention in class, but who spend hours working on a stamp collection or repairing a carburetor.

  Teachers can identify these interests by having their students complete interest inventories at the beginning of the school year. The information gathered from these surveys can help teachers design lessons that include references to student interests as often as possible. Guidance counselors can provide information on the types and sources of interest inventories.

- **Establish Accountability.** When learners believe they will be held accountable for new learning, processing time increases. High school students have little difficulty staying on task in driver education classes. Not only do they have interest but they also know they will be legally accountable for their knowledge and skills long after they complete the license tests.

– Continued –

Increasing Processing Time Through Motivation—Continued

● **Provide Feedback.** When students get prompt, specific, and corrective feedback on the results of their thinking, they are more likely to continue processing, making corrections, and persisting until successful completion. Frequent brief quizzes that are carefully corrected and returned promptly are much more valuable learning tools than the unit test, and are more likely to help students be successful. This success will improve self-concept and encourage them to try more difficult tasks. Computers are motivating because they provide immediate and objective feedback and allow students to evaluate their progress and understand their level of competence.

Another effective strategy suggested by Hunter (1982) for increasing processing time through motivation is called *level of concern*. This refers to how much the student cares about the learning. We used to think that if the students had anxiety about learning, then little or no learning occurred, but there is helpful anxiety (desire to do well) and there is harmful anxiety (feeling threatened). Having anxiety about your job performance will usually get you to put forth more effort to obtain positive results. When you are concerned about being more effective (helpful anxiety), you are likely to learn and try new strategies. This is an example of how emotions can increase learning.

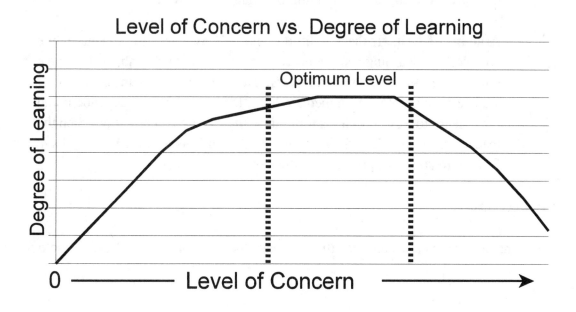

– Continued –

Increasing Processing Time Through Motivation—Continued

The graph shows that as the level of concern increases, so does the degree of learning. Of course, if the stress level gets too high, we go past the optimum level. We shift our focus to the emotions generated by the stress, and learning fades.

Students also need a certain level of concern to stimulate their efforts to learn. When there is no concern, there is little or no learning. If there is too much concern, anxiety shuts down the learning process and adverse emotions take over. The teacher then has to seek the level of concern that produces the optimum processing time and learning. Hunter (1982) offers four ways to raise or lower the level of concern in a learning situation.

- **Consequences.** Teachers raise the level of concern when they say "This is going to be on the test," and lower it with, "Knowing this will help you learn the next set of skills more easily."

- **Visibility.** Standing next to a student who is off-task will raise that student's concern; moving away from an anxious student will lower concern. Telling students their work will be displayed can also raise concern.

- **Amount of Time.** Giving students only a little time to complete a learning task will raise concern; extending the time will lower it.

- **Amount of Help.** If there is little or no help available to students while completing a learning task, concern rises. On the other hand, if they have quick access to help, concern lowers. This can be a problem, however. If students can always get immediate help, they may become dependent and never learn to solve problems for themselves. There comes a time when the teacher needs to reduce the help and tell the students to use what they have learned to solve the problem on their own.

Reflections

A. What are some class activities that **increase** the level of concern beyond the optimum level?

B. What strategies **lower** the level of concern raised by the activities in your answers to A above?

PRACTITIONER'S CORNER

Creating Meaning in New Learning

Meaning refers to the relevancy that students attach to new learning. Meaning isn't inherent in content, but rather is the result of how the students relate it to their past learnings and experiences. Questions like "Why do I need to know this?" reveal a learner who is having difficulty determining the relevancy of the new topic. Here are a few ways teachers can help students attach meaning to new learning.

- **Modeling**. Models are examples of the new learning that the learner can perceive in the classroom rather than relying on experience. Models can be concrete (an engine) or symbolic (a map). To be effective, a model should:

  – Accurately and unambiguously highlight the critical attribute(s) of new learning. A dog is a better example of a mammal than a whale.

  – Be given first by the teacher to ensure that it is correct during this period of prime time when retention is highest.

  – Avoid controversial issues that can evoke strong emotions and redirect the learner's attention.

- **Using Examples From Students' Experience.** These allow students to bring previous knowledge into working memory to accelerate making sense and attaching meaning to the new learning. Make sure that the example is clearly relevant to the new learning. This is not easy to do on the spot, so examples should be thought out in advance when planning the lesson.

- **Creating Artificial Meaning.** When it is not possible to identify exemplary elements from student experience to develop meaning, we can resort to other methods. Mnemonic devices help students associate material so they can remember it. Examples are HOMES to remember the Great Lakes and "Every good boy does fine" for the musical notes *e, g, b, d,* and *f* (See Chapter 3).

PRACTITIONER'S CORNER

Using Closure to Enhance Sense and Meaning

Closure describes the covert process whereby the learner's working memory summarizes for itself its perception of what has been learned. It is during closure that a student often completes the rehearsal process and attaches sense and meaning to the new learning, thereby increasing the probability that it will be retained in long-term storage.

- **Initiating Closure:** The teacher gives directions that focus the student on the new learning, such as "I'm going to give you about two minutes to think of the three causes of the Civil War that we learned today; be prepared to discuss them briefly." In this statement, the teacher is providing adequate quiet time for the cerebral summarizing to occur and has included a following overt activity (discussion) for student accountability. During the discussion, the teacher can assess the quality and accuracy of what occurred during closure and make any necessary adjustments in teaching.

- **Closure Is Different From Review.** In review, the teacher does most of the work, repeating key concepts made during the lesson and rechecking student understanding. In closure, the student does most of the work by mentally rehearsing and summarizing those concepts and deciding whether they make sense and have meaning.

- **When to Use Closure.** Closure can occur at various times in a lesson.

  - It can start a lesson: "Think of the two causes of the Civil War we talked about yesterday and be prepared to discuss them."
  - It can occur during the lesson (called *procedural closure)* when the teacher moves from one sublearning to the next: "Review those two rules in your mind before we learn the third rule."
  - It should also take place at the end of the lesson (called *terminal closure)* to tie all the sublearnings together.

Closure is an investment that can pay off dramatically in increased retention of learning.

PRACTITIONER'S CORNER

Testing Whether Information Is in Long-Term Storage

Information that the learner processes during a lesson remains in working memory where it eventually will be dropped out or saved for long-term storage. Just because students act as if they have learned the new information or skill doesn't mean it will be transferred to long-term storage. Extensive research on retention indicates that 70 percent to 90 percent of new learning is forgotten 18 to 24 hours after the lesson. Consequently, if the new learning survives this time period intact, it is probably destined for long-term storage and will not deteriorate further.

This time requirement confirms that the processing and transfer between working memory and long-term storage needs adequate time for the encoding and consolidation of the new information into the storage networks. Thus, tomorrow is the earliest reliable time we can confirm that what was learned today has been indeed retained.

How to Test. If teachers want to test whether information actually has been transferred to long-term storage, the test needs to

- Be given no sooner than 24 hours after the learning

- Test precisely what should have been retained

- Come as a surprise to the learner, with no warning or preparation time

Rationale. If the learners have warning about the test, they are likely to review the material just before the test. In this case, the test may determine the amount of information the learners were able to cram and hold in working memory and not what they have recalled from long-term storage. While testing without warning may seem insensitive, it is the only way teachers can be sure that long-term storage was the source of the test information that the learners provided. Unannounced quizzes, then, should help students assess what they have remembered, rather than be a classroom management device to get students back on task.

– Continued –

Testing Whether Information Is in Long-Term Storage—Continued

Misuse of Tests. Some teachers use unannounced tests as punishment to get students back on task. This is a misuse of a valuable tool. Another approach is for teachers to

- **Establish** sense and meaning to increase the probability that retention will occur.

- **Explain** to students that unannounced tests help them see *what* as well as *how much* they have retained and learned over a given period of time.

- **Ensure** that the test or quiz matches the rehearsal when it was first taught. If the learning required essentially rote rehearsal, give a rote type of test. If it required elaborate rehearsal, use a test that allows the students more flexibility in their responses.

Using the Test Results. It is important that teachers

- **Analyze** immediately the results of the test to determine what areas need to be retaught or practiced. If some students forgot parts, consider forming cooperative learning groups that focus on reteaching the forgotten areas.

- **Record** the grades of only a small portion of these unannounced assessments. Rather, ask students to share their results and discuss in a think-pair-share format what strategies the students used to remember their correct responses. In this way, students talk about their memory processes and have a better understanding of how they learn and remember.

- **Decide** whether memory strategies such as concept maps, mnemonics, or chunking (see following chapters) can help in retention.

The analysis might also reveal areas of the curriculum to be reworked or updated for relevance, or it might show that the lesson should be retaught in a different way. A task analysis on a failed lesson is a good way to detect false assumptions about learning that the teacher may have made, and it recasts the lesson into a new presentation that can be more successful for both students and teacher.

Using tests as tools to help students to be right, rather than to catch them being wrong, will create a supportive learning climate that results in improved student performance.

PRACTITIONER'S CORNER

Using Synergy to Enhance Learning

Synergy describes how the joint actions of people working together increase each other's effectiveness. This strategy gets students moving and talking while learning. It is effective because it is multisensory, uses active participation, is emotionally stimulating, and encourages socialization. Each participant ends up having a better understanding as a result of this interaction (synergy). It can be used from the primary grades to graduate school. Here are the guidelines:

- **Provide Adequate Time for Reflection**. After teaching a concept, ask students to quietly review their notes and be prepared to explain what they have learned to someone else. Be sure to allow sufficient time for this mental rehearsal to occur (usually 1 to 3 minutes).

- **Model the Activity**. Working with a student, show the students how you want them to behave and interact during the activity.

- **Get Students to Stand, Move, and Deliver**. Ask students to walk across the room and pair up with someone they don't usually work with or know very well. They stand face-to-face and take turns explaining what they have learned. They add to their notes anything their partners have said that they don't have. When done, all students end up with more information and ideas than they would have had if they worked alone. If they cannot agree or don't understand something, they are to ask the teacher about it when the activity is over. (Note: Make sure students stand face-to-face—rather than just looking at each other's notes—so that they must talk to their partners. Allow pairs only—one trio, if you have an uneven number of students.)

- **Keep in Motion**. Move around the room using proximity to help students stay on task. Answer questions to get them back on track, but avoid re-teaching the lesson. Otherwise, students will become dependent on your re-teaching rather than on each other's explanations.

– Continued –

Using Synergy to Enhance Learning—Continued

- **Provide Enough Time and Adjust As Needed**. Allow adequate time for this process to be effective. Start with a few minutes, adding more time if they are still on task and reducing the time when you sense they are done.

- **Ensure Accountability**. To help keep students on task, tell them that you will call on several students at random when the activity is over to explain what they discussed.

- **Clarify Any Misunderstandings**. Ask if there were any misunderstandings or items that need further explanation, and clarify them. An inviting statement would be "Is there anything I need to clarify?" rather than "Is there anything you didn't understand?"

- **Use Variety for the Pairing**. You can pair by birth week or month, hair or eye color, height, musical cues, similar first names, etc. Aim for random pairing as much as practicable to enhance socialization (because students tend to work more with their friends) and to avoid monotony.

Some Barriers to Using Synergy

- **"The Teacher Should Be Talking."** The long-standing practice of the teachers being the "deliverer" of information is tough to overcome. For that reason, some teachers are uncomfortable with this activity because they are not "working" (read "talking"). But shifting the work to the students' brains increases the likelihood that they will find sense and meaning in the new learning.

- **"It Takes Too Much Time."** The question is: What would the teacher be doing otherwise? More talking? This is a useful investment of time because the students are talking about the lesson, thereby enhancing learning and retention.

- **"The Students Will Get Off Task."** This is a common and realistic concern. However, off-task behavior can be reduced significantly if the teacher continually moves around the room, asks questions of the student pairs, and holds them accountable for the learning at the end of the activity.

PRACTITIONER'S CORNER

NeuroBingo

Directions: In this activity the entire group gets up and moves around. Each person tries to find someone who can answer one of the questions in a box. The person who answers the question initials the box. The object is to get a bingo pattern (horizontally, vertically, or diagonally). No person may initial the same sheet twice. Time limit: 15 to 20 minutes, depending on the size of the group.

Find a person who is able to

Explain the function of the sensory register	Explain the importance of sense and meaning to learning	Define "windows of opportunity"	Explain how the brain prioritizes incoming information	Name the senses
State the two functions of the hippocampus	Tell you the function of immediate memory	Explain the function of the amygdala	Explain what is meant by the "novel" brain	Provide an example of how self-concept affects learning
Relate the cognitive belief system to learning	Tell you the functions of the cerebellum	Tell you the functions of the cerebrum	Describe the time limits of working memory	Explain synapses
Explain the meaning of sensory preferences	Describe the capacity limits of working memory	Explain what is meant by emotional control	Explain the function of neuro-transmitters	Explain the function of long-term memory
Explain the value of humor in learning	Explain chunking	Describe the sources of brain research	Explain closure	Describe a neuron

Chapter 2—How the Brain Processes Information

Key Points to Ponder

Jot down on this page key points, ideas, strategies, and resources you want to consider later. This sheet is your personal journal summary and will help to jog your memory.

CHAPTER 2 – NOTES

1. Apart from the five classical senses of sight, hearing, smell, touch, and taste, our body has special sensory receptors that detect internal signals. For example, we have receptors inside the ear and body muscles that detect the body's movement and position in space; sensory hairs in the ear that detect balance and gravity; stretch receptors in muscles to help the brain coordinate muscular contraction; and pain receptors throughout the body. For the purposes of the model, however, I have focused on the classical senses because they are the major receptors of *external* stimuli.

2. Squire and Kandel (1999), pp. 84–85.

3. The numbers used in this chapter are averages over time. There are always exceptions to these values as a result of human variations or pathologies.

4. The older literature calls this area short-term memory. The two terms for the same area will cause confusion until they become standardized in newer writings.

5. For the original research on working memory capacity, see the work of Miller (1956).

6. Maquire, Frith, and Morris (1999).

CHAPTER 3

MEMORY, RETENTION, AND LEARNING

The study of memory might also affect pedagogy by suggesting new methods of teaching based upon how the brain stores knowledge.
> – Larry Squire and Eric Kandel,
> *Memory: From Mind to Molecules*

Chapter Highlights: This chapter probes the nature of memory. It explains why our ability to retain information varies within a learning episode and with the teaching method used. It also discusses the value and pitfalls of practice, as well as techniques for increasing the capacity of working memory.

Memory gives us a past and a record of who we are and is essential to human individuality. Without memory, life would be a series of meaningless encounters that have no link to the past and no use for the future. Memory allows individuals to draw on experience and use the power of prediction to decide how they will respond to future events.

For all practical purposes, the capacity of the brain to store information is unlimited. That is, with about 100 billion neurons, each with thousands of dendrites, the number of potential neural pathways is incomprehensible. The brain will hardly run out of space to store all that an individual learns in a lifetime. Learning is the process by which we *acquire* new knowledge and skills; memory is the process by which we *retain* the knowledge and skills for the future. Most of what makes up our cognitive belief system, we have learned. Investigations into the neural mechanisms required for different types of learning are revealing more about the interactions between learning new information, memory, and changes in brain structure. Just as muscles improve with exercise, the brain seems to improve with use. While learning does not increase the number of brain cells, it does increase their size, their branches, and their ability to form more complex networks.

The brain goes through physical and chemical changes when it stores new information as the result of learning. Storing gives rise to new neural pathways and strengthens existing pathways. Thus, every time we learn something, our long-term storage areas undergo anatomical changes that, together with our unique genetic makeup, constitute the expression of our individuality.

How Memory Forms

What is a memory? Is it actually located in a piece of the brain at a specific spot? Are memories permanent? How does the brain manage to store a lifetime of memories in an organ the size of a melon? The definitive explanation for memory is still elusive. Nevertheless, neuroscientists have discovered numerous mechanisms that occur in the brain that, taken together, define a workable hypothesis about memory formation.

The Temporary Stimulus

You will recall from Chapter 1 that a stimulus (say, the color red, a whiff of perfume, or a musical note) causes nerve impulses to travel down the axon to the gap, or synapse, where neurotransmitter chemicals are released. These chemicals cross the synapse to the dendrite of the other neuron. As the chemical messages enter the neighboring neuron, they spark a series of electrochemical reactions that cause

> **The brain goes through physical and chemical changes each time it learns.**

this second neuron to generate a signal, or "fire." The reaction continues and causes more receptor sites on other neurons to fire as well. This sequence forms a pattern of neuronal connections firing together.

The firing may last only for a brief time, after which the memory decays and is lost. If the second neuron is not stimulated again, it will stay in a state of readiness for hours, or days. What is created here is a perception, and even recognition, of an outside stimulus that quickly passes. We are bombarded with thousands of such events each day.

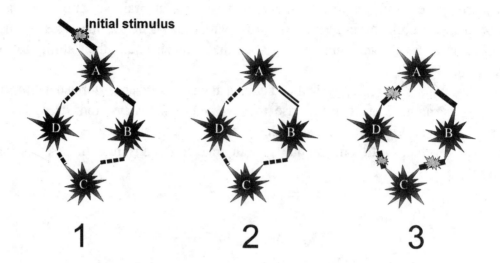

Figure 3.1 *Memories are formed when a group of neurons fires together when activated. (1) Neuron A receives a stimulus, which causes it to set off neuron B. (2) If neuron A fires again soon, a link is established. Later, neuron A can just fire weakly to set off neuron B. (3) The firing of neurons A and B may set off neighboring neurons C and D. If this happens repeatedly, the four cells become a network and will fire together in the future—forming a memory.*

Repetition of the Stimulus Forms the Memory

On the other hand, if the pattern is repeated during this standby period (through rehearsal and practice), the tendency for the associated group to fire together is increased. The faster a neuron fires, the greater the electrical charge it generates and the more likely it is to set off its neighbors. As the neighbors fire, the surfaces of their dendrites change to make them more sensitive to stimulation. This process of synaptic awareness and sensitivity is called *long-term potentiation* or *LTP*. Eventually, repeated firing of the pattern binds the neurons together so that if one fires, they all fire, ultimately forming a new memory trace, or *engram*. These individual traces associate and form networks so that whenever one is triggered, the whole network is strengthened, thereby consolidating the memory and making it more easily retrievable.[1] Drugs may soon be available that enhance the ability of the neurons to form and recall these engrams. Although researchers are aiming to develop drugs that will help patients with memory disorders, these same drugs will help normal people perform memory tasks, such as test taking, with greater success. This prospect will pose some interesting ethical questions for classroom teachers.[2]

Memories are not stored intact. Instead, they are stored in pieces and distributed in sites throughout the cerebrum. The shape, color, and smell of an orange, for example, are categorized and stored in different sets of neurons. Activating these sites simultaneously brings together a recollection of our thoughts and experiences involving an orange.

There is also some evidence that the brain stores an extended experience in more than one network. Which sites to select for storage could be determined by the number of associations that the brain makes between the new learning and past learnings. The more connections that are made, the more understanding and meaning the learner can attach to the new learning, and the more likely it is that it will be stored in different networks. This process now gives the learner multiple opportunities to retrieve the new learning.

Stages and Types of Memory

Stages of Memory

The stages of memory are the following: immediate, working, and long-term. In Chapter 2, I described the nature of immediate and working memories, which you will recall are temporary memories. Some stimuli that are processed in these temporary memories are eventually transferred to long-term memory sites where they actually change the structure of the neurons so they can last a lifetime. Although neuroscientists are not in total agreement with psychologists as to all of the

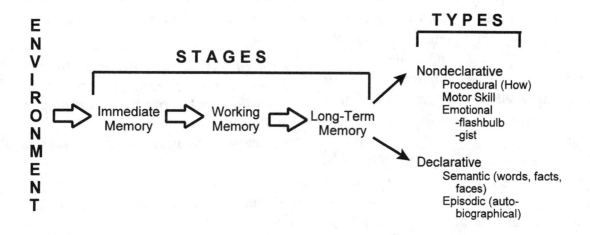

Figure 3.2 The diagram shows the stages and types of memory.

characteristics of long-term memory, there is considerable agreement on some of their types, and their description is important to understand before setting out to design learning activities accordingly. Long-term memory can be divided into two categories, *nondeclarative memory* and *declarative memory*. Figure 3.2 shows the stages of memory and the various types of long-term memory.

Nondeclarative Memory

Nondeclarative memory (sometimes called implicit memory) exists in several different forms, including procedural memory, motor skill memory, and emotional memory.

Procedural Memory. Procedural memory refers to remembering *how* to do something, like riding a bicycle, driving a car, swinging a tennis racket, and tying a shoelace. As practice of the skills continues, these memories become more efficient and can be performed with little conscious thought or recall. The brain process shifts from *reflective* to *reflexive*. For example, you may remember the first time you drove an automobile by yourself. No doubt you gave a lot of conscious attention to your speed, maneuvering the vehicle, putting your foot on the correct pedal, and observing surrounding traffic (reflective thought). However, as you continued to practice this routine, the skills were stored in procedural memory and became more automatic (reflexive activity). Now, you can drive from home to work and not even recall what happened on the road ("Did I really stop at that stop sign?" "What was that thump?"). Procedural memory was driving the car while working memory was planning your day.

Procedural memory helps us to learn things that don't require conscious attention and to habituate ourselves to the environment. Thus, we can become accustomed to the clothes we wear, the daily noisy traffic outside the school, a ticking clock in the den, or the sounds of construction. This adjustment to the environment allows the brain to screen out unimportant stimuli so it focus on those that matter.

> *Procedural memory helps us to learn things that don't require conscious attention and to habituate ourselves to the environment.*

We also learn *perceptual skills*, such as reading, discriminating colors, and identifying tones in music, and *cognitive skills*, such as figuring out a *procedure* for solving a problem. Cognitive skills are different from cognitive concept building in that cognitive skills are performed automatically and rely on procedural memory rather than declarative memory. Perceptual and cognitive skill acquisition involve some different brain processes and memory sites from cognitive concept learning. If they are learned differently, should they be taught differently?

Motor Skill Memory. Much of what we do during the course of a day involves the performance of skills. We go through the morning grooming and breakfast rituals, read the newspaper, get to work, and shake the hand of a new acquaintance. We do all of these tasks without realizing that we have learned them and without being aware that we are using our memory. Although learning a new skill involves conscious attention, skill performance later becomes unconscious and relies essentially on nondeclarative memory.

Emotional Memory. In Chapter 2, we learned how emotions can positively or negatively affect the acquisition of new learning. Emotions associated with a learning become part of the nondeclarative memory system. These emotions can return and change how students *feel* about what they learned. This unconscious response can turn them toward or away from a similar learning experience.

A powerful emotional experience can cause an instantaneous and long-lasting memory of an event called a *flashbulb memory*. An example is remembering where you were and what you were doing when President Kennedy was assassinated or when the *Challenger* space shuttle exploded. Although these memories are not always accurate, they do attest to the brain's ability to record emotionally significant experiences. This ability most likely results from the stimulation of the amygdala and the release throughout the body of emotion-arousing substances, such as adrenalin.[3]

Sometimes, an experience is stored merely as an emotional *gist* or summary of the event, that is, we remember whether we liked it or not. A year after seeing a movie, for example, we might be able to recall only bits of the storyline and perhaps its mood. Students often can remember whether they liked a particular topic, but cannot recall many details about it.

Declarative Memory

Declarative memory (also called *conscious* or *explicit* memory) describes the remembering of names, facts, music, and objects (e.g., where you live and the kind of car you own), and is processed by the hippocampus and cerebrum. Think for a moment about a person who is now important in your life. Try to recall that person's image, voice, and mannerisms. Then think of an important event you both attended, one with an emotional connection, such as a concert, wedding, or funeral. Once you have the context in mind, note how easily other components of the memory come together. This is declarative memory in its most common form—a conscious and almost effortless recall.

Declarative memory can be further divided into *episodic memory* and *semantic memory*. Episodic memory refers to the memory of events in one's own life history. It helps a person identify the time and place when an event happened. Semantic memory is knowledge of facts and data that may not be related to any event. A veteran knowing that there was a Vietnam War in the 1970s is using semantic memory; remembering his experiences in that war is episodic memory.

It seems that procedural and declarative memories are stored differently. Studies of brain-damaged and amnesia victims show that they may still be perfectly capable of riding a bicycle (procedural) without remembering the word, *bicycle* or when they learned to ride (declarative). Procedural and declarative memory seem to be stored in different regions of the brain, and declarative memory can be lost while procedural is spared.[4]

Implications for Teaching

How the learner processes new information presented in school has a great impact on the quality of what is learned and is a major factor in determining whether and how it will be retained. Memories, of course, are more than just information. They represent fluctuating patterns of associations and connections across the brain from which the individual extracts order and meaning. Teachers with a greater understanding of the types of memory and how they form can select strategies that are more likely to improve the retention and retrieval of learning.

Learning and Retention

Learning and retention are different. Learning involves the brain, the nervous system, and the environment, and the process by which their interplay acquires information and skills. Sometimes, we need information for just a short period of time, like the telephone number for a pizza delivery, and then the information decays in just a few seconds. Thus, learning does not always involve long-term retention.

> *Learning and retention are different. We can learn something for just a few minutes and then lose it forever.*

A good portion of the teaching done in schools centers on delivering facts and information to build concepts that explain a body of knowledge. We teach numbers, arithmetic operations, ratios, and theorems to explain mathematics. We teach about atoms, momentum, gravity, and cells to explain science. We talk about countries, famous leaders, and their trials and battles to explain history, and so on. Students may hold on to this information in working memory just long enough to take a test, after which it readily decays and is lost. (See the **Practitioner's Corner** in Chapter 2 on testing whether information is in long-term storage, p. 71.) Retention, however, requires that the learner not only give conscious attention but also build conceptual frameworks that have sense and meaning for eventual consolidation into the long-term storage networks.

Factors Affecting Retention of Learning

Retention refers to the process whereby long-term memory preserves a learning in such a way that it can locate, identify, and retrieve it accurately in the future. As explained earlier, this is an inexact process influenced by many factors including the degree of student focus, the length and type of rehearsal that occurred, the critical attributes that may have been identified, the student's learning style, and, of course, the inescapable influence of prior learnings.

The information processing model in Chapter 2 identifies some of these factors and sets the stage for finding ways to transfer what we know into daily classroom practice. Let us look more specifically at the way the brain processes and retains information during a learning episode, how the nature of that processing affects the degree of retention, and how the degree of retention varies with the length of the episode.

Rehearsal

The assignment of sense and meaning to new learning can occur only if the learner has adequate time to process and reprocess it. This continuing reprocessing is called *rehearsal* and is a critical component in the transference of information from working memory to long-term storage. The concept of rehearsal is not new. Even the Greek scholars of 400 BC knew its value. They wrote:

> *Repeat again what you hear; for by often hearing and saying the same things, what you have learned comes complete into your memory.*
>
> – from the *Dialexeis*

Two major factors should be considered in evaluating rehearsal: The amount of time devoted to it, which determines whether there is both initial and secondary rehearsal, and the type of rehearsal carried out, which can be rote or elaborative.

Time for Initial and Secondary Rehearsal

Time is a critical component of rehearsal. Initial rehearsal occurs when the information first enters working memory. If the learner cannot attach sense or meaning, and if there is no time for further processing, then the new information is likely to be lost. Providing sufficient time to go beyond the initial processing to secondary rehearsal allows the learner to review the information, to make sense of it, to elaborate on the details, and to assign value and relevance, thus increasing significantly the chance of long-term storage. When done at the end of a learning episode, this rehearsal is called *closure*.

Scanning studies indicate that the frontal lobe is very much involved during the rehearsal process and, ultimately, in long-term memory formation. This makes sense because working memory is also located in the frontal lobe. Several studies using fMRI scans of humans showed that during longer rehearsals the amount of activity in the frontal lobe determined whether items were stored or forgotten.[5]

Students carry out initial and secondary rehearsal at different rates of speed and in different ways, depending on the type of information in the new learning and their learning styles. As the learning task changes, learners automatically shift to different patterns of rehearsal.

Rote and Elaborative Rehearsal

Rote Rehearsal. This type of rehearsal is used when the learner needs to remember and store information exactly as it is entered into working memory. This is not a complex strategy, but it is necessary to learn information or a skill in a specific form or sequence. We use rote rehearsal to remember a poem, the lyrics and melody of a song, multiplication tables, telephone numbers, and steps in a procedure.

Elaborative Rehearsal. This type of rehearsal is used when it is not necessary to store information exactly as learned, but when it is more important to associate the new learnings with prior learnings to detect relationships. This is a more complex thinking process in that the learner reprocesses the information several times to make connections to previous learnings and assign meaning. Students use rote rehearsal to memorize a poem, but elaborative rehearsal to interpret its message. When

> **There is almost no long-term retention of cognitive concepts without rehearsal**.

students get very little time for, or training in, elaborative rehearsal, they resort more frequently to rote rehearsal for nearly all processing. Consequently, they fail to make the associations or discover the relationships that only elaborative rehearsal can provide. Also, they continue to believe that learning is merely the recalling of information as learned rather than its value for generating new ideas, concepts, and solutions.

When deciding on how to use rehearsal in a lesson, teachers need to consider the time available as well as the type of rehearsal appropriate for the specific learning objective. Keep in mind that rehearsal only contributes to, but does not guarantee that information will transfer into long-term storage. However, there is almost no long-term retention *without* rehearsal.

Test Question No. 4: Increased time on task increases retention of new learning.

Answer: False. Simply increasing a student's time on a learning task does not guarantee retention if the student is not allowed the time and help to personally interact with the content through rehearsal.

Retention During a Learning Episode

When an individual is processing new information, the amount of information retained depends, among other things, on *when* it is presented during the learning episode. At certain time intervals during the learning, we will remember more than at other intervals. Let's try a simple activity to illustrate this point. You will need a pencil and a timer. Set the timer to go off in 12 seconds. When you start the timer, look at the list of 10 words below. When the timer sounds, cover the list and write as many of the 10 words as you remember on the lines to the right of the list. Write each word on the line that represents its position on the list (i.e., the first word on line one, etc.). Thus, if you cannot remember the eighth word, but you remember the ninth, write it on line number nine.

Ready? Start the timer and stare at the word list for 12 seconds. Now cover the list and write the words you remember on the lines to the right. Don't worry if you did not remember all the words.

KEF	1.	_____
LAK	2.	_____
MIL	3.	_____
NIR	4.	_____
VEK	5.	_____
LUN	6.	_____
NEM	7.	_____
BEB	8.	_____
SAR	9.	_____
FIF	10.	_____

Turn to your list again and circle the words that were correct. To be correct, they must be spelled correctly and be in the proper position on the list. Look at the circled words. Chances are you remembered the first 3 to 5 words (lines 1 through 5) and the last 1 to 2 words (lines 9 and 10), but had difficulty with the middle words (lines 6-8). Read on to find out why.

Primacy-Recency Effect

Your pattern in remembering the word list is a common phenomenon that is referred to as the *primacy-recency effect*. In a learning episode, we tend to remember best that which comes first, and remember second best that which comes last. We tend to remember least that which comes just past the middle of the episode. This is not a new discovery. Ebbinghaus published the first studies on this effect in the 1880s.

> *During a learning episode, we remember best that which comes first, second best that which comes last, and least that which comes just past the middle.*

Later studies help to explain why this is so. The first items of new information are within the working memory's functional capacity so they command our attention, and are likely to be retained in semantic memory. The later information, however, exceeds the capacity and is lost. As the learning episode concludes, items

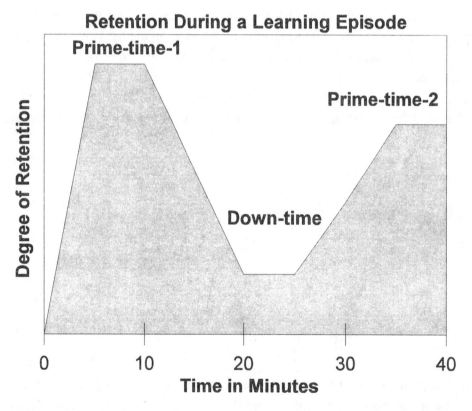

Retention During a Learning Episode

Figure 3.3 The degree of retention varies during a learning episode.

in working memory are sorted or chunked to allow for additional processing of the arriving final items, which are likely held in immediate memory unless further rehearsed.

Figure 3.3 shows how the primacy-recency effect influences retention during a 40-minute learning episode.[6] The times are approximate and averages. Note that it is a bimodal curve, each mode representing the degree of greatest retention during that time period. For future reference, I will label the first or primary mode *prime-time-1,* and the second or recency mode *prime-time-2.* Between these two modes is the time period in which retention during the lesson is least. I will refer to that area as the *down-time.* This is not a time when no retention takes place, but a time when it is most difficult for retention to occur.

Implications for Teaching

Teach New Material First

> **When you have the students' focus, teach the new information. Don't let prime-time get contaminated with wrong information.**

There are important implications of the primacy-recency effect for teaching a lesson. The learning episode begins when the learner focuses on the teacher with intent to learn (indicated by "0" in the Figure 3.3 graph). New information or a new skill should be taught first, during prime-time-1, because it is most likely to be remembered. Keep in mind that the students will remember almost any information coming forth at this time. It is important, then, that only *correct* information be presented. This is not the time to be searching for what students may know about something. I remember watching a teacher of English start a class with, "Today, we are going to learn about a new literary form called *onomatopoeia.* Does anyone have any idea what that is?" After several wrong guesses, the teacher finally defined it. Regrettably, those same wrong guesses appeared in the follow-up test. And why not? They were mentioned during the most powerful retention position, prime-time-1. The new material being taught should be followed by practice or review during the down-time. At this point, the information is no longer new, and the practice helps the learner organize it for further processing. Closure should take place during prime-time-2, since this is the second most powerful learning position and an important opportunity for the learner to determine sense and meaning. Adding these activities to the graph in Figure 3.4 shows how we can take advantage of research on retention to design a more effective lesson.

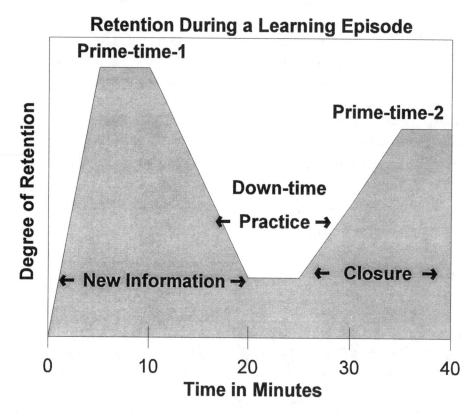

Figure 3.4 New information and closure are best presented during the prime-time periods. Practice is appropriate for the down-time segment.

Misuse of Prime-Time

Even with the best of intentions, teachers with little knowledge of the primacy-recency effect can do the following: After getting focus by telling the class the day's lesson objective, the teacher takes attendance, distributes the previous day's homework, collects that day's homework, requests notes from students who were absent, and reads an announcement about a club meeting after school. By the time the teacher gets to the new learning, the students are already at the down-time. As a finale, the teacher tells the students that they were so well-behaved during the lesson that they can do anything they want during the last 5 minutes of class (that is, during prime-time-2) as long as they are quiet. I have observed this scenario, and I can attest that the next day those students remembered who was absent and why, which club met after school, and what they did at the end of the period. The new learning, however, was difficult to remember because it was presented at the time of least retention. (See the **Practitioner's Corner** on p. 120 on using the primacy-recency effect in the classroom.)

Retention Varies With Length of Teaching Episode

Another fascinating characteristic of the primacy-recency effect is that the proportion of prime-times to down-time changes with the length of the teaching episode. Look at Figure 3.5 below. Note that during a 40-minute lesson, the two prime-times total about 30 minutes, or 75 percent of the teaching time. The down-time is about 10 minutes, or 25 percent of the lesson time. If we double the length of the learning episode to 80 minutes, the down-time increases to 30 minutes, or 38 percent of the total time period.

As the lesson time lengthens, the percentage of down-time increases faster than for the prime-times. The information is entering working memory faster than it can be sorted or checked, and it accumulates. This cluttering interferes with the sorting and chunking processes and reduces the learner's ability to attach sense and meaning, thereby decreasing retention. Think back to some of those college classes that lasted for two hours. After the first 20 minutes or so, didn't you find yourself concentrating more on taking notes rather than on learning what was being presented?

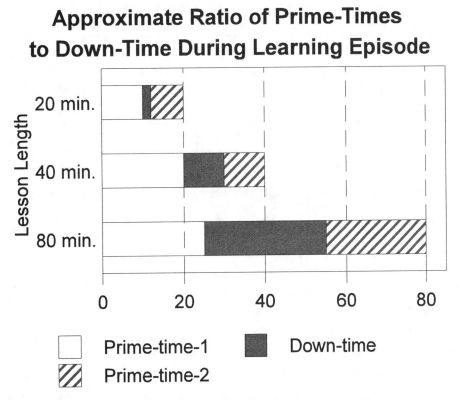

Figure 3.5 *The proportion of down-time to prime-times for 20-, 40-, and 80-minute learning episodes, when taught as one lesson.*

Figure 3.5 also shows what happens when we shorten the learning time to 20 minutes. The down-time is about 2 minutes, or 10 percent of the total lesson time. As we shorten the learning episode, the down-time decreases faster than the prime-times. This finding indicates that there is a higher probability of effective learning taking place if we can keep the learning episodes short and, of course, meaningful. Thus, teaching two 20-minute lessons provides 20 percent more prime-time (approximately 36 minutes) than one 40-minute lesson (approximately 30 minutes). Note, however, that a time period shorter than 20 minutes may not give the learner sufficient time to determine the pattern and organization of the new learning, and is thus of little benefit.

Table 3.1 below summarizes the approximate number of minutes in the prime-times and down-times of the learning cycle for episodes of 20, 40, and 80 minutes. Remember that the times are averages over many episodes. Nonetheless, these data confirm what we may have suspected: More retention occurs when lessons are shorter.

Table 3.1 Average Prime- and Down-times in Learning Episodes				
	Prime-Times		Down-Time	
Episode Time	Total Number of Minutes	Percentage of Total Time	Number of Minutes	Percentage of Total Time
20 minutes	18	90	2	10
40 minutes	30	75	10	25
80 minutes	50	62	30	38

Shorter Is Better: Impact on Block Scheduling

Because today's students are accustomed to quick change and novelty in their environment, many find it difficult to concentrate on the same topic for long periods of time. They fidget, drift, or get into off-task conversations. This is particularly true if the teacher is doing most of the work, such as lecturing. The primacy-recency effect has a particularly important impact in block scheduling, in which an 80-minute period can be a blessing or a disaster, depending on how the time is used. Figure 3.6 shows that a block containing four 20-minute segments will often be much more productive than one continuous lesson. Further, only one or two of the four block segments should be teacher directed. (See the **Practitioner's Corner** on p. 122 on block scheduling.)

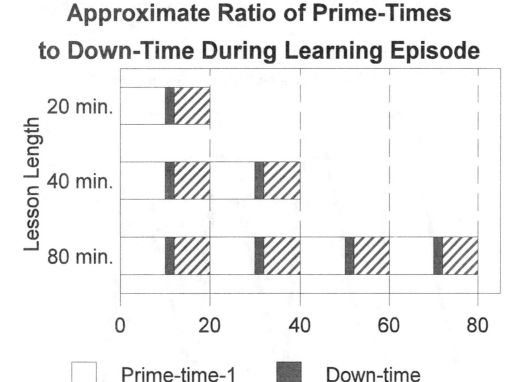

Figure 3.6 *By dividing each learning episode into 20-minute segments, there is proportionately more prime-time to down-time.*

Rest Between Block Lesson Segments

Most teachers believe that staying on-task throughout the learning period is best. In recent years, I have asked secondary teachers to conduct action research projects in their block schedule classrooms to determine if going off-task between lesson segments (e.g., telling a joke or story, playing music, or just taking a quiet rest break) resulted in more, less, or the same amount of attending (measured by the speed with which the students returned to task) than if they had stayed continuously on-task.[7]

Figure 3.7 is the compilation of their results, which are similar to Tony Buzan's (1989) findings in the 1980s. The graph suggests that teachers are more likely to keep students focused *during* the lesson segments if they go off-task *between* the segments. Granted, this is not a scientifically controlled study, but the results are not surprising given the higher novelty-seeking behavior of today's students. Teachers in nonblock classes (that is, 40 to 45 minutes in length) who take an off-task break about half-way through the period have reported similar results.

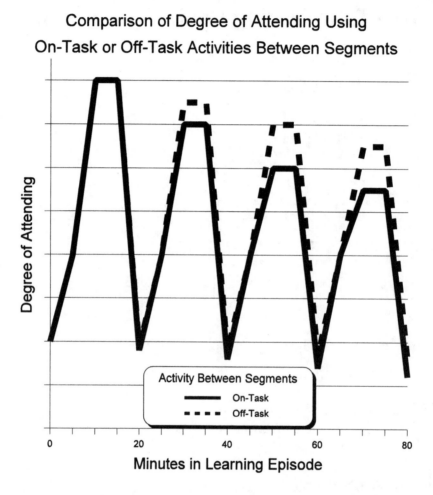

Comparison of Degree of Attending Using On-Task or Off-Task Activities Between Segments

Degree of Attending

Activity Between Segments
— On-Task
▪ ▪ ▪ ▪ Off-Task

Minutes in Learning Episode

Figure 3.7 *Compilation of 18 action research studies in secondary school classrooms comparing the degree of attending (focus) to on-task and off-task behavior between lesson segments of a block period.*

Retention Varies With Teaching Method

The learner's ability to retain information is also dependent on the type of teaching method used. Some methods result in more retention of learning than others. The learning pyramid shown

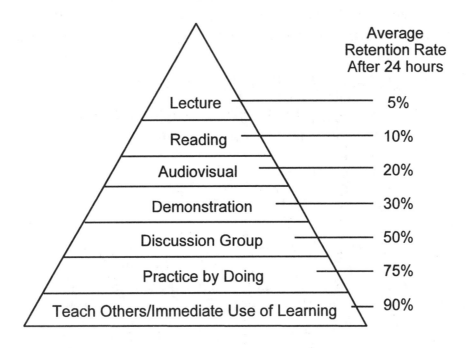

Figure 3.8 *The diagram shows the average percentage of retention of material after 24 hours for each of the instructional methods.*

in Figure 3.8, devised in the 1960s by the National Training Laboratories of Bethel, Maine (now the NTL Institute of Alexandria, Virginia), comes from studies on retention of learning after students were exposed to different teaching methods. The pyramid shows the percentage of new learning that students can recall after 24 hours as a result of being taught *primarily* by the teaching method indicated. (Note: Information recalled after 24 hours is presumed to be in long-term storage.)

The percentages are rounded to the nearest 5 percent and are not additive. At the top of the pyramid is lecture—the teaching method that results in an average retention of only 5 percent of learning after 24 hours. This result is not surprising because lecture usually involves little student active participation or mental rehearsal. In this format, the teacher is telling and the students

> *Lecture continues to be the most prevalent teaching mode in secondary and higher education, despite overwhelming evidence that it produces the lowest degree of retention for most learners.*

are listening just enough to convert the teacher's auditory output into written notes. Rote rehearsal predominates and elaborative rehearsal is minimal or nonexistent. Despite the impressive amount of evidence about how little students retain from lecture, it continues to be the most prevalent mode of teaching, especially in secondary and higher education.

Moving down the pyramid, students become more involved in the learning process, and retention increases. The method at the bottom of the pyramid involves having the students teach others or use the new learning immediately. This results in over 90 percent retention after 24 hours. We have known for a long time that the best way to learn something is to prepare to teach it. In other words, whoever explains, learns. This is one of the major components of cooperative learning groups and helps to explain the effectiveness of this instructional technique.

Learning Motor Skills

Scanning studies show that a person uses the frontal lobe and motor cortex to learn a new physical skill, and the cerebellum to store it. Learning a skill involves following a set of procedures and can be carried out largely without conscious attention. In fact, too much conscious attention directed to a motor skill while performing it can diminish the quality of its execution.

Brain Activity During Motor Skill Acquisition

Of course, when first learning the skill, attention and awareness are required. The frontal lobe is engaged because working memory is needed, and the motor cortex of the cerebrum (located across the top of the brain) is activated to control muscle movement. As practice continues, the activated areas of the motor cortex become larger as nearby neurons are recruited into the new skill network. However, the memory of the skill isn't established (i.e., stored) until after practice stops. It takes about 6 hours for this consolidation to take place in the cerebellum. Once the skill is mastered, brain activity shifts to the cerebellum, which organizes and coordinates the movements and the timing to perform the task. Procedural memory is the mechanism, and the brain no longer needs to use its higher-order processes as the performance of the skill becomes automatic.[8]

Continued practice of the skill changes the brain structurally, and the younger the learner is, the easier it is for these changes to occur. Most music and sports prodigies began practicing their skills very early in life. Because their brains were most sensitive to the structural changes needed to acquire the skills, they can perform them masterfully. These skills become so much a part of the individual that they are difficult to change later in life. Michael Jordan tried to become a major league baseball player at the age of 31 after a stellar career as a lead basketball scorer for the Chicago Bulls. Despite much effort, his attempt at baseball failed. Jordan had started playing basketball at the age of 8 and had developed a finely tuned set of motor skills in procedural memory that allowed him to be an expert basketball player. Trying to learn a new set of motor and perceptual skills to be a successful baseball player in a short period of time was just not possible.

The Problem of Learning Two Similar Skills

A surprising finding from these studies was that if the person practiced a very similar skill during the 6-hour down-time, the second skill interfered with the mastery of the first skill—and vice versa. Consequently, the person was not able to perform either skill well. This appears to be evidence that negative transfer can occur during the learning of motor skills as well as during the learning of cognitive concepts. Think of the implications that this has for teaching, wherein similarity is one of the major criteria we use to decide the sequence for presenting information and skills. (See the **Practitioner's Corner** at the end of the chapter on p. 116 on how similarity can interfere with new motor skill learning.)

> *Learning two skills that are too similar at the same time causes memory interference so that the student learns neither skill well.*

Test Question No. 5: Two very similar concepts or motor skills should be taught at the same time.

Answer: False. Teaching two very similar concepts or skills at the same time can cause interference so that the student learns neither.

Does Practice Make Perfect?

Practice refers to learners repeating a skill over time. It begins with the rehearsal of the new learning in working memory. Later, the memory is recalled from long-term storage and additional rehearsal follows. The quality of the rehearsals and the learner's knowledge base will largely determine the outcome of each practice.

Over the long term, repeated practice causes the brain to assign extra neurons to the task, much as a computer assigns more memory for a complex program. The assignment of these additional neurons is more or less on a permanent basis. Professional keyboard and string musicians, for example, have larger portions of the motor cortex devoted to controlling finger and hand movements. Furthermore, the earlier their training started, the bigger the motor cortex.[9] If practice is stopped altogether, the neurons that are no longer being used are eventually assigned to other tasks and skill mastery will decline.[10] In other words, use it or lose it!

The old adage that "practice makes perfect" is rarely true. It is very possible to practice the same skill repeatedly with no increase in achievement or accuracy of application. Think of the people you know who have been driving, cooking, or even teaching for many years with no improvement in their skills. I am a self-taught bowler, and although I have been bowling for 20 years, I do not improve. My bowling scores are embarrassingly low and remain there despite years of repeated bowling. Why is this? How is it possible for one to continuously practice a skill with no resulting improvement in performance?

Conditions for Successful Practice

For practice to *improve* performance, four conditions must be met (Hunter, 1982):

1.   The learner must be sufficiently motivated to *want* to improve performance.

2.   The learner must have all the knowledge necessary to understand the different ways that the new knowledge or skill can be applied.

3.   The learner must understand how to apply the knowledge to deal with a particular situation.

4.   The learner must be able to analyze the results of that application and know what needs to be changed to improve performance in the future.

Teachers help learners meet these conditions when they do the following:

●   Start by selecting the smallest amount of material that will have maximum meaning for the learner.

●   Model the application process step-by-step.

●   Insist that the practice occur in their presence over a short period of time while the student is focused on the learning.

- Watch the practice and provide the students with prompt and specific feedback on what variable needs to be altered to correct and enhance the performance.

Guided Practice, Independent Practice, and Feedback

Practice does make permanent, thereby aiding in the retention of learning. Consequently, we want to ensure that students practice the new learning correctly from the beginning. This early practice (referred to as *guided practice),* then, is done in the presence of the teacher, who can now offer corrective feedback to help students analyze and improve their practice. When the practice is correct, the teacher can then assign *independent practice,* in which the students can rehearse the skill on their own to enhance retention.

> **Practice does not make perfect. Practice makes permanent. However, perfect practice makes perfect.**

This strategy leads to perfect practice, and, as Vince Lombardi said, "Perfect practice makes perfect." In my case, I go bowling every few months to be with the same close friends, who are very busy professionals. Bowling is simply the means that allows us to catch up on our lives. Thus, I have no *motivation* to improve—and, believe me, I don't.

Teachers should avoid giving students independent practice before guided practice. Because practice makes permanent, allowing students to rehearse something for the first time while away from the teacher is very risky. If they unknowingly practice the skill incorrectly, then they will learn the incorrect method well! This will present serious problems for both the teacher and learner later on because it is very difficult to change a skill that has been practiced and remembered, even if it is not correct.

Unlearning and Relearning a Skill. If a learner practices a skill incorrectly but well, unlearning and relearning that skill is very difficult. The degree to which the unlearning and relearning processes are successful will depend on the

- Age of the learner (i.e., the younger, the easier to relearn)

- Length of time the skill has been practiced incorrectly (i.e., the longer, the more difficult to change)

- Degree of motivation to relearn (i.e., the greater the desire for change, the easier to change).

Sometimes, students who are young, and who have practiced the skill wrong for only a brief time, are so annoyed at having wasted their time with the incorrect practice that they lose motivation to learn the skill correctly.

Practice Over Time Increases Retention

Hunter (1982) suggested that teachers use two different types of practice over time, massed and distributed. Practicing a new learning during time periods that are very close together is called *massed practice*. This produces fast learning, as when you may mentally rehearse a new telephone number if you are unable to write it down. Immediate memory is involved here and the information can fade in seconds if it is not rehearsed quickly.

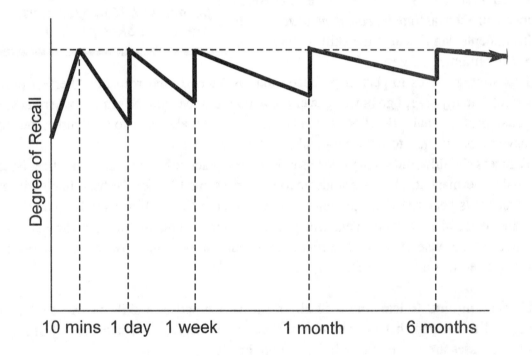

Figure 3.9 *Practice over time (distributed practice) increases the degree of recall of learnings.*

Teachers provide massed practice when they allow students to try different examples of applying new learning in a short period of time. Cramming for an exam is an example of massed practice. Material can be quickly chunked into working memory but can also be quickly dropped or forgotten if more sustained practice does not follow soon. This happens because the material has no further meaning and thus the need for long-term retention disappears. Sustained practice over time, called *distributed practice,* is the key to retention. If you want to remember that new telephone number later on, you will need to use it repeatedly over time. Thus, practice that is distributed over longer periods of time sustains meaning and consolidates the learnings into long-term storage in a form that will ensure accurate recall and applications in the future. The graph in Figure 3.9 shows that recall after periodic review improves over time. This is the rationale behind the idea of the spiral curriculum, whereby critical information and skills are reviewed at regular intervals within and over several grade levels.

Effective practice, then, starts with massed practice for fast learning and proceeds to distributed practice later for retention. This means that the student is continually practicing previously learned skills throughout the year(s). Each test should not only test new material but also allow students to practice older learnings. This method not only helps in retention but reminds students that the learnings will be useful for the future, not just for the time when they were first learned and tested.

How Daily Biological Rhythms Affect Teaching and Learning

Circadian Rhythms

Many of our body functions and their components, such as temperature, breathing, digestion, hormone concentrations, etc., go through daily cycles of peaks and valleys. These daily cycles are called *circadian* (from the Latin, "about a day") rhythms. The rhythms are thought to be controlled by just 10,000 neurons in a tiny region of the brain located in the limbic system. The timing of these cycles is determined by the brain's exposure to daylight.

One of these rhythms regulates our ability to focus on incoming information. It can be referred to as the psychological-cognitive cycle. This cycle has drawn the attention of several research studies on the awake-and-asleep cycles of students.[11] The findings show that the cognitive rhythm is about the same for a preadolescent and an adult, but starts later in an adolescent. This is because the onset of puberty shifts this particular cycle roughly an hour later than the preadolescent. It returns to its previous level when the adolescent enters adulthood.

Figure 3.10 shows a comparison of the preadolescent/postadolescent, and adolescent cycles. Note the trough that occurs for both groups just past the middle of the day. This is a low point of focus. Learning can still occur during this 20- to 60-minute period, but it will require more *effort.* I refer to the trough as the "dark hole of learning." Some cultures refer to it as the "siesta," having recognized long ago how difficult it is to accomplish much learning during this time.

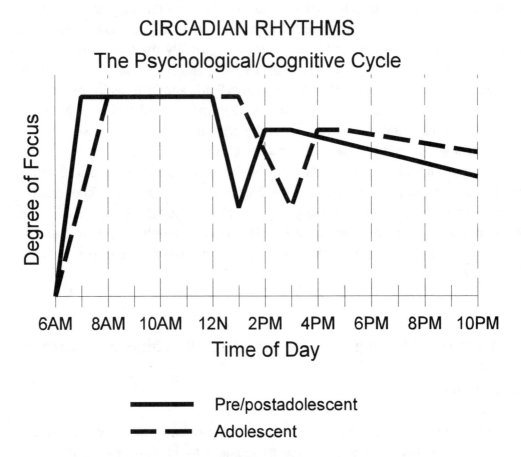

Figure 3.10 *A comparison of the typical pre/postadolescent and adolescent cognitive cycles during the day.*

Note that the adolescent cycle has shifted and that these students don't reach their peak until about an hour later. Note, too, that the second peak is flatter than for the other groups. This graph explains why adolescents are sleepier in the morning and tend to stay up later at night.

What Are the Implications? The different rhythms among preadolescents, adolescents, and their teachers have several implications. For example, how do the start times at elementary and secondary schools compare to the times when the students they serve are at their cognitive peak? Can the performance of students on standardized tests be affected when we test the whole K–12 population of students at the same time—usually in the morning? Can classroom climate in high schools be affected in the early afternoon when the teacher is in the trough and the students at their peak? Can starting high schools later in the morning when students are more apt to be attentive result in lowering the drop-out rate? And would alternative high schools be more successful if they started in the afternoon? (See also the **Practitioner's Corner** on p. 126 on the impact of circadian rhythms on schools and classrooms at the end of this chapter.)

The Importance of Sleep in Learning and Memory

The encoding of information into the long-term memory sites occurs during sleep, more specifically, during the rapid-eye movement (REM) stage. This is a slow process that can flow more easily when the brain is not preoccupied with external stimuli. What we think and talk about while awake very likely influences the nature and shape of the memory consolidation that occurs during sleep.

Adequate sleep is vital to the memory storage process, especially for young learners. Most teenagers need about nine hours of sleep each night. Many teenagers are not getting enough sleep. Several factors are responsible for eroding sleep time. In the morning, high schools start earlier, teens spend more time grooming, and some travel long distances to school. At the end of the day, there are athletic and social events, part-time jobs, and homework. Add to this the shift in teens' body clocks that tends to keep them up later (Figure 3.10), and the average sleep time is more like five to six hours.

> *Teenagers are not getting enough sleep. This sleep deprivation affects their ability to store information, increases irritability, and leads to fatigue which can cause accidents.*

Delayed Sleep Phase Disorder. This problem is becoming so prevalent in middle and high schools that some neuroscientists and psychiatrists are convinced that it is a chronic disorder of the adolescent population. Called Delayed Sleep Phase Disorder (DSPD), it is characterized by a persistent pattern that includes difficulty falling asleep at night and getting up in the morning, fatigue during the day, and alertness at night. Caused mainly by the shift in the adolescent's circadian rhythm (Figure 3.10), DSPD is aggravated by other conditions.

Figure 3.11 shows the stages and cycles of sleep for teenagers and adults. Long-term storage is believed to occur during the rapid-eye movement (REM) phases. During the normal sleep time of eight to nine hours, five REM cycles occur. Adolescents getting just five to six hours of sleep lose out on the last two REM cycles, thereby reducing the amount of time the brain has to consolidate information and skills into long-term storage. This sleep deprivation not only disturbs the memory storage process but can lead to other problems as well. Students may nod off in class or become irritable. Worse, their decreased alertness due to fatigue can lead to accidents.[12]

Some studies show that students who get less sleep are more likely to get poorer grades in school than students who sleep longer. Sleep-deprived students also had more daytime sleepiness and depressed moods.[13] It is important to remind students of the significance of sleep to their mental and physical health and to encourage them to reexamine their daily activities to provide for adequate sleep.

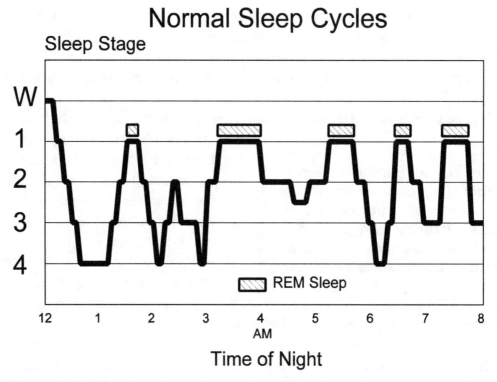

Figure 3.11 *The chart shows the cycles of sleep from Waking through Stage 1 (Transitional), Stage 2 (Light Sleep), and Stages 3 to 4 (Deep Sleep). Long-term storage occurs during the rapid-eye movement (REM) phase.*

Intelligence and Retrieval

Intelligence

Multiple Intelligences and Brain Research. Our modern notion of what constitutes human intelligence is growing increasingly complex. At the very least, it represents a combination of varied abilities and skills. The work of researchers such as Howard Gardner and Robert Sternberg has changed our concept of intelligence from a singular entity to a multifaceted aptitude that varies even within the same person. In 1983, Howard Gardner defined intelligence as an individual's ability to use a learned skill, create products, or solve problems in a way that is valued by the society of that individual. He also proposed that at least seven different intelligences exist for each individual; he recently added an eighth.[14]

This theory suggests that at the core of each intelligence is an information-processing system (similar perhaps to that in Chapter 2) unique to that intelligence. The intelligence of an athlete is different from that of a musician or physicist. He also suggests that each intelligence is semiautonomous. A person who has abilities in athletics but who does poorly in music has enhanced athletic intelligence. The presence or absence of music capabilities exists separately from the individual's athletic prowess.

PET scans and fMRIs do show some localization of brain activity for certain tasks. However, there is no scientific basis for equating the task with a particular intelligence. For example, visual stimuli are processed first in the visual cortex at the rear of the brain, and then in other parts of the brain for spatial perception and recognition. If anything, recent brain scans and case studies are revealing how remarkably integrated brain activity is when performing even the simplest task. Although most neuroscientists agree that there are areas that are specialized for certain tasks, these areas rarely, if ever, work in isolation in the normal brain.

Gardner's suggestion that the eight intelligences are semiautonomous systems that can learn independently of each other gains little support from neuroscience research at this time. Rather, it appears that eight is much too small a number to describe the categories of complex and integrated activities that the brain carries out while learning. However, we are indebted to Gardner for moving us away from the traditional model of intelligence a singular entity, fixed at birth, and best measured by vocabulary and reading. He helped us understand that the environment can have significant impact on intelligence, and that human beings can be smart in different ways.

> *Intelligence is a multifaceted aptitude that varies even within the same individual. It can be defined simply as the rate of learning something.*

Perhaps the next step is to realize that each of the eight intelligences has many skills contained within it, and thus, there are *innumerable* ways that each brain can manipulate information and skills during the learning process. Expanding our view beyond separate intelligences to an integrated wealth of intelligences is supported by neuroscience, and it also reduces the chances that we will label kids as "word smart" or "music dumb." Rather, we can accept that the best teaching and learning occurs when we use the greatest variety of techniques thereby making it more likely that all learners will succeed.[15]

Working Definition of Intelligence

We need a working definition of intelligence that reflects modern theory and is useful for practitioners. I offer this one: Intelligence is the *rate of learning* something. Although we are defining this complex concept with only three words, we need to understand them thoroughly. *Rate* is the amount of learning per unit of time. *Learning* is acquiring the information or skill through the application level of Bloom's Taxonomy (Chapter 7), so that it can be used to solve problems. Thus, *rate of learning* means the number of units of time one needs to acquire information or a skill at a level that can be used to solve problems correctly. By applying Gardner's concept of multiple intelligences, an individual can acquire different types of learning at different rates. One could learn to play several musical instruments quickly and competently but have difficulty learning mathematics, for example.

Using the rate of learning as the major criterion implies that intelligence is primarily a matter of neural efficiency. Could it be that intelligence describes the speed of the process whereby the brain eventually learns to use fewer neurons or networks to accomplish a repetitive task? If so, think of the implications this concept has for altering the way we allocate learning time and design and deliver lessons. It suggests, at the very least, that we should vary learning time to accommodate the task at hand and move learners to intensive practice as soon as comprehension is established.

Evidence of this neural efficiency exists in PET scans taken of the brain while playing a computer game. When first learning the game there is a large amount of neural activity. As the player masters the game, the amount of brain activity diminishes significantly. Further, the higher the IQ of the player, the more quickly the neural activity drops while learning the game.

Retrieval

It takes less than 50 milliseconds (a millisecond is 1/1,000th of a second) to retrieve an item from working memory. Retrieving a memory from long-term storage, however, can be complicated and comparatively time-consuming. The brain uses two methods to retrieve information from the long-term storage sites.

Recognition. Recognition matches an outside stimulus with stored information. For example, the questions on a multiple-choice test involve recognizing the correct answer (assuming the learner stored it originally) among the choices. This method helps explain why even poor students almost always do better than expected on multiple-choice tests.

Recall. Recall is quite different and more difficult. It describes the process whereby cues or hints are sent to long-term memory, which must search and retrieve information from the long-term storage sites, then consolidate and decode it back into working memory.

Both methods require the firing of neurons along the neural pathways to the storage site(s) and back again to working memory. The more frequently we access a pathway, the less likely it is to be obscured by other pathways. Information we use frequently, such as our name and telephone number, are quickly retrieved because the neural impulses to and from those storage sites keep the pathways clear. When the information is moved into working memory, we reprocess it to determine its validity and, in effect, relearn it.

Factors Affecting Retrieval. The rate at which the retrieval occurs depends on a number of factors.

- **Adequacy of the Cues**. The cue used to stimulate the retrieval of a memory may prompt a fully accurate recall or an ambiguous one. Since memory is not a videocassette recorder, the rememberer must reconstruct the memory based on the information retrieved by that cue. Having a strong memory does not seem to be as important as the retrieval cues.[16]

- **Mood of the Retriever**. Studies show that people in a sad mood more easily remember negative experiences, while those in a happy mood tend to recall pleasant experiences.

- **Context of the Retrieval**. Accurate recall is more likely to occur if the context during retrieval is very similar to the context of the period during which it was learned. Thus, testing for information in the same location in which it was learned is likely to result in better retrieval.

- **System of Storage**. Declarative memories get stored across brain structures, most likely in the areas that perceive and process incoming stimuli. Thus, the interests and past experiences of the learner will influence the type of cerebral networks that are constructed to contain the memory.

Students store the same item of information in different networks, depending on how they link the information to their past learnings. These storage decisions affect the amount of time it will later take to retrieve the information. This explains why some students need more time than others to retrieve the same information. When teachers call on the first hands that go up, they inadvertently

> *Whenever we retrieve something from long-term storage into working memory we relearn it.*

signal to the slower retrievers to stop the retrieval process. This is an unfortunate strategy for two reasons: First, the slower retrieving students feel that they are not getting teacher recognition, thereby lowering their self-concept. Second, by not retrieving the information into working memory, they miss an opportunity to relearn it.

Rates of Learning and Retrieval. In the information processing model in Chapter 2, the rate of learning (our working definition of intelligence) is represented by the data arrows flowing from left to right (from the senses through the sensory register) to immediate memory and into working memory. The rate of retrieval is represented by the recall arrow moving information from right to left (i.e., from long-term storage to working memory). *These two rates are independent of each other.* This notion

> *Calling on the first hands that go up signals the slower retrievers to stop the retrieval process.*

is quite different from classic doctrine which holds that the retrieval rate is strongly related to intelligence and, thus, anchored in genetic inheritance. The doctrine is further fueled in our society by timed tests and quiz programs that use the speed of retrieving answers as the main criterion for judging success and intelligence. The disclosure that the rate of retrieval is linked to the nature of the learner's storage method—a learned skill—rather than to intelligence is indeed significant. Because it is a *learned* skill, it can be taught. There is now great promise that techniques can be developed for helping us refine our storage methods for faster and more accurate retrieval. (See the **Practitioner's Corners** on retention on pp. 117 and 129 at the end of this chapter.)

Because the rate of learning and the rate of retrieval are independent, individuals can be fast or slow learners, fast or slow retrievers, and every combination in between. Although most people tend to fall midrange, some are at the extremes. Actually, not only have we had experience

> *The rate of learning and the rate of retrieval are independent of each other.*

with learners possessing the extreme combinations of these two rates but we have also (unwittingly) made up labels to describe them. An individual who is a fast learner and a fast retriever we call a *genius.* Such students retrieve answers quickly. Their hands go up first. Their responses are almost always correct, and they get reputations as "brains." Teachers call on them when they want to keep the lesson moving.

A student who is a fast learner but slow retriever we call an *underachiever.* Teachers say to these students, "Come on, John, I know you know this ... keep trying." We often run out of patience and admonish them for not studying enough. A slow learner and fast retriever, we call an *overachiever.* These students respond quickly, but their answers may be incorrect. Teachers sometimes mistakenly view them as trying too hard to learn something that may be beyond them.

Test Question No. 6: The rate at which a learner retrieves information from memory is closely related to intelligence.

Answer: False. The rate of retrieval is independent of intelligence. It is more closely tied to how and where the information was stored originally.

For the student who is a slow learner and slow retriever, we have a whole list of uncomplimentary labels. More regrettable is that too often we interpret "slow learner" to mean "unable to learn." What being a slow learner really means is that the student is unable to learn

> *Too often we interpret "slow learner" to mean "unable to learn."*

something in the amount of time we have arbitrarily assigned for that learning. All these labels are unfortunate because they perpetuate the mistaken notion that the major factors promoting successful learning are beyond the control of the learner and teacher.

Chunking

There are three limits to our power of reasoning and thinking: our limited attention span, working memory, and long-term memory. Is it possible to consciously increase the number of items that working memory can handle at one time? The answer is yes, through a process called *chunking*. Chunking occurs when working memory perceives a set of data as a single item, much as we perceive *information* as one word (and, therefore, one item) even though it is composed of 11 separate letters. Going back to the number exercise in Chapter 2, some people may have indeed remembered all 10 digits in the right sequence. These may be people who spend a lot of time on the telephone. When they see a 10-digit number, their experience helps them to group it by area code, prefix, and extension. Thus, they see the second number, 4915082637, as (491) 508-2637, which is in three chunks, not 10. Since three are within the working memory's functional capacity, the digits can be remembered accurately.

Chunking allows us to deal with a few large blocks of information rather than many small fragments. Problem solving involves the ability to access large amounts of relevant knowledge from long-term memory for use in working memory. The key to that skill is chunking. The more a person is able to chunk in a particular area, the more expert the person becomes. These experts have the ability to use their experiences to group or chunk all kinds of information into discernable patterns.

This ability to chunk is much more a reflection of how the expert's knowledge base is organized rather than a superior perceptual ability. Experience has changed the experts' brains so that they can encode relevant information in greater detail and more fully than the nonexperts. As they gain experience, more patterns are chunked and linked and the expertise becomes less conscious and more intuitive. Here are some examples:

- An experienced physician takes much less time to diagnose a medical condition than an intern.

- Expert waiters remember meal combinations rather than single menu items.

- Expert musicians recall long passages, not single notes.

- Chess masters recall board layouts as functional clusters rather than separate pieces.

- Expert readers take in phrases, not individual words.

Test Question No. 7: The amount of information a learner can deal with at one time is genetically linked.

Answer: False. The amount of information a learner can deal with at one time is linked to the learner's ability to add more items to the chunks in working memory—a learned skill.

Effect of Past Experiences

Let's show how past experiences affect chunking. First, look at the following sentence:

Grandma is buying an apple.

This sentence has 22 letters, but only five chunks (or words) of information. Because the sentence is one complete thought, most people treat it as just one item in working memory. In this example, 22 bits of data (letters) become one chunk (complete thought). In addition, visual learners probably formed a mental image of a grandmother buying that apple.

Now let's add more information to working memory. Stare at the next sentence below for about 10 seconds. Now close your eyes and try recalling the two sentences.

Hte plpae si edr.

Having trouble with the second? That's because the words make no sense and working memory is treating each of the 13 letters and three spaces as 16 individual items (plus the first sentence as 1 item, for a total of 17). The 5 to 9 item functional capacity range of working memory is quickly exceeded.

Let's rearrange the letters in each word of the second sentence to read as follows:

The apple is red.

Stare at this sentence for 10 seconds. Now close your eyes again and try to remember the first sentence and this sentence. Most people will remember both sentences because they are now just 2 items instead of 17 and their meanings are related. Experience, once again, helps the working memory decide how to chunk items.

Here's a frequently used example of how experience can help in chunking information and improving achievement. Get the pencil and paper again. Now stare at the letters below for 10 seconds. Then look away from the page and write them down in the correct sequence and groupings. Ready? Go.

LSDN BCT VF BIU SA

Check your results. Did you get all the letters in the correct sequence and groupings? Probably not, but that's OK. Most people would not get 100 percent by staring at the letters in such a short period of time.

Let's try it again. Same rules: Stare at the letters below for 10 seconds and write the letters down. Ready? Go.

LSD NBC TV FBI USA

How did you do this time? Most people do much better on this example. Now compare the two examples. Note that the letters in both examples are *identical and in the same sequence*! The only difference is that the letters in the second example are grouped—or chunked—in a way that allows past experience to help working memory process and hold the items. Working memory usually sees the first example as 14 letters plus 4 spaces (i.e., the grouping is important) or 18 items—much more than its functional capacity. But the second example is quickly seen as only 5 understandable items (the spaces no longer matter) and, thus, within the limits of its capacity. Some people may even pair NBC with TV, and FBI with USA, so that they actually deal with just

3 chunks. These examples show the power of past experience in remembering—a principle of learning called *transfer,* which we will discuss in the next chapter.

Chunking is a very effective way of enlarging working memory's capacity. It can be used to memorize a long string of numbers or words. Most of us learned the alphabet in chunks—for

> *Chunking is an effective way of enlarging working memory's capacity and for helping the learner make associations that establish meaning.*

some it may have been *abcd, efg, hijk, lmnop, qrs, tuv, wxyz.* Chunking reduced the 26 letters to a smaller number of items that working memory could handle. Even people can be chunked, such as couples (e.g., Romeo and Juliet, Abbott and Costello, Bonnie and Clyde), in which recalling the name of one immediately suggests the name of the other. Although working memory has a functional capacity limit as to the number of chunks it can process at one time, there appears to be no limit to the number of items that can be combined into a chunk. Teaching students (and yourself) how to chunk can greatly increase learning and remembering.

Test Question No. 8: It is usually not possible to increase the amount of information that the working memory can deal with at one time.

Answer: False. By increasing the number of items in a chunk, we can increase the amount of information that our working memory can process simultaneously.

Cramming

Cramming for a test or interview is another example of chunking. The learner loads into working memory as many items as can be identified as needed. Varying degrees of temporary associations are made among the items. With sufficient effort and meaning, the items can be carried in working memory, even for days, until needed. If the source of the crammed items was outside the learner, that is, from texts or class notes, then it is possible for none of the crammed items to be transferred to long-term storage. This practice (which many of us have experienced) explains how a learner can be conversant and outwardly competent in the items tested on one day (while the items were in working memory) and have little or no understanding of them several days later after they drop out of working memory into oblivion. We cannot recall what we have not stored. (See the **Practitioner's Corner** on p. 71 of Chapter 2 on "Testing Whether Information Is in Long-Term Storage.")

Forgetting

What happens to memories in long-term storage over time? Surely, some sites deteriorate naturally over time due to subtle changes in the structure and orientation of the molecules at the dendrite spines located in the memory site synapses. As these changes continue, more of the memory is distorted or lost, resulting in forgetting. Recent studies of brain-damaged patients (Rose, 1992) suggest that forgetting may be due to *losing the pathways* to the sites. Apparently, this happens when we do not retrieve a memory for a long time. Other similar experiences create new pathways and interfere with our ability to recall the older memory. The older memory may or may not remain unchanged throughout the life of the individual.

Forgetting may be frustrating, but it is most likely a survival adaptation of memory. There is little value in remembering everything that has happened to us. By forgetting the trivial, we leave room for the more important and meaningful experiences that shape who we are and establish our individuality.

Some memories actually strengthen over time. When memories are continually recalled, the neural networks strengthen with each rehearsal. This process is called *consolidation* and can occur over short periods, such as just after new learning, yet can also operate over decades if there is frequent recall.[17]

> **By forgetting the trivial, we leave room for the more important and meaningful experiences that shape who we are and establish our individuality.**

Does it make a difference whether forgetting is the deterioration of the memory sites or losing the pathways? Is not the result the same, the inability to recall the memory? Sure, the result is the same, but since our understanding of the storage process has changed, so has the method for trying to recall it. We can use a therapy that helps us to find the original pathway, or an alternate pathway, to the memory sites.

Here is an example. Suppose you try to recall the name of the teacher you had when you were in second grade. Unless you have thought recently about that teacher, the pathway to that name has not been used for a long time. It is blocked by newer pathways, and you will have difficulty finding it. The name is still there, but it may take you as long as several days to find it. It will probably come to you when you least expect it.

Another example: Suppose you start thinking about finding an old sweater that you have not seen in several years. If you believe you gave it away, you will not even begin to look for it. That is the same as if you believe that your forgotten memory has been destroyed over time; you will not even try to recall it. On the other hand, if you are convinced that the sweater is somewhere in that big attic, then it is just a matter of time before your hunt pays off and you find it. You'll probably start by thinking of the last time you wore it.

This is the same process of memory therapy that is used with brain-damaged individuals. The therapy helps the patient seek other neural connections to find the original or an alternate pathway to the memory sites. (We'll discuss this storage process more in Chapter 4 when we look at the transfer of learnings.)

Confabulation

Have you ever been discussing an experience with someone who had shared it with you and started arguing over some of the details? As described earlier, long-term memory is the process of searching, locating, retrieving, and transferring information to working memory. Rote recall, especially of frequently used information, such as your name and address, is actually simple. These pathways are clear and retrieval time is very short. Retrieving more complex and less frequently used concepts is much more complicated. It requires signaling multiple storage sites through elaborate, cluttered pathways for intermediate consolidation and ultimate decoding into working memory. It is less accurate. First, most of us do not retain 100 percent of elaborate experiences, such as an extensive vacation. Second, we store parts of the experience in many storage areas.

> *Our brain fabricates information and experiences that we believe to be true.*

When retrieving such an experience, the long-term memory may not be able to locate all the events being requested, either because of insufficient time or because they were never retained. Moreover, older memories can be modified or distorted by the acquisition of new information. During the retrieval process, memory can unconsciously fabricate the missing or incomplete information by selecting the next closest item it can recall. This process is called *confabulation* and occurs because the brain is always active and creative, and seems to abhor incompleteness. This is not unlike the way the brain completes visual patterns that do not exist, as in optical illusions. Take a look at Figure 3.12. Although you may see a white triangle in the diagram, it does not exist it. It is the result of confabulation as the brain seeks to make sense of the pattern.

Confabulation is *not* lying, because it is an unconscious rather than a deliberate process, and the individual believes the fabricated information to be true. This explains why two people who participated in the same experience will later recall slightly—or even significantly—

Figure 3.12 The white triangle you may see does not exist. It is a result of confabulation.

114

different versions of the same event. Neither individual stored 100 percent of the experience. If each stored 90 percent, it would not be the *same* 90 percent for both. Their missing and different 10 percent will be fabricated and will cause each to question the accuracy of the other's memory. The less of the experience remembered, the more the brain must fabricate.

Over time, the fabricated parts are consolidated into the memory network. As we systematically recall this memory, minor alterations may continue to be made through confabulation. Gradually the original memory is transformed and encoded into a considerably different one that we believe to be true and accurate.[18] The left hemisphere seems to be the driving force behind confabulation. Experiments show that the left hemisphere is so intent on looking for order that it will find it even when there is none.[19] (See more about this in Chapter 5.)

Implications. Confabulation also happens in the classroom. When recalling a complex learning, the learner is unaware of which parts are missing and, thus, fabricated. The younger the learner, the more inconsistent the fabricated parts are likely to be. The teacher may react by thinking the student is inventing answers intentionally and may discipline accordingly. In another situation, a list of similar words or concepts may induce the confabulation of words or concepts *not* on the list. Studies show that this is a common phenomenon.[20] In these cases, the teacher should be aware of confabulation as a possibility, identify the fabricated parts, and provide the feedback needed to help the student correct the inaccurate material. Through practice, the learner will then incorporate the corrected material into memory and transfer it to long-term storage.

Confabulation has implications for the justice system. This tendency for the brain to fabricate information rather than admit its absence can have serious consequences in court trials where eyewitnesses, under the pressure of testifying, feel compelled to provide complete information. Confabulation also raises questions about the accuracy of witnesses recalling very old memories of unpleasant events, such as a childhood accident or abuse. Experiments have shown how easy it is to distort a person's recollection of even recent events, or to "implant" memories. In the absence of independent verification, it is impossible to decide what events in the recalled "repressed memory" actually occurred and which are the result of confabulation.[21]

PRACTITIONER'S CORNER

Avoid Teaching Two Very Similar Motor Skills

When a learner practices a new skill (in this example, swinging a baseball bat), the motor cortex (across the top of the cerebrum) coordinates with the cerebellum to establish the pathways that will consolidate the movements to perform the skill. After the learner stops the practice, it takes about six hours (down-time) for this consolidation to occur. Further memory pathways are established as the learner sleeps. Practicing the skill the next day will be much easier and more accurate.

If, during the six-hour down-time, the learner practices a second skill (in this example, swinging a golf club) that is very similar to the first skill, the pathways for the two skills get confounded. As a result, the learner is able to perform *neither* skill well.

Implications for Practice:

- Avoid teaching two motor skills that are very similar to each other in the same day. When in doubt, make a list of their similarities and differences. If the similarities far outweigh the differences, it is best not to teach them together.

- When the time comes to teach the second skill, teach the *differences* first. This ensures that the differences are recognized during prime-time-1, which is the most powerful position for remembering.

PRACTITIONER'S CORNER

Using Rehearsal to Enhance Retention

Rehearsal refers to the learner's reprocessing of new information in an attempt to determine sense and meaning. It occurs in two forms. Some information items have value only if they are remembered *exactly* as presented, such as the letters and sequence of the alphabet, spelling, poetry, telephone numbers, notes and lyrics of a song, and the multiplication tables. This is called *rote rehearsal*. Sense and meaning are established quickly, and the likelihood of long-term retention is high. Most of us can recall poems and telephone numbers that we learned years ago.

More complex concepts require the learner to make connections and to form associations and other relationships in order to establish sense and meaning. Thus, the information may need to be reprocessed several times as new links are found. This is called *elaborative rehearsal*. The more senses that are used in this elaborative rehearsal, the more reliable the associations. Thus, when visual, auditory, and kinesthetic activities assist the learner during this rehearsal, the probability of long-term storage rises dramatically. That is why it is important for students to talk about what they are learning *while* they are learning it, and to have visual models as well.

Rehearsal is teacher initiated and teacher directed. Recognizing that rehearsal is a necessary ingredient for retention of learning, teachers should consider the following when designing and presenting their lessons:

Rote Rehearsal Strategies

- **Simple Repetition.** For remembering short items (telephone numbers, names, and dates), this is simply repeating a set of items over and over until it can be recalled in correct sequence.

- **Cumulative Repetition.** For longer sets of items (song, poem, list of battles) the learner rehearses the first few items. Then the next set of items in the sequence is added to the first set and rehearsed, and so on. For example, to remember a poem of four stanzas, the learner rehearses the first stanza, then rehearses the second stanza alone, then the two together, then rehearses the third stanza, then the three stanzas together, etc.

– Continued –

Using Rehearsal to Enhance Retention—Continued

Elaborative Rehearsal Strategies

- **Paraphrasing**. Students orally restate ideas in their own words, which then become familiar cues for later storage. Using auditory modality helps the learner attach sense, making retention more likely.

- **Selecting and Note Taking**. Students review texts, illustrations, and lectures, deciding which portions are critical and important. They make these decisions on the basis of criteria from the teacher, authors, or other students. Students then paraphrase the idea and write it into their notes. Adding the kinesthetic exercise of writing furthers retention.

- **Predicting**. After studying a section of content, the students predict the material to follow or what questions the teacher might ask about that content. Prediction keeps students focused on the new content, adds interest, and helps them apply prior learnings to new situations, thus aiding retention.

- **Questioning**. After studying content, students generate questions about the content. To be effective, the questions should range from lower-level thinking of recall, comprehension, and application to higher-level thinking of analysis, synthesis, and evaluation (see Bloom's Taxonomy in Chapter 7). When designing questions of varying complexity, students engage in deeper cognitive processing, clarify concepts, and predict meaning and associations—all contributors to retention.

- **Summarizing**. Students reflect on and summarize in their heads the important material or skills learned in the lesson. This is often the last and critical stage where students can attach sense and meaning to the new learning. Summarizing rehearsal is also called *closure* (see the **Practitioner's Corner** on closure on p. 70 in Chapter 2 for further explanation).

– Continued –

Using Rehearsal to Enhance Retention—Continued

General Guidelines

If the retention of new information or skills beyond the immediate lesson is an important expectation, then rehearsal must be a crucial part of the learner's processing. The considerations below should be incorporated into decisions about using rehearsal.

- **Teach** students rehearsal activities and strategies. As soon as they recognize the differences between rote and elaborative rehearsal, they can understand the importance of selecting the appropriate type for each learning objective. With practice, they should quickly realize that fact and data acquisition require rote rehearsal, whereas analysis and evaluation of concepts require elaborative rehearsal.

- **Remind** students to continuously practice rehearsal strategies until they become regular parts of their study and learning habits.

- **Keep** rehearsal relevant. Effective elaborative rehearsal relies more on making personally meaningful associations to prior learning than on time-consuming efforts that lack these student-centered connections. Any associations that center in the teacher's experiences may not be relevant to students.

- **Remember** that time alone is not a trustworthy indicator of the effectiveness of rehearsal. The degree of meaning associated with the new learning is much more significant than the time allotted.

- **Have** learners verbalize their rehearsal to peers or teachers while they are learning new material, as this increases the likelihood of retention.

- **Provide** more visual and contextual clues to make rehearsal meaningful and successful. Students with limited verbal competence will focus on visual and concrete lesson components to assist in their rehearsal. This will be particularly true of students whose first language is not English.

- **Vary** the rehearsal strategies that you initiate to ensure that there is plenty of novelty in the process. Students will bore quickly if the same method of rehearsal (e.g., sharing with the same partner) is used all the time.

PRACTITIONER'S CORNER

Using the Primacy-Recency Effect in the Classroom

The primacy-recency effect describes the phenomenon whereby, during a learning episode, we tend to remember best that which comes first (prime-time-1), second best that which comes last (prime-time-2), and least that which comes just past the middle (down-time). Proper use of this effect can lead to lessons that are more likely to be remembered.

Below is a sketch of two lessons. One is taught by Mr. Blue and the other by Mr. Green. Study their lesson sequences and look for any application of the primacy-recency effect.

Mr. Blue	Lesson Sequence	Mr. Green
"Get ready to tell me the two causes of the Civil War we discussed yesterday." After getting this he then says, "Today we will learn the third and most important cause as we are still living with its aftereffects 130 years later." "Before I tell you, let me give back some homework, collect today's homework, collect the notes from Bill and Mary who were absent yesterday, take attendance, and read a brief announcement."	Prime-time-1	"Get ready to tell me the two causes of World War I we discussed yesterday." After getting this he then says, "Today we will learn the third and most important cause as it set the stage for another world war just 30 years later." "And here is the third cause!" (He presents third cause, gives examples, and relates it to yesterday's two causes.)
"Here is the third cause." (He presents third cause, gives examples, and relates it to yesterday's two causes.)	Down-time	"Go into your discussion groups and discuss this third cause. Not only tie it to the two causes we learned yesterday but also to other wars we have learned so far. What are the similarities and differences?"
"OK, we've got only 5 minutes to the end of the period. You've listened attentively so you can do anything you want as long as you are quiet."	Prime-time-2	"Take 2 minutes to review quietly to yourself what you learned about this third cause. Be prepared to share your thoughts with the class."

– Continued –

Using the Primacy-Recency Effect in the Classroom—Continued

If these sequences are representative of what happens most of the time in these two teachers' classes, whose students are more likely to remember what they have learned over time? Why? What are some other implications of using the primacy-recency effect in the classroom?

Here are some other considerations for using this effect in the classroom.

- **Teach the new material first** (after getting the students' focus) during prime-time-1. This is the time of greatest retention.

- **Avoid asking students** at the beginning of the lesson if they know anything about a *new* topic being introduced. If it is a new topic, the assumption is that most students do not know it. However, there are always some students ready to take a guess—no matter how unrelated. Because this is the time of greatest retention, almost anything that is said, including incorrect information, is likely to be remembered. Give the information and examples yourself to ensure that they are correct.

- **Avoid using precious prime-time** periods for classroom management tasks, such as collecting absence notes or taking attendance. Do these before you get focus, or during the down-time.

- **Use the down-time** portion to have students practice the new learning or to discuss it by relating it to past learnings.

- **Do closure during prime-time-2**. This is the learner's last opportunity to attach sense and meaning to the new learning, to make decisions about it, and to determine where and how it will be transferred to long-term storage. It is important, then, that the student's brain do the work at this time. If you wish to do a review, then do it *before* closure to increase the chances that the closure experience is accurate. Doing review *instead* of closure is of little value to retention.

- **Try to package lesson objectives** (or sublearnings) in teaching episodes of about 20 minutes. Link the sublearnings according to the total time period available (e.g., two 20-minute lessons for a 40-minute teaching period, three for an hour period, and so on).

PRACTITIONER'S CORNER

Strategies for Block Scheduling

More high schools (and some middle schools, too) are converting from the standard 40- to 45-minute daily period to a block schedule consisting of longer teaching periods, usually 80 to 90 minutes. Although there are various formats for the blocks, the main goal of this change is to allow more time for student participation in the learning process.

The benefits of this approach are many: There is less fragmentation to the school day, more time to dig into concepts and allow for transfer to occur, and more time to develop hands-on activities, such as projects. It also allows for more performance-based assessments of student learning, reducing the reliance on paper-and-pencil tests.

The block experience is likely to be more successful if the teacher recognizes the value and need for novelty, and resists the temptation to be the focus of the block during the entire time period. Here are some suggestions for a brain-compatible block lesson.

- **Remember the primacy-recency effect**. Teaching a 90-minute episode as one continuous lesson will mean a down-time of about 35 minutes. Plan for four 20-minute learning segments and your down-time is reduced substantially to about 10 minutes. This down-time can also be productive if the students are engaged in discussions about the new learning.

- **Be in direct control of just one segment**. You may wish to do some direct instruction during one of the lesson segments. If so, use the first segment for this, and then shift the work burden to the students for the other segments. Remember that the brain that does the work is the brain that learns.

- **Go off-task between segments**. Figure 3.7 (p. 94) shows how going off-task between the lesson segments can increase the degree of focus when the students return to task. This is because of the novelty effect. If you prefer to stay on-task, however, then use a joke, story, or cartoon that is related to the learning. You still get the novelty effect without losing focus.

– Continued –

Strategies for Block Scheduling—Continued

● **Eliminate the unnecessary**. Block scheduling is designed to give students a chance to dig deeper into concepts. To get the time to do this, scrap less important items that sneak into the curriculum over time. We all know that everything in the curriculum is not of equal importance. This selective abandonment is necessary on a regular basis.

● **Work with your colleagues**. Block activities offer an excellent opportunity for teachers to work together in planning the longer lessons. This collegial process can be very productive and interesting, especially when teachers deliver lessons together. Such planning can be within or across subject areas.

● **Vary the blocks**. Novelty means finding ways to make each of the segments different and multisensory. Here are just a few examples of block activities that you can use for the lesson segments:

> Teacher talk (maximum of two segments of 10 to 15 minutes each)
> Research
> Cooperative learning groups
> Reading
> Student peer coaching
> Laboratory experiences
> Computer work
> Journal writing
> Guest speakers
> Videos/movies/slides
> Audiotapes
> Reflection time
> Jigsaw combinations
> Discussion groups
> Role-playing/simulations
> Instructional games/puzzles

PRACTITIONER'S CORNER

Using Practice Effectively

Practice does not make perfect, it makes *permanent*. Practice allows the learner to use the newly learned skill in a new situation with sufficient accuracy so that it will be correctly remembered. Before students begin practice, the teacher should model the thinking process involved and guide the class through each step of the new learning's application.

Since practice makes permanent, the teacher should monitor the students' early practice to ensure that it is accurate and to provide timely feedback and correction if it is not. This guided practice helps eliminate initial errors and alerts students to the critical steps in applying new skills. Here are some suggestions by Hunter (1982) for guiding initial practice:

- **Amount of Material to Practice.** Practice should be limited to the smallest amount of material or skill that has the most relevancy for the students. This allows for sense and meaning to be consolidated as the learner uses the new learning.

- **Amount of Time to Practice.** Practice should take place in short, intense periods of time when the student's working memory is running on prime-time. When the practice period is short, students are more likely to be intent on learning what they are practicing.

- **Frequency of Practice.** New learning should be practiced frequently at first so that it is quickly organized. This is called *massed practice*. If we expect students to retain the information in active storage and to remember how to use it accurately, it should continue to be practiced over longer time intervals. This is called *distributed practice*, and it is the real key to accurate retention and application of information and skills over time.

- **Accuracy of Practice**. As students perform guided practice, the teacher should give prompt and specific feedback on whether the practice is correct or incorrect and why. This process gives the teacher valuable information about the degree of student understanding and whether it makes sense to move on or reteach portions that may be difficult for some students.

PRACTITIONER'S CORNER

Relearning Through Recall

Every time we recall information from long-term storage into working memory, we relearn it. Therefore, teachers should use classroom strategies that encourage students to recall previously learned information regularly so they will relearn it. One strategy for doing this is to maintain learner participation throughout the lesson. Called *active participation*, this principle of learning attempts to keep the mind of the student consistently focused on what is being learned or recalled through covert and overt activities.

The covert activity involves the teacher asking the students to recall previously learned information and to process it in some way. It could be, "Think of the conditions that existed in America just after the Civil War that we learned yesterday, and be prepared to discuss them in a few minutes." This statement informs the students that they will be held accountable for their recall. This accountability increases the likelihood that the students will recall the desired item and, thus, relearn it. It also alleviates the need for the teacher to call on every student to determine if the recall has occurred. After sufficient wait time (see the **Practitioner's Corner** on wait time, p. 128), overt activities are used to determine the quality of the covert recall.

Some suggestions follow on how to use active participation strategies effectively:

- **State the question** and allow thinking time *before* calling on a student for response. This holds all students accountable for recalling the answer until you pick your first respondent.

- **Give clear and specific directions** as to what the students should recall. Focus on the lesson objectives and not on the activities unless they were a crucial part of the learning. Repeat the question using different words and phraseology. This increases the number of cues that the learners have during their retrieval search.

- **Avoid predictable patterns** when calling on students, such as alphabetical order, up and down rows, or raised hands. These patterns signal the students *when* they will be held accountable, thereby allowing them to go off-task before and after their turns.

PRACTITIONER'S CORNER

Impact of Circadian Rhythms on Schools and Classrooms

This chapter explained the differences in circadian rhythms of adolescents compared to pre/postadolescents (Figure 3.10, p. 102). The adolescent rhythm is about an hour later, and these differences have implications for secondary schools. Here are four things to consider:

- **School Start Times**. Because of this shift in rhythm, teenagers are sleepier in the morning and tend to stay up later at night. They come to school sleep deprived (i.e., many suffer from Delayed Sleep Phase Disorder), and often with an inadequate breakfast (i.e., lacking glucose, the brain's fuel). Meanwhile, students often face a long bus ride to get to high schools that are starting earlier. District leaders should consider realigning opening times and course schedules more closely with the students' biological rhythms to increase the chances of successful learning. School districts that have adopted later starting times for their high schools are reporting positive results. These same positive results apply to elementary schools that start earlier than the traditional time of 9:00 a.m.[22]

- **Classroom Lighting**. Adolescents with Delayed Sleep Phase Disorder have a high amount of melatonin (the hormone that induces sleep) in their bodies. One of the best ways to reduce melatonin levels is with bright light. Keep classroom lights on, open blinds, lift shades, and look for ways to get the students into outdoor light, especially in the morning.[23]

- **Testing**. School districts usually give standardized tests to all students in the morning. However, high school students tend to perform better in problem-solving and memory tasks later in the day rather than earlier. It is probable that a number of high school students do not do as well on these tests as they could because of the testing times. Testing later in the morning and early afternoon could improve their performance and scores.

– Continued –

Impact of Circadian Rhythms on Schools and Classrooms—Continued

- **Classroom Climate**. Classroom climate problems can arise in high schools if the teacher is in the postnoon trough while the students are still at their pretrough peak. The teacher is likely to be irritable, and minor discipline annoyances can easily escalate into major confrontations. High school administrators in charge of discipline have reported to me a marked rise in student referrals in the early afternoon.

PRACTITIONER'S CORNER

Using Wait Time to Increase Student Participation

Wait time is to the period of teacher silence that follows the posing of a question before the first student is called on for a response. Regrettably, studies first conducted by Mary Budd Rowe (1974) and others indicate that high school teachers had an average wait time of just over one second. Elementary teachers waited an average of three seconds. This is hardly enough time for slower retrievers, many of whom may know the correct answer, to locate that answer in long-term storage and retrieve it into working memory. And as soon as the teacher calls on the first student, the remaining students **stop the retrieval process** and lose the opportunity to relearn the information. Rowe found that the following happened when teachers extended the wait time to at least **five** seconds or more:

- The length and quality of student responses increased.

- There was greater participation by slower learners.

- Students used more evidence to support inferences.

- There were more higher-order responses.

These results occurred at all grade levels and in all subjects.

Rowe also noted positive changes in the behavior of teachers who consistently used longer wait times. Specifically, she observed that these teachers

- Used more higher-order questioning

- Demonstrated greater flexibility in evaluating responses

- Improved their expectations for the performance of slower learners

One effective method for using wait time is Think-Pair-Share. In this strategy, the teacher asks the students to think about a question. After adequate wait time, the students form pairs and exchange the results of their thinking. Some students then share their ideas with the entire class.

PRACTITIONER'S CORNER

Using Chunking to Enhance Retention

Chunking is the process whereby the brain perceives several items of information as a single item. Words are common examples of chunks. *Elephant* is composed of eight letters, but the brain perceives them as one item of information. The more items we can put into a chunk, the more information we can process in working memory and remember at one time. Chunking is a learned skill and, thus, can also be taught. There are different types of chunking.

Pattern Chunking: This is most easily accomplished whenever we can find patterns in the material to be retained.

- Say we wanted to remember the number 3421941621776. Without a pattern, these 13 digits are treated as separate items and exceed working memory's functional capacity of about seven items. But we could arrange the numbers in groups that have meaning. For example, 342 (my house number), 1941 (when the U.S. entered World War II), 62 (my father's age), and 1776 (the Declaration of Independence). Now the number is only four chunks with meaning: 342 1941 62 1776.

- The following example, admittedly contrived, shows how chunking can work at different levels. The task is to memorize the following string of words:

COW GRASS FIELD TENNIS NET SODA DOG LAKE FISH

We need a method to remember the sequence, because nine is more than the typical functional capacity of seven. We can chunk the sequence of items by using a simple story. First, we see a **cow** eating **grass** in a **field**. Also in the field are two people playing **tennis**. One player hits the ball way over the **net**. They are drinking **soda** while their **dog** runs after the ball that went into the **lake.** The dog's splashing frightens the **fish**. `

– Continued –

Using Chunking to Enhance Retention—Continued

- Learning a step-by-step procedure for tying a shoelace and copying a computer file from a floppy to a hard disk are examples of pattern chunking. We group the items in a sequence and rehearse it mentally until it becomes one or a few chunks. Practicing the procedure further enhances the formation of chunks, and subsequent performance requires little conscious attention.

Categorical Chunking: This is a more sophisticated chunking process in that the learner establishes various types of categories to help classify large amounts of information. The learner reviews the information looking for criteria that will group complex material into simpler categories or arrays. The different types of categories can include

- **Advantages and Disadvantages**. The information is categorized according to the pros and cons of the concept. Examples include energy use, abortion, and capital punishment.

- **Similarities and Differences**. The learner compares two or more concepts using attributes that make them similar and different. Examples are comparing the Articles of Confederation to the Bill of Rights, mitosis to meiosis, and the U.S. Civil War to the Vietnam War.

- **Structure and Function**. These categories are helpful with concepts that have parts with different functions, such as identifying the parts of an animal cell, a short story, or the human digestive system.

- **Taxonomies**. This system sorts information into hierarchical levels according to certain common characteristics. Examples are biological taxonomies (kingdom, phylum, class, etc.), taxonomies of learning (cognitive, affective, and psychomotor), and governmental bureaucracies.

- **Arrays**. These are less ordered than taxonomies in that the criteria for establishing the array are not always logical, but are more likely based on observable features. Human beings are classified, for example, by learning style and personality type. Dogs can be grouped by size, shape, or fur length. Clothing can be divided by material, season, and gender.

PRACTITIONER'S CORNER

Using Mnemonics to Help Retention

Mnemonics (from the Greek "to remember") are very useful devices for remembering unrelated information, patterns, or rules. They were developed by the ancient Greeks to help them remember dialogue in plays and for passing information to others when writing was impractical. There are many types of mnemonic schemes. Here are two that can be easily used in the classroom. Work with students to develop schemes appropriate for the content.

- **Rhyming Mnemonics.** Rhymes are simple yet effective ways to remember rules and patterns. They work because if you forget part of the rhyme or get part of it wrong, the words lose their rhyme or rhythm and signal the error. To retrieve the missing or incorrect part, you start the rhyme over again, and this helps you to relearn it. Have you ever tried to remember the fifth line of a song or poem without starting at the beginning? It is very difficult to do because each line serves as the auditory cue for the next line.

    Common examples of rhymes we have learned are "*I* before *e*, except after *c* ...," "Thirty days hath September ...," and "Columbus sailed the ocean blue ...". Here are some rhymes that can help students learn information in other areas:

    The Spanish Armada met its fate
    In fifteen hundred and eighty-eight.

    Divorced, beheaded, died;
    Divorced, beheaded, survived.
    (the fate of Henry VIII's six wives, in chronological order)

    The number you are dividing by,
    Turn upside down and multiply.
    (rule for dividing by fractions)

    – Continued –

Using Mnemonics to Help Retention—Continued

This may seem like a clumsy system, but it works. Make up your own rhyme, alone or with the class, to help you and your students remember more information faster.

- **Reduction Mnemonics:** In this scheme, you reduce a large body of information to a shorter form and use a letter to represent each shortened piece. The letters are either combined to form a real or artificial word or are used to construct a simple sentence. For example, the real word **HOMES** can help us remember the names of the great lakes (Huron, Ontario, Michigan, Erie, and Superior). The name **ROY G BIV** aids in remembering the seven colors of the spectrum (red, orange, yellow, green, blue, indigo, and violet). The artificial word NATO recalls North Atlantic Treaty Organization. The sentence **My Very Earnest Mother Just Served Us Nine Pizzas** can help us remember the nine planets of the solar system in order from the sun (Mercury, Venus, Earth, Mars, Jupiter, Saturn, Uranus, Neptune, and Pluto). Here are other examples:

  Please Excuse My Dear Aunt Sally.
  (the order for solving algebraic equations: Parenthesis, Exponents, Multiplication, Division, Addition, Subtraction)

  Frederick Charles Goes Down And Ends Battle.
  (F, C, G, D, A, E, B: the order that sharps are entered in key signatures; reverse the order for flats)

  In Poland, Men Are Tall.
  (the stages of cell division in mitosis: Interphase, Prophase, Metaphase, Anaphase, and Telophase)

  Krakatoa Positively Casts Off Fumes, Generally Sulfurous Vapors.
  (the descending order of zoological classifications: Kingdom, Phylum, Class, Order, Family, Genus, Species, Variety)

  King Henry Doesn't Mind Drinking Cold Milk.
  (the descending order of metric prefixes: Kilo, Hecto, Deca, (measure), Deci, Centi, and Milli)

Chapter 3—Memory, Retention, and Learning

Key Points to Ponder

Jot down on this page key points, ideas, strategies, and resources you want to consider later. This sheet is your personal journal summary and will help to jog your memory.

_____

_____

_____

_____

_____

_____

_____

_____

_____

_____

_____

CHAPTER 3 – NOTES

1. This process is explained in greater detail in Squire and Kandel (1999) and Carter (1998).

2. Several pharmaceutical companies (e.g., Helicon Therapeutics and Cortex Pharmaceuticals) are working on "smart drugs," several of which are being tested on humans. One approach is to affect long-term potentiation to increase synaptic transmission. Another is to enhance the effectiveness of certain neurotransmitters during memory formation. This is an area to watch closely.

3. Cahill and McGaugh (1998).

4. These fascinating case studies are described in Rose (1992), Schacter (1996), and Squire and Kandel (1999).

5. See Buckner, Kelley, and Petersen (1999) and Wagner et al. (1998).

6. Many of the original studies used for Figures 3.3, 3.4, and 3.5 and Table 3.1 can be found in Buzan (1989) and Thomas (1972).

7. These action research projects were conducted by graduate students who attended my classes at Seton Hall University in New Jersey, 1994–1997.

8. Shadmehr and Holcomb (1997).

9. Schlaug, Jancke, Huang, and Steinmetz (1995).

10. Amunts et al. (1997).

11. Carskadon, Acebo, Wolfson, Tzischinsky, and Darley (1997).

12. Acebo, Wolfson, and Carskadon (1997) and Schacter (1996).

13. Wolfson and Carskadon (1998).

14. Gardner's eight intelligences are musical, logical-mathematical, spatial, bodily-kinesthetic, linguistic, interpersonal, intrapersonal, and naturalist.

15. For an excellent discussion of multiple intelligences and brain research, see Kagan and Kagan (1998).

16. Schacter (1996), pp. 79–81.

17. Schacter (1996), pp. 81–84.

18. Although we all fall victim to confabulation at one time or another, damage to certain brain areas can cause chronic and extreme confabulation where the recalled memories deviate significantly from reality. See Shallice (1999).

19. Gazzaniga (1998a), pp. 156–158.

20. Roediger and McDermott (1995).

21. Loftus (1997).

22. Among the first school districts to change to later high school start times were Minnetonka and Edina, Minnesota.

23. Kripke, Youngstedt, and Elliot (1997).

CHAPTER 4

THE POWER OF TRANSFER

Transfer is the basis of all creativity, problem solving and the making of satisfying decisions.
— Madeline Hunter,
Mastery Teaching

Chapter Highlights: This chapter explains the components of the most powerful principle of learning, transfer. It examines the factors that affect transfer and how teachers can use past learnings effectively to enhance present and future learning.

The brain is a dynamic creation that is constantly organizing and reorganizing itself when it receives new stimuli. More networks are formed as raw items merge into new patterns. Just as musicians in an orchestra join the individual sounds of their instruments in new and melodious ways, so does the brain unite disconnected ideas with wonderful harmony. We can add beauty and clarity, and forge isolated ideas into spectacular visions. Transfer is one process that allows this amazing inventiveness to unfold. It encompasses the ability to learn in one situation and then use that learning, possibly in a modified or generalized form, in other situations. Transfer is the core of problem solving, creative thinking, and all other higher mental processes, inventions, and artistic products.

What Is Transfer?

The most powerful principle of learning, called *transfer*, describes a two-part process: (1) the effect that past learning has on the processing of new learning, and (2) the degree to which the new learning will be useful to the learner in the future.[1] The process goes something like this: Whenever new learning moves into working memory, long-term memory (most likely stimulated by a signal from the hippocampus) simultaneously searches the long-term storage sites for any past

136

learnings that are similar to, or associated with, the new learning. If the experiences exist, the memory networks are activated and also move into working memory.

The degree to which past learning affects the learner's ability to acquire new knowledge or skills in another context describes one phase of the powerful phenomenon called transfer. In other words, the information processing system depends on past learnings to associate with, make sense of, and treat new information. This recycling of past information into the flow not only reinforces and provides additional rehearsal for already-stored information but also aids in assigning meaning to new information. The degree of meaning attributed to new learning will determine the connections that are made between it and other information in long-term storage. These connections and associations give the learner more options to cope with new situations in the future (Figure 4.1).

Transfer can be referred to as the "so what?" phase of learning. The context in which students learn information and skills is often different from the context where they will apply that learning. If students do not perceive how the information or skill can be used for the future, they will tend to pay little attention and exert even less effort.

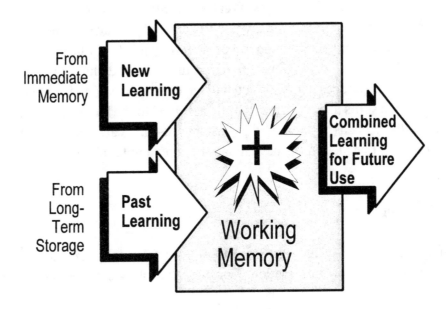

Figure 4.1 *New learning and past learning coming together in working memory is one part of transfer. The learner's understanding of how the combined learning can be used in the future is the other part of transfer.*

Types of Transfer

Positive Transfer

When past learning *helps* the learner deal with new learning, it is called *positive transfer*. Suppose a violin player and a trombone player both want to learn to play the viola, an instrument similar to the violin. Who will learn the new instrument more easily? The violin player already possesses the skills and knowledge that will help in learning the viola. The trombone player, on the other hand, may be a very accomplished trombonist but possesses few skills that will help to play the viola. Similarly, Michelangelo, DaVinci, and Edison were able to transfer a great deal of their knowledge and skills to create magnificent works of art and invention. Their prior learnings made greater achievement possible.

Negative Transfer

Sometimes past learning *interferes* with the learner's understanding of new learning, resulting in confusion or errors. This process is called *negative transfer*. If, for example, you have been driving cars with only automatic shift, you will have quite a surprise the first time you drive a standard-shift car. You were accustomed to keeping your left foot idle or using it to brake. In either case, the left foot has a very different function in a standard-shift car. If it keeps doing its automatic-shift functions (or does nothing), you will have great difficulty driving the standard-shift car. In other words, the skills that the driver's brain assigned to the left foot for the automatic-shift car are not the skills it needs to cope with the standard-shift car. The skill it used before is interfering with the skill needed in the new situation, an example of negative transfer.

Transfer and Meaning

Meaning often results when past learning moves from long-term storage into working memory and interacts with new information. Consider the following pieces of information:

1. There are seven days in the week.
2. Force = mass **X** acceleration.
3. Iraq is an evil country.
4. ...They also serve who only stand and wait.
5. Jesus is the son of God.
6. There's a sucker born every minute.

In each instance, the meaning of the information depends on the experience, education, and state of mind of the reader. The third and last statements can arouse passionate agreement or disavowal. The second and fourth statements would be meaningless to a second grader, but not the first statement. The fifth could provoke an endless debate among adherents of different religions.

Meaning is often context dependent. The transfer process not only provides interpretation of words, but often includes nuances and shadings that can result in very different meanings. "He is a piece of work!" can be either a compliment or a sarcastic comment, depending on tone and context.

Transfer in the Curriculum

A review of any curriculum reveals that transfer is an integral component and expectation of the learning process. Every day, teachers deliberately or intuitively refer to past learning to make new learning more understandable and meaningful. For the long term, students are expected to transfer the knowledge and skills they learn in school to their daily routines, jobs, and ventures outside the school. Writing and speaking skills should help them communicate with others, scientific knowledge should inform their decisions on environmental and health issues, and their understanding of history should guide their responses to contemporary problems at personal, social, and cultural levels. It is almost axiomatic that the more

> **Thematic units and an integrated curriculum enhance the transfer process.**

information students can transfer from their schooling to the context of everyday life, the greater the probability that they will be good communicators, informed citizens, critical thinkers, and successful problem solvers.

Yet studies continue to show that students are not successful in recognizing how the skills and knowledge they learned in school apply to new situations they encounter outside school.[2] Apparently, we are doing little in schools to deliberately make the transfer connections to enhance new learning. The more connections that students can make between past learning and new learning, the more likely they are to determine sense and meaning and thus retain the new learning. Moreover, when these connections can be extended across curriculum areas, they establish a framework of associative networks that will be recalled for future problem solving. Successful transfer can be enhanced by educators who advocate thematic units and an integrated curriculum. This approach helps students to see commonalities among diverse topics and reinforces understanding and meaning for future applications.

Transfer in the Classroom

During a lesson, students are dealing continually with transfer as they process and practice new information and skills. Because students' experiences vary, the extent of what transfers also varies. Whether that transfer aids or impedes the acquisition of new learning is a major factor in determining the degree of success each student has in accomplishing the lesson objective.

For example, teachers who teach Romance languages to native English speakers are frequently helped by positive transfer and plagued by negative transfer. Words like *rouge* in French and *mucho* in Spanish help to teach *red* and *much*, respectively, but when students see the French *librairie* and are told it is a place where books are found, experience prompts them to think that it means "library." It really means "bookstore."

Transfer Provoked by Environment

Another interesting characteristic of transfer is that it is more frequently provoked by the environment than consciously by the learner. Have you ever heard a song that brings back a flood of memories? You could not really control that recall unless something else in your present environment now demanded your immediate attention, such as your crying baby or a ringing fire alarm. Now, who represents a large portion of the environment for students in school? Yes, the teachers! Teachers are the instruments of transfer for students. If teachers are not aware of that, they can inadvertently provoke negative transfer during learning situations just as easily as they can provoke positive transfer. To use transfer effectively, teachers need to identify factors that facilitate learning (positive transfer) while minimizing or eliminating factors that can cause interference (negative transfer).

> **Teachers are frequently the provokers of transfer for their students.**

Test Question No. 9: Most of the time, the transfer of information from long-term storage is under the conscious control of the learner.

Answer: False. The transfer process is more often provoked by the learner's present environment.

Example of Transfer in an English Class. The following anecdote illustrates how transfer can impede or promote a lesson objective. A few years ago, I observed a senior class in British literature in a large urban high school. It was late April, and as the students entered the class, they were discussing the upcoming final examinations, the prom, and preparations for graduation. After the opening bell rang, the teacher admonished the students to pay attention and said, "Today, we are going to start another play by William Shakespeare." The moans and groans were deafening and abated only after the teacher used every threat short of ripping up their forthcoming diplomas. Judging from their reactions and unsolicited comments, the students' perceptions of past experiences with Shakespeare were hardly positive. Without realizing it, the teacher's brief introduction had provoked negative transfer; getting the students to focus constructively on the new play now would not be easy.

Later that afternoon, I found myself in a different teacher's British literature class. A large television monitor and a videocassette recorder in the front of the classroom attracted the students as they entered. The teacher asked the students to watch a videotape and be prepared to discuss what they saw. What unfolded over the next 15 minutes was a cleverly edited collection of scenes from the movie *West Side Story*. There was enough to get the plot and enough of the music to maintain interest. The students were captivated; some even sang along. As the showdown between Tony and Maria's brother came on the screen, the teacher stopped the tape. The students complained, wanting to see who won the fight. The teacher noted that this was really an old story set in modern times, and that she had the script of the original play. The characters' names and the location were different, but the plot was the same. While the students were discussing what they had seen, she distributed Shakespeare's *Romeo and Juliet*. Many students eagerly flipped through the pages trying to find the outcome of the fight scene! The teacher's understanding of positive transfer was evident, and she had used it magnificently.

Knowledge is power. Understanding how transfer helps or impedes learning gives teachers opportunities to use positive transfer and avoid negative transfer.

Factors Affecting Transfer

How quickly transfer occurs during a learning situation depends on the rate of retrieval. As noted earlier, the rate of retrieval is largely dependent on the storage system that the learner has created and how the learning was originally stored. Designing the filing system in long-term storage is a *learned* skill and can run the gamut from very loose connections to a highly organized series of networks. Working memory uses a sensory cue that it encodes with the material and files it in a network containing similar items.

The cue helps long-term memory locate, identify, and select the material for later retrieval, similar to the way the label on a file folder helps to locate and identify what is in the file. If the learner is recalling a complex concept, information has to come from various storage areas to a convergence zone for assembly, verification, and decoding into working memory. Many factors in a learning system affect the nature of this transfer process. Hunter and others have identified four of these: similarity, critical attributes, association, and the context and degree of original learning. No factor is more important than the others, and they often work together.[3]

Similarity

Transfer is generated by the similarity of the situation in which something is being learned and the situation to which that learning may transfer. Thus, behavior in one environment tends to transfer to other environments that are similar. For example, commercial jet pilots are first trained in flight simulators before they sit in the cockpit of the actual plane. All the training and learnings they acquired in the simulator, an exact replica of the actual plane, will transfer to the real flying situation. This positive transfer helps the pilot get accustomed quickly to the actual plane, and it reduces errors.

If you have ever rented a car, you realize that it does not take you very long to get accustomed to it and drive away. The environment is similar to your own car, and most of the important components are in familiar places. You may need a few moments, however, to locate the windshield wiper and light switches.

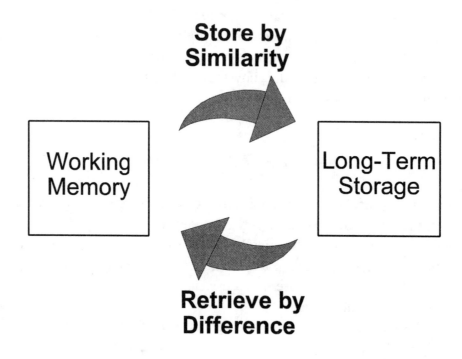

Figure 4.2 *We tend to store information in networks by similarity but retrieve it back into working memory by difference.*

Teachers often use similarity when introducing new material. They may have students learn words with similar spelling patterns, such as *beat, heat, meat,* and *neat.* Students may use their skills at finding locations on a road map to help place ordered numbers on a graph grid. However, as we shall discuss shortly, presenting two items of information at the same time that are *too* similar can cause retention problems.

Other examples of using similarity are fire and tornado drills. Even giving students major tests in the room where they learned the material being tested uses similarity of the environment for positive transfer.

Similarity of sensory modes is another form of transfer. Using the color red to represent danger can alert us to traffic lights, the location of fire alarm boxes, or hazardous areas. Sensory similarity can also cause error. Students may confuse *there, their,* and *they're* because they sound alike, or they may not be able to pronounce *read* until they know the word's context.

The more specific the cue that working memory attaches to a new learning, the easier it is for long-term memory to identify the item being sought. This process leads to an interesting phenomenon regarding long-term storage and retrieval: **We store by similarity, but we retrieve by difference.** That is, long-term memory most often stores new learnings into a network that contains learnings with similar characteristics or associations, as perceived by the learner. This network identification is one of the connections made in working memory during rehearsal and closure. To retrieve an item, long-term memory identifies how it is *different* from all the other items in that network (Figure 4.2).

A simple example is: How would you recognize your best friend in a crowd? It is not because he has two arms, two legs, a head, and a torso. These characteristics make him *similar* to all the others. Rather, it is his more subtle *differences,* such as facial features, walk, and voice, that allow you to distinguish him from everyone else. His unique characteristics are called his *critical attributes.* If your friend is an identical twin, however, you might have difficulty picking him out from his brother if both are in the crowd. Similarly, the high degree of similarity between two concepts, coupled with few differences, makes it difficult for the learner to tell them apart.

Take, for example, the concepts of latitude and longitude. The similarities between these two ideas far outweigh their differences. Both use identical units of measure, deal with all four compass points, are imaginary lines, locate points on the

> *Two concepts that are very similar to each other ordinarily should not be taught at the same time.*

Earth's surface, and are similar in sound and spelling. Their only real difference is their orientation in space. Teaching them together can be very difficult because their many similarities obscure their singular difference. The problem of similarity can be pervasive because curriculums are often written with the most alike concepts taught together.[4] (See the **Practitioner's Corner** at the end of this chapter, p. 151, for precisely when this can be a problem and how to deal with it.)

Critical Attributes

Critical attributes, characteristics that make one idea unique from all others, are the cues of *difference* that learners can use as part of their storage process. Statements like *Amphibians live both on land and in water, Homonyms are words that sound alike but have different spellings and meanings*, and *To produce sound, something must vibrate* are examples of identifying critical attributes.

Identifying the critical attributes of a concept is not an easy task. We live in a culture driven by a quest for equality for all. This culture places a higher value on similarities than on differences. Thus, our cerebral networks are organized around similarity from an early age, and teachers frequently use similarity in the classroom to introduce new ideas. Successful retrieval from mental storage areas is accomplished by identifying differences among concepts. Consequently, teachers can help learners process new learnings accurately by having them identify the unique characteristics that make one concept different from all others. For example, what are the critical attributes of an explorer? Will these attributes help to separate Vasco da Gama from Napoleon? Students can use critical attributes to sort concepts so that they are stored in logical networks with appropriate cues. This will facilitate long-term memory's searches and increase the probability that it will accurately identify and retrieve the concept being sought.

Association

Whenever two events, actions, or feelings are learned together, they are said to be *associated,* or bonded, so that the recall of one prompts the spontaneous recall of the other. The word *Romeo* elicits *Juliet,* and *Batman* gets *Robin.* A song you hear being played at a mall may elicit memories of some event that are associated with that song. The odor of a cologne once worn by a close friend from the past triggers the emotions of that relationship. Trademarks and product symbols, such as McDonald's golden arches, are designed to recall the product. Although there is no similarity between the two items, they were learned together and are, therefore, recalled together.

Here is a simple example of transfer. Look at the words listed below. On the lines to the right, write one or two words that come to mind as you read each word in the list.

Monday	_____	_____
dentist	_____	_____
Mom	_____	_____
vacation	_____	_____
babies	_____	_____

emergency	_____	_____
money	_____	_____
Sunday	_____	_____

What you wrote down represents thoughts that you have associated with each word in the list. Here are some responses that others have written for Monday: *work, blues, quarterback, beginning.* For Mom, others have written: *love, apple pie, caring, important, security, dad.* Were your words anything like these? Maybe they were, or maybe not. Show the list to your family and friends and note their responses. Each of us makes different connections with concepts based on our unique experiences; this activity points out the variety of associations that different people can make with the same thought.

Making associations expands the brain's ability to retain information. New connections are formed between neurons and new insights are encoded. Much like a tree growing new branches, everything we remember becomes another set of branches to which memories can be attached. The more we learn and retain, the more we *can* learn and retain.

> **The more we learn, the more we can learn.**

Emotions. Association is particularly powerful when feelings or emotions are associated with a learning. We mentioned earlier that the brain's amygdala encodes emotional messages when they are strong and bonds them to learnings for long-term storage. We also noted that emotions usually have a higher priority than cognitive processing for commanding our attention. Words like *abortion, Holocaust,* and *capital punishment* often evoke strong feelings. Math anxiety is an example of a strong feeling (probably failure) associated with mathematics. Some students will avoid new situations involving learning mathematics to avoid the negative feelings that are recalled with the content. On the other hand, people devote hours to their hobbies because they associate feelings of pleasure and success with the activity. Thus, teachers should strive to bond positive feelings to new learnings so that students feel competent and can enjoy the process.

Context and Degree of Original Learning

The quality of transfer that occurs during new learning is largely dependent on the quality of the original learning. Most of us can recall easily our Social Security number or even a poem we learned in our early school years. If the original learning was well-learned and accurate, its influence on new learning will be more constructive and help the student toward greater achievement. Students who did not learn the scientific method well, for example, will not be very effective in laboratory analysis, and they will not be able to transfer this learning to future success.

> *Today's learning is tomorrow's transfer. Therefore, if something is worth teaching, it is worth teaching well.*

If something is worth teaching, it is worth teaching well. If we teach students to be conscious of both the new learning and the context into which it fits, we are helping them forge strong associations for future recall. When using transfer, we ask students to bring learnings from their past forward to today. If the past learning was taught well, it should help the students acquire today's learning. What is taught today becomes past learning tomorrow. If it is taught well today, the positive transfer will enhance tomorrow's learning, and so forth. In other words, today's learning is tomorrow's transfer.

Teaching for Transfer

Teachers should not assume that transfer will automatically occur after students acquire a sufficient base of information. Significant and efficient transfer occurs only if we teach to achieve it. Hunter (1982), Perkins and Salomon (1988), and others have suggested that when teachers understand the factors that affect transfer, they can plan lessons that use the power of positive transfer to help students learn faster, solve problems, and generate creative and artistic products that enrich the learning experience.

To teach for transfer, we need to consider two major factors: The time sequence and the complexity of the transfer link between the learnings. The time sequence refers to the way the teacher will use time and transfer in the learning situation. Transfer can occur from past to present or from present to future.

Transfer From Past to Present

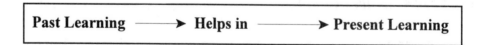

Past Learning ⟶ Helps in ⟶ Present Learning

In this, the teacher links something from the learner's past that helps add sense and meaning to the new learning. It is important to select an experience that is clear, unambiguous, and closely relevant (not just related) to the new learning. Some examples are as follows:

- An English teacher uses *West Side Story* to introduce *Romeo and Juliet* so that students transfer their knowledge about street gangs and feuds to help them understand Shakespeare's plot.

- A science teacher asks students to recall what they have learned about plant cells to study the similarities and differences in animal cells.

- A social studies teacher asks students to think of the causes of the U.S. Civil War to see if they can also explain the causes of the Vietnam War.

Transfer From Present to Future

> **Present Learning ———→ Helps in ———→ Future Learning**

The teacher makes the present learning situation as similar as possible to a future situation to which the new learning should transfer. For the transfer to be successful, students must attain a high degree of original (current) learning and be able to recognize the critical attributes and concepts that make the situations similar and different. For example,

- Students learn the critical attributes of fact and opinion so they can transfer that learning in the future when evaluating advertising, news reports, election campaigns, and the like.

- Students learn how to read graphs, pie charts, and tables so that in the future they can evaluate data presented to them for analysis and action.

- Students learn safe personal and interpersonal hygiene practices to protect their health throughout their lives.

Teaching techniques, such as *bridging* and *hugging*, are designed to help students make transfer links from past to present, and present to future. They can be used in all subject areas and for learning both cognitive concepts and psychomotor skills. (Examples of these techniques are found in the **Practitioner's Corners** at the end of this chapter; see pp. 157 and 159.)

Complexity of the Link Between Learnings

The way that transfer occurs during a learning situation can range from a very superficial similarity to a sophisticated, abstract association. For example, when renting a car, it takes just a few minutes to get accustomed to the model, find the windshield wiper and light controls, and drive off. Interpreting a pie chart in the school budget requires the recall of graph analysis skills from a prior mathematics course. The new learning environments are perceived as being *similar* to others that the learner has practiced, and that similarity automatically triggers the same learned behaviors.

Metaphor, Analogy, and Simile. The transfer connection can also be much more complex, requiring the learner to make an abstract application of knowledge and skills to the new situation. Metaphors, analogies, and similes are useful devices for promoting abstract transfer. The *metaphor* is the application of a word or phrase to an object or concept that it does not literally denote to suggest a comparison with another object or concept. A person may say "It's raining cats

> **Metaphors can convey meaning of abstract material as well and as rapidly as literal language.**

and dogs outside. I'm drowned!" Obviously, it is not raining animals and the person did not drown. He is speaking figuratively and the metaphor compares things that are essentially dissimilar. An *analogy* compares partial similarity between two things, such as comparing a heart to a pump. The *simile* compares two unlike things: *She is like a rose.*

Metaphors can often convey meaning of abstract material as well and as rapidly as literal language. Metaphors help to explain complex concepts or processes. A geologist explains the movement of glaciers as flowing like batter on a griddle, and that the glacier was like an enormous plow upon the land. Comparing life to taking a long trip also is a metaphor. We ask the learner to reflect on how the situations encountered on the road compare to those encountered in life. How can the meaning of bumps, detours, road signs and billboards, places we have visited, passed through, or stayed in for a while all compare to life situations? Complex transfer patterns can reach back to the past: *How does the thinking strategy I used when I encountered a major detour help me to decide what course to choose in life now?* They can also transfer to the future: *The planning I used in preparing for the trip should help me prepare for other major decisions I need to make in my life that require extensive planning.*

These strategies are rich in imagery and enhance the thinking process by encouraging students to seek out associations and connections that they would not ordinarily make (See more on imagery in Chapter 5; see also the **Practitioner's Corner** on p. 161 on using metaphors to enhance transfer). They gain insights into relationships among ideas that help to forge a more thorough understanding of new learning.

Journal Writing for Transfer

Transfer is more likely to occur when students have an opportunity to reflect on their new learning. This reflection time can occur during closure, and is more likely to take place if the student is given a specific task. Journal writing is a very useful technique for closure because the specific steps help students to make connections to previous knowledge and

> **Journal writing is a highly effective strategy for closure and transfer.**

organize concepts into networks for eventual storage. The strategy takes but a few minutes, but it can have enormous payback in terms of increased understanding and retention of learning. See the **Practitioner's Corner** on p. 163 for the specific steps that are likely to make this a successful effort.

Transfer and Constructivism

The proper and frequent use of transfer greatly enhances the constructivist approach to learning. Constructivist teachers are those who[5]

- Use student responses to alter their instructional strategies and content

- Foster student dialogue

- Question student understanding before sharing their own

- Encourage students to elaborate on their initial responses

- Allow students time to construct relationships and create metaphors

All these strategies have been discussed here and in previous chapters and are characteristic of teachers who are proficient in using transfer deliberately throughout their lessons.

149

PRACTITIONER'S CORNER

Strategies for Connecting to Past Learnings

Transfer helps students make connections between what they already know and the new learning. It is important to remember that the connections are of value only if they are relevant to the *students'* past, not the teacher's. This process also helps the teacher find out what the students already know about the new material. If students already have knowledge of what is planned for the new lesson, then teachers should make some adjustments and move on. (The curriculum is notably cluttered with too much repetition at every grade level and in every subject area.) This method also alerts the teacher to any prior knowledge that may interfere with new learning (negative transfer). Here are a few suggestions to discover what students already know so that prior learnings can help facilitate new learning (positive transfer). Note that the activities use novelty and shift the task burden to the student. Choose those that are grade-level appropriate.

- **Short Story**. Students write short stories to describe what they already know about a given topic. This can be used in any subject area because writing is a skill that should be continually practiced. (Note: This activity is not journal writing, which serves a different purpose.)

- **Interviews**. In a think-pair-share format, students interview their partners to determine their knowledge levels.

- **Graphic Organizers**. Students select an appropriate graphic organizer to explain and relate their past learning.

- **Mural or Collage**. Students make a mural or collage to communicate their current knowledge.

- **Music Activity**. Students write a song that tells of their prior knowledge.

- **Models**. Students build or draw models to express what they know.

- **Student Ideas**. Students may suggest other ways of showing what they know, such as writing a poem, painting a picture, creating a quiz show, etc.

PRACTITIONER'S CORNER

Avoid Teaching Concepts That Are Very Similar

Teachers often use similarity to introduce new topics. They say, "You already learned something about this topic when we ..." This helps students to use positive transfer by recalling similar items from long-term storage that can assist in learning new information. But as we saw in the Chapter 3 discussion on learning motor skills, similarity can also be a problem. Whenever two concepts have many more similarities than differences, such as latitude and longitude, mitosis and meiosis, or simile and metaphor, there is a high risk that the learner cannot tell them apart. In effect, the similarities overwhelm the differences, resulting in the learner attaching the same retrieval cues to both concepts. Thus, when the learner uses that cue later to retrieve information, it could produce either or both concepts and the learner may not recognize which is correct.

How to Deal With This Problem. When planning a lesson with two very similar concepts, list their similarities and differences. If the number of similarities and differences is about the same, there is less chance the students will be confused, but if the number of similarities is far greater than the differences, confusion is likely. In that case, try the following:

- **Teach the Two Concepts at Different Times.** Teach the first concept; make sure that the students thoroughly understand it and can practice it correctly. Then teach a related concept to give the first concept time to be consolidated accurately and fully into long-term storage. Teach the second concept a few weeks later. Now information from the first concept acts for positive transfer in learning the second concept.

- **Teach the Difference(s) First.** Another option is to start by teaching the difference(s) between the two concepts. This works better with older students because they have enough prior learnings to recognize subtle differences. For example, teach that the only real difference between latitude and longitude is their orientation in space. Focusing on and practicing the difference gives learners the warnings and the cues they need to separate the two similar concepts and identify them correctly in the future.

– Continued –

Avoid Teaching Concepts That Are Very Similar—Continued

It seems so logical that two concepts that have many similarities should be taught at the same time. And so, for years, teachers have struggled with introducing concepts like the following in the same lesson: latitude and longitude; mitosis and meiosis; simile, analogy, and metaphor; complementary and supplementary angles; monarchy, oligarchy, plutocracy; writing lower-case b, d, p, and q, and many others. But the very fact that they are *so* similar can lead to retrieval problems.

To see how similarity may affect your work, try this activity:

A. Think about and list two or more concepts that are so similar they could cause confusion.

_____

_____

_____

_____

_____

B. How could these concepts be presented to minimize confusion?

_____

_____

_____

_____

_____

PRACTITIONER'S CORNER

Identifying Critical Attributes for Accurate Transfer

Critical attributes are characteristics that make one concept *unique* among all others. Teachers need to help students identify these attributes so students can use them for eventual and accurate retrieval. Hunter (1982) suggested a five-step process:

1. **Identify the Critical Attributes.** Suppose the learning objective is for the students to understand how mammals are different from all other animals. The two critical attributes of mammals are that (a) they nurse their young through mammary glands, and (b) they have hair.

2. **Teacher Gives Simple Examples.** The teacher offers some simple examples, such as the human being, cat, dog, and gerbil, to establish the concept. The teacher gives the examples at this point, not the students. Because this new learning is occurring in prime-time-1 when retention is highest, the examples must be correct. Be sure to match the example to the two critical attributes.

3. **Teacher Gives Complex Examples.** Now the teacher gives more complex examples, such as the porpoise and whale, which, unlike most mammals, live in water. It is important here to show again how the critical attributes apply.

4. **Students Give Examples.** Here the teacher checks for student understanding to ensure that the critical attributes are used correctly and that the concept is firmly in place. The students must also prove that the attributes apply to their examples.

5. **Teach the Limits of the Critical Attributes.** The learner must recognize that critical attributes may have limits and not apply in every instance. In this lesson, these attributes will accurately identify all mammals, but may incorrectly identify some nonmammals. There is a small group of animals called *platypuses*, that exhibit not only mammalian characteristics but also those of amphibians and birds. They are in a separate classification.

Take each major concept you teach and use the five-step process above to identify its critical attributes. These attributes help students clearly recognize what makes this concept *different* from all others. These attributes become valuable cues for accuracy and later retrieval.

– Continued –

Identifying Critical Attributes for Accurate Transfer—Continued

By identifying the critical attributes, the student learns how one concept is different from all other similar concepts. This leads to clearer understanding, concept attainment, the ability to relate the new concept properly to others, and the likelihood that it will be stored and remembered accurately. All subject areas have major concepts whose critical attributes should be clearly identified. Here are a few simple examples:

Social Studies

Law	Rule made by a government entity that is used for the control of behavior, is policed, and carries a penalty if broken.
Culture	The common behavior of a large group of people who can be identified by specific foods, clothing, art, religion, and music.

Science

Mammal	An animal that has hair and mammary glands.
Planet	A natural heavenly body that revolves around a star, rotates on its axis, and does not produce its own light.

Mathematics

Triangle	A two-dimensional figure that is closed and three-sided.
Prime	An integer with a value greater than 1 whose only positive factors are itself and 1.

Language Arts

Sonnet	A poem of 14 lines, written in iambic pentameter with a specific rhyming pattern.
Simile	A figure of speech that compares two unlike things.

Try the activity on the next page to help identify the critical attributes of important concepts from your own teaching or learning experiences.

– Continued –

Identifying Critical Attributes for Accurate Transfer—Continued

A. Work with a partner to complete the worksheet on the next page, *Identifying Unique and Unvarying Elements*. Begin by using the Analogy Map to help you decide on the differences between two similar concepts.

Analogy Map

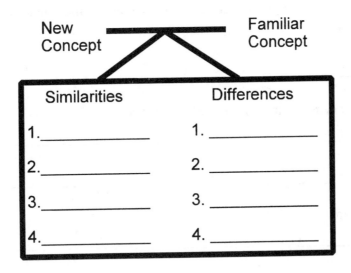

B. After completing the worksheet, decide what benefits are provided to the learner by identifying the unique and unvarying elements/critical attributes.

C. List here some concepts in your curriculum that would be good candidates for this strategy.

– Continued –

Identifying Critical Attributes for Accurate Transfer—Continued

**Identifying
Unique and
Unvarying
Elements**

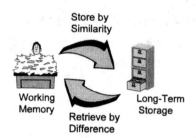

Identify a major concept and decide on its unique and unvarying elements (critical attributes):

Concept:_____

1. Its unique and unvarying elements (critical attributes) are

_____

_____

2. Simple examples are

_____

_____

3. Complex example(s) are

_____

_____

4. Student examples could be

_____

_____

5. Limits of the unique and unvarying elements (if any) are

_____

PRACTITIONER'S CORNER

Teaching for Transfer: Bridging

Perkins and Salomon (1988), among others, have suggested various techniques for teachers to use to achieve positive transfer. In the technique called *bridging,* the teacher invokes transfer by helping students see the connection and abstraction from what the learner knows to other new learnings and contexts. There are many ways this can be accomplished. Here are a few:

- **Brainstorming.** When introducing a new topic, ask students to brainstorm ways this new learning can be applied in other situations. For example, can students use the skills they have just learned in analyzing charts, tables, and graphs? How else can they use their understandings about the law of supply and demand? What future value is there in knowing about nuclear power generation and alternative energy sources?

- **Analogies.** After learning a topic, use an analogy to examine the similarities and differences between one system and another. For example, ask students to make comparisons: How was the post–Vietnam War period in Vietnam similar to and different from the post–U.S. Civil War period? How is the post–Soviet Union period in Russia today similar to and different from the U.S. post–Revolutionary War period?

- **Metacognition.** When solving problems, ask students to investigate ways of approaching the solutions and discuss the advantages and disadvantages of each. For example, what solutions are there to meet the increased demand for electrical power in a densely populated area? What power sources could be used and which would be safest, most economical, most practical, etc.? What are the ways in which governments could regionalize to improve their effectiveness and economy of services? What impact might this have on local government and the democratic process? After applying their solutions, the students discuss how well their approaches worked and how they might change their approaches next time to improve their success.

– Continued –

Teaching for Transfer: Bridging (Transfer of Past to Present)—Continued

The Brooklyn Bridge

Bridging: Invoking transfer by connecting what the learner knows to other new learning and contexts. Select a concept (e.g., energy, democracy, equilibrium, allegory) and use the strategies below to link that concept to the learner's past knowledge. Look at the **Practitioner's Corner** on concept mapping in Chapter 5, p. 196 for help with this task.

Brainstorming (applying new learning in other situations):

_____

_____

Analogies (examining similarities and differences):

The Analogy Map could help here (see p. 185).

_____

_____

_____

Metacognition (solving problems by investigating advantages and disadvantages of alternative solutions):

Advantages	Disadvantages

PRACTITIONER'S CORNER

Teaching for Transfer: Hugging

Hugging, suggested by Perkins and Salomon (1988), uses similarity to make the new learning situation more like future situations to which transfer is desired. This is a lower form of transfer and relies on an almost automatic response from the learner when the new situation is encountered. Teachers should ensure that the similarity of a situation actually involves the student using the skill or knowledge to be transferred. When students use a word search puzzle to identify certain French verbs written forward or backward, this does not mean that they will be able to understand these verbs in written or spoken French. *Hugging* means keeping the new instruction as close as possible to the environment and requirements that the students will encounter in the future. Here are a few ways to design hugging:

● **Simulation Games.** These are useful in helping students practice new roles in diverse situations. Debates, mock trials, and investigating labor disputes are ways that students can experiment with various approaches to solving complex legal and social issues.

● **Mental Practice.** When a student is unable to replicate an upcoming situation, it is very useful for the student to mentally practice what that situation could be like. The student reviews potential variations of the situation and devises mental strategies for dealing with different scenarios. Suppose a student is to interview a political candidate for the school newspaper. In addition to the prepared questions, what other questions could the student ask, depending on the candidate's response? What if the candidate is reticent or changes the course of the questioning?

● **Contingency Learning.** Here the learner asks what other information or skill must be acquired to solve a problem, and then learns it. For example, if the student is building a model to demonstrate gas laws, what else must the student learn in order to design and construct the apparatus at a reasonable cost so that it shows the desired gas relationships effectively?

– Continued –

Teaching for Transfer: Hugging (Transfer of Present to Future)—Continued

Hugging: Invoking transfer by making the new learning situation more like future situations to which transfer is desired. Select a concept (or the same one you chose in Bridging) and use the strategies that follow to show how the concept can be useful in future circumstances.

Simulation games (practicing new roles in diverse situations):

_____

_____

_____

_____

Be prepared to present the simulation to the group.

Mental practice (devising mental strategies for dealing with different scenarios):

_____

_____

_____

_____

Contingency learning (secondary learnings needed to accomplish primary learning):

_____

_____

_____

PRACTITIONER'S CORNER

Using Metaphors to Enhance Transfer

Metaphors can convey meaning as well and as rapidly as literal language. They are usually rich in imagery, are useful bridging strategies, and can apply to both content and skill learnings. West, Farmer, and Wolff (1991) suggest a six-step process for using metaphors in lesson design.

1. **Select the Metaphor.** The criteria for selecting the appropriate metaphor center on goodness of fit (how well the metaphor explains the target concept or process), degree or richness of imagery, familiarity that the students will have with it, and its novelty.

2. **Emphasize the Metaphor.** The metaphor must be emphasized consistently throughout the lesson. Students should be alerted to interpret the metaphor figuratively and not literally.

3. **Establish Context.** Proper interpretation of the metaphor requires that the teacher establish the context for its use. Metaphors should not be used in isolation, especially if the students lack the background to understand them.

4. **Provide Instructions for Imagery.** Provide students with the instructions they will need to benefit from the rich imagery usually present in metaphors. "Form a mental picture of this" is good advice (See the **Practitioner's Corner** on imagery in Chapter 6, p. 237).

5. **Emphasize Similarities and Differences.** Because the metaphor juxtaposes the similarities of one known object or procedure with another, teachers should emphasize the similarities and differences between the metaphor and the new learning.

6. **Provide Opportunities for Rehearsal.** Use rote and elaborate rehearsal strategies to help students recognize the similarities and differences between the metaphor and the new learning, and to enhance their depth of understanding and types of associations.

7. **Beware Mixed Metaphors.** Because metaphors are such powerful learning devices, make sure you choose them carefully. Mixed metaphors cause confusion and lead to inaccuracy.

– Continued –

Using Metaphors to Enhance Transfer—Continued

We used metaphors in designing the Information Processing Model (See the **Practitioner's Corner** in Chapter 2 on redesigning the model, p. 56) to help remember the important stages in the process. Now, let's practice it with a different concept.

Directions: Working with a partner, select a concept and decide what metaphor(s) would help you or your students remember it.

Concept:_____

Metaphor(s):

_____

_____

_____

_____

_____

_____

_____

_____

_____

PRACTITIONER'S CORNER

Using Journal Writing to Promote Transfer and Retention

Journal writing can be a very effective strategy to promote positive transfer and increase retention. It can be done in nearly all grade levels and subject areas and is particularly effective when used as a closure activity.

Teachers may be reluctant to use this technique because they believe it takes up too much class time while adding more papers for them to evaluate. However, this strategy takes just three to five minutes, two or three times a week. That is, the teacher only spot checks journals periodically. The gain in student understanding and retention will be well worth the small amount of time invested. Here are some suggestions for using journal writing for maximum effectiveness:

- Students should keep a different journal for each class or subject area.

- To use this as a closure activity, ask students to write down their responses to these three questions:

  1. **"What did we learn today about** … (insert the *specific* learning objective)?" Avoid questions like, "Write down what we did today," because younger students are likely to focus on activities rather than on the learning. This question helps to establish *sense*.

  2. **"How does this connect or relate to what we already know about** … (insert some past learning that will help students with positive transfer)?" It is permissible to give hints to guide student thinking. After all, we want to facilitate accuracy. This question can help the learner *chunk* new learning into existing networks.

  3. **"How can this help us, or how can we use this information/skill in the future?"** Give hints if necessary. This question aids in finding *meaning*.

- You can use one day's journal entry as a prefocus activity for the following day, provided the new day's lesson is related.

Chapter 4—The Power of Transfer

Key Points to Ponder

Jot down on this page key points, ideas, strategies, and resources you want to consider later. This sheet is your personal journal summary and will help to jog your memory.

CHAPTER 4 – NOTES

1. Hunter (1982) and Perkins and Salomon (1988).

2. Perkins and Salomon (1988).

3. Hunter (1982).

4. A useful task for a committee rewriting a curriculum is to list those concepts that students find the most difficult. Then determine if the difficulty is that two very similar concepts or motor skills are taught together, resulting in confusion.

5. Brooks and Brooks (1993).

CHAPTER 5

BRAIN SPECIALIZATION
AND LEARNING

Despite myriad exceptions, the bulk of split-brain research has revealed an enormous degree of lateralization—that is, specialization in each of the hemispheres.

> – Michael Gazzaniga,
> *The Split Brain Revisited*

Chapter Highlights: This chapter explores the research on how areas of the brain are specialized to perform certain tasks. It examines hemispheric specialization and debunks some myths that have obscured the value of this work. You will be able to determine whether you have a hemispheric preference and what that means about how you learn and think. The chapter also examines language specialization, how we learn to speak and read, and the implications of this research for classroom instruction and for the curriculum and structure of schools.

One of the intriguing characteristics of the human brain is its ability to integrate disparate and seemingly disconnected activities going on in specialized areas of the brain into a unified whole. Brain scans reveal how certain areas of the brain get involved in processing and performing specific tasks. For example, the auditory cortex responds to sound input, the frontal lobe to cognitive rehearsal, and sections of the left hemisphere to spoken language. The ability of certain areas of the brain to perform unique functions is known as *lateralization* or *specialization*.

More evidence is accumulating that the brain has a much greater amount of specialization than was previously thought. Researchers are suggesting the idea that the brain is a set of modular units that carry out specific tasks. According to this *modular model*, the brain is a collection of units that supports the mind's information-processing requirements, and not a singular unit whose every part is capable of any function.[1]

Hemisphere Specialization

The first indications of brain specialization were discovered long before scanning technologies were developed. During the late 1950s, neurosurgeons decided that the best way to help patients with severe epileptic seizures was to sever the *corpus callosum* (Figure 1.2), the thick cable of nerve fibers that connects the two cerebral hemispheres. This last-ditch approach isolated the hemispheres so that seizures in the damaged hemisphere would not travel to the other side. The surgery had been tried on monkeys with epilepsy, and the results were encouraging. By the early 1960s, surgeons were ready to try the technique on human beings. One of the pioneers was Dr. Roger Sperry of the California Institute of Technology. Between 1961 and 1969, surgeons Joseph Bogen and Phillip Vogel successfully performed several operations under Sperry's guidance.

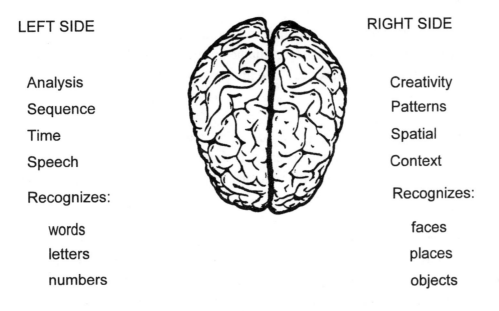

LEFT SIDE

Analysis

Sequence

Time

Speech

Recognizes:

   words

   letters

   numbers

RIGHT SIDE

Creativity

Patterns

Spatial

Context

Recognizes:

   faces

   places

   objects

Figure 5.1 The left and right hemispheres of the human brain are specialized and process information differently.

Although the operations resulted in a substantial reduction or elimination of the seizures, no one was sure what effect cutting this bridge between the hemispheres would have on "split-brain" patients.

Sperry and his student Michael Gazzaniga conducted a series of experiments with these patients and made a remarkable discovery.[2] Splitting the brain seemed to result in two separate domains of awareness. When a pencil was placed in the left hand (controlled by the right hemisphere) of a blindfolded patient, the patient could not name it. When the pencil was shifted to the right hand, however, the patient named it instantly. Neither hemisphere seemed to know what the other was doing and they acted, as Sperry said, "each with its own memory and will, competing for control."

As the tests progressed, Sperry charted the characteristics each hemisphere displayed. He concluded that each hemisphere seems to have its own separate and private sensations; its own perceptions; and its own impulses to act. This research showed that the right and left hemispheres have distinctly different functions that are not readily interchangeable. It also solved the mystery of the corpus callosum. Its purpose is largely to unify awareness and allow the two hemispheres to share memory and learning. Sperry won the 1981 Nobel Prize in medicine in part for this work.

Left and Right Hemisphere Processing (Hemisphericity)

Continued testing of split-brain patients and brain scans of normal (whole-brained) individuals have revealed considerable consistency in the different ways the two halves of the brain store and process information (Figure 5.1). This cerebral specialization is also called *hemisphericity*.

Left Hemisphere. The left brain is the *logical* hemisphere. It monitors the areas for speech, is analytical, and evaluates factual material in a rational way. It understands the literal interpretation of words and detects time and sequence. It also recognizes words, letters, and numbers written as words.

Right Hemisphere. The right brain is the *intuitive* hemisphere. It gathers information more from images than from words and looks for patterns. It interprets language through context—body language, emotional content, and tone of voice—rather than through literal meanings. It specializes in spatial perception and is capable of creativity. It also recognizes places, faces, and objects.

More recent research on the kind of processing done by each hemisphere has expanded our understanding of this remarkable division of labor.[3] Table 5.1 specifies these and other functions that the hemispheres seem to perform as they deal with the vast amount of new and past information that must be assessed every second.

168

Table 5.1 Functions of the Left and Right Cerebral Hemispheres		
LEFT HEMISPHERE FUNCTIONS		**RIGHT HEMISPHERE FUNCTIONS**
Connected to right side of the body	**C**	Connected to the left side of the body
Processes input in a sequential and analytical manner	**O** **R**	Processes input more holistically and abstractly
Time-sensitive	**P** **U**	Space-sensitive
Generates spoken language	**S**	Interprets language through gestures, facial movements, emotions, and body language
Does invariable and arithmetic operations	**C** **A**	Does relational and mathematical operations
Specializes in recognizing words and numbers (as words)	**L** **L**	Specializes in recognizing faces, places, objects, and music
Active in constructing false memories	**O** **S**	More truthful in recall
Seeks explanations for why events occur	**U** **M**	Puts events in spatial patterns
Better at arousing attention to deal with outside stimuli		Better at internal processing
Sources: Carter (1998); Gazzaniga (1998a,1998b)		

What Causes Specialization? No one knows why the brain is specialized although it does seem that such a capacity enables it to deal with a great amount of sensory data without going on overload. How it *becomes* specialized is another question. The key to answering this may lie in the brain's structure and wiring. There is general agreement among neuroscientists now that the brain is hardwired for certain functions, such as spoken language, and that this hardwiring is localized.

Another factor may be that left and right hemispheres are physically different. The hemispheres are made up of the cortex (the thin but tough surface) called *gray matter* and the support tissue below it called *white matter*. The left hemisphere has more gray matter, while the right has more white. The left hemisphere's more tightly-packed neurons are better able to handle intense, detailed work. The right hemisphere's white matter contains neurons with longer axons that can connect with modules further away. These long-range connections help the right to come up with broad but rather vague concepts. The information from each hemisphere is then pooled by sending signals across the corpus callosum.[4]

> *Although each hemisphere has specialized functions, both usually work together when learning.*

Specialization Does Not Mean Exclusivity

The research data support the notion that each hemisphere has its own set of functions in information processing and thinking. However, these functions are not always *exclusive* to only one hemisphere, and in even some simple tasks, it is possible for both hemispheres to be involved. In a normal individual, the results of the separate processing are exchanged with the opposite hemisphere through the corpus callosum. There is harmony in the goals of each, and they complement one another in almost all activities. Thus, the individual benefits from the integration of the processing done by both hemispheres and is afforded greater comprehension of whatever situation initiated the processing. For example,

- Logic is not confined to the left hemisphere. Some patients with right-brain damage fail to see the lack of logic in their thinking when they propose to take a walk even though they are completely paralyzed.

- Creativity or intuition is not solely in the right hemisphere. Creativity can remain, though diminished, even after extensive right-hemisphere damage.

- Because the two hemispheres do not function independently in a normal brain, it is impossible to educate only one hemisphere.

- Specialization does not mean **exclusivity**. There is no evidence that people are purely left or right brained. One hemisphere may be more active in most people, but only in varying degrees.

- Both hemispheres are capable of synthesis, that is, putting pieces of information together into a meaningful whole.

Hemispheric Preference: A Question of Learning Style

Since the work of Sperry, case studies and additional testing procedures have enabled researchers to understand more about the functions of each hemisphere.[5] These tests include anesthetizing one hemisphere, PET imaging scans, electroencephalographs (which record electrical impulses), and hemisphere-specific vision and hearing tests. The research shows that most people have a preferred hemisphere, and that this preference affects personality, abilities, and learning style. The preference runs the gamut from neutral (no preference) to strongly left or right. Those who are left-hemisphere preferred tend to be more verbal, analytical, and able to solve problems. Right-hemisphere-preferred individuals paint and draw well, are good at math, and deal with the visual world more easily than with the verbal.

Once again, the preference for either hemisphere does not mean that we do not use both hemispheres. In doing a simple task, we use the hemisphere that will accomplish it more efficiently. When we are faced with a task that is more complex, the preferred hemisphere will take the lead, although the nonpreferred hemisphere will likely get involved as well.[6]

Preference and Consciousness. One of the more fascinating revelations from the continued studies of split-brain patients is the realization that their left and right hemispheres can give different answers to questions about themselves. It is as though they have a distinct consciousness residing

> *Most people have a preferred hemisphere. This preference affects their personality, abilities, and learning style.*

in each hemisphere. For example, the inventive left hemisphere's consciousness surpasses that of the right. But the mind-boggling suggestion here is that even though our consciousness reflects that of the preferred hemisphere, another—and perhaps very different—consciousness lurks hidden in the nonpreferred hemisphere.[7] Sperry, himself, suspected as much of his split-brain patients. He wrote, "Everything we have seen indicates that the surgery has left these people with two separate minds ... that is, two separate spheres of consciousness."[8]

Examples of Preference. Suppose you are right-handed. A pen is on the table just next to your left hand, and someone asks you to pass the pen. Because this is a simple task, you will pick up the pen with your left hand in a smooth motion and pass it. You are not likely to stretch your right hand across your body or twist your torso to hand it over. If the person asks you to throw the pen, however, you will probably use your right hand because this task is more difficult.

During learning, both hemispheres are engaged, processing the information or skill according to their specializations and exchanging the results with the opposite hemisphere through the corpus callosum. So if someone were to toss a pen to you, your likelihood of successfully catching it would increase greatly if you used *both* hands, not just the right (dominant) hand.

Knowing the difference between how the left and right hemispheres process information explains why we succeed with some tasks but not with others, especially when we are trying to do them simultaneously. For instance, most of us can carry on a conversation (left-hemisphere activity) while driving a car (right-hemisphere and cerebellar activity). In this case, each task is controlled by different hemispheres, but trying to carry on a conversation on the telephone while

171

talking to someone in the room at the same time is very difficult because these are functions of the same (left) hemisphere and can interfere with each other.

Implications of Preference for Teachers. Hemispheric preference is one component of learning style. Because teachers tend to teach the way they learn, they need to know as much about their own learning style as possible. Besides telling them something about themselves, this knowledge also helps them to understand learners with very different styles. To determine your hemispheric preference, see the **Practitioner's Corner** at the end of this chapter on p. 187.

So What? Cautions About Interpreting Hemispheric Preference

Perhaps no single piece of brain research has received so much attention and controversy as the notion that the two hemispheres of the brain process information differently. Although a substantial body of evidence suggests that each hemisphere has its specialized abilities, we should not jump to the conclusion that normal people have two brains or are functioning with only half a brain. The differences are not all-or-nothing. Quite the contrary, normal people have one integrated and magnificently differentiated brain that generates a single mind and self.

Unfortunately, some people have misused this research, referring to themselves, or worse, to students as "too left-brained" or "too right-brained." What is important to remember is that the two hemispheres work together as an integrated whole, sharing their different stimuli through the corpus callosum. Nevertheless, misinformation about the specialization of the hemispheres and several popular myths persist.

Some Myths About Hemispheric Preference

Several myths connecting hemispheric preference to other variables have evolved and endured during the past two decades. The myths have obscured the benefit of this research and undermined its value to the teaching and learning process. Here are three common myths we can debunk.

Handedness (lateral preference). Because the hemispheres of the brain control the opposite sides of the body, many have speculated that hemispheric preference is directly connected to handedness, or lateral preference. There is evidence that more right-hemisphere-preferred individuals are left-handed than right-handed. Scanning evidence also shows that most right-handers (about 93 to 95 percent) have left-hemisphere language preference,[9] whereas only 70 percent of left-handers have left-hemisphere language preference; the other 30 percent have language preference in the right or in both hemispheres.[10] However, no direct cause-and-effect connection between handedness and hemispheric preference has been established. Thus, it is incorrect to assume that most right-handed people are left-hemisphere preferred and vice versa.[11]

Intelligence. There is no research to support the notion that those with one hemispheric preference are any more or less intelligent than those with the opposite preference. Individuals who are strongly and oppositely preferred will exhibit vastly different personalities and learning styles, but this has no connection to intelligence, as we have defined it, or the ability to learn.

Genetics. There is no evidence that hemispheric preference is inherited. Studies of several generations of many families show mixed, unpredictable preference patterns.

The Gender Connection

Are male and female brains different? If so, what are the structural and performance natures of those differences? Studies begun in the early 1970s by Jerre Levy at the University of Chicago, and subsequent studies by other researchers have shown some gender differences in brain characteristics and capabilities.[12] PET scans and fMRIs, for instance, indicate that males and females use different areas of their brains when accomplishing similar tasks.

Structural Differences

- Males have a higher percentage of gray matter (the thin cortex layer) in the left hemisphere than females. In females, the percentage of gray matter is the same in both hemispheres.[13]
- Males have more neurons in the cerebral cortex, while females have more connections between the neurons.[14]
- For most males and females, the language areas are in the left hemisphere. But females also have an active language processor in the right hemisphere.

Performance Differences

- Females perform better on tests of perceptual speed, verbal fluency, determining the placement of objects (sequence), identifying specific attributes of objects, precision manual tasks, and arithmetic calculations. Males perform better on spatial tasks, such as mentally rotating three-dimensional objects; at target-directed motor skills; at spotting shapes embedded in complex diagrams; and in mathematical reasoning.
- When recalling emotions, females use a larger portion of their limbic system than do males. Females are also better at recognizing different types of emotions in others.

- Analysis of a large number of adolescent test scores showed boys scored better on mathematics, science, and social studies questions; girls scored better on reading comprehension, perceptual speed, and remembering associated facts and concepts. The boys had a wider range of high-low scores, and their writing scores were significantly lower.[15]

These and other studies further indicate that more females are left-hemisphere preferred and more males are right-hemisphere preferred. Why is this so? To what extent do nature (genetic makeup) and nurture (environment) contribute to these structural and performance differences? Although no one knows the answer for sure, several theories exist that attempt to explain these results.

The Hormone Theory. One possibility is that hormones, such as testosterone and androgen, influence brain development differently in the sexes. Testosterone seems to delay the development of the left hemisphere in boys. Thus, girls get a head start in using the left hemisphere; boys are forced to rely more on their right hemisphere. The early exposure to these hormones seems to alter other brain functions (such as language acquisition and spatial perception) permanently for the individual.[16] The resurgence of hormones with the onset of puberty may further reconfigure the mental organization of teens, especially as new social pressures emerge with their accompanying emotional shifts.

> *More girls than boys are left-hemisphere preferred; more boys than girls are right-hemisphere preferred. The reasons are not as important as our response.*

The Natural Selection Theory. A related theory suggests that natural selection affected our brain characteristics as we evolved. For thousands of years, the division of labor between the sexes was distinct. In prehistoric times, men were responsible for hunting large game over long distances, making weapons, and defending the group from predators, animal and otherwise. Women took care of the home and the children, prepared food, and made clothing. Such specialization required different cerebral operations from men and woman. Men needed more route-finding and spatial abilities and better targeting skills; women needed more fine-motor and timing skills to maintain the household. The individual males and females who could perform their respective tasks well survived to pass their genes on to their children. Moreover, any new genetic combinations eventually led to structural changes in the brain—and other parts of the body—that were gender specific.

The Environment Theory. Another prevailing explanation, popular in the 1980s, looks to a combination of the different ways the sexes develop and interact with their environment. First, studies of infant boys and girls demonstrate that the acuity of senses does not develop identically in both genders. That is, hearing and touch (left-hemisphere controlled) develop more quickly in girls. Spatial vision (right-hemisphere controlled), however, develops more rapidly in boys. Second, parents tend to treat baby boys differently from baby girls. And third, boys and girls between the ages of 6 and 12 typically spend their out-of-school time quite differently as they are growing up. Girls are more likely to spend their free time indoors. In this structured environment, girls are exposed to more language through radio and television, and they are more conscious of time because of clocks, media, and other family members who may be coming home. This environment, psychologists argue, enhances left-hemisphere processes. On the other hand, more boys spend their free time outdoors. In this unstructured environment, boys rely more on space (location) than time, design their own games, use more visual than verbal skills during play, and use little language and only in context to accomplish a task. This behavior enhances right-hemisphere processes.

> **The brains of males and females organize differently from very early in their development through their formative years, leading to different preferences in learning.**

The theories and evidence suggest that we no longer think in terms of nature versus nurture. Rather, we should see the relationship of these forces as more circular. Genes influence behavior, and behavior can influence how genes function as a child grows and develops. Thus, a combination of nature and nurture factors causes the brains of males and females to organize differently from very early in their development through their formative years, leading, among other things, to different preferences in learning.

However, during the past decade, technology, such as video games and computers, has had significant impact on how and where children occupy their spare time. It is possible that this impact has already begun to narrow the current differences in the hemispheric preferences of the genders and will continue to do so in the coming years.

Regardless of the source of these preferences, **we should avoid using hemispheric preference to stereotype individuals**, to assume that one preference is better than another, or that persons cannot accomplish certain tasks because of their preference. The cause of hemispheric preference, for all practical purposes, is not relevant. It is our response that really matters. We can use this research to understand better how hemispheric preference affects learning and what teachers can do about it in their classrooms.

Schools and Hemispheric Preference

Recognizing that hemispheric preference is a contributor to learning style, the question arises as to whether school climate and classroom instruction are designed to embrace different styles so that all learners can succeed. Is it possible that schools may be inadvertently designed to favor one type of learning style over another?

Left-Hemisphere Schools? Take a moment to think about the entire schooling process that takes place from kindergarten through grade 12. During this mental review, look again at the list of left- and right-hemisphere functions. Is K–12 schooling best described by the characteristics listed for the left hemisphere, the right hemisphere, or both equally? Most educators readily admit that schools are predominantly left-hemisphere oriented. Schools are structured environments that run according to time schedules, favor facts and rules over patterns, and offer predominantly verbal instruction, especially at the secondary level.

This means that left-hemisphere preferred learners (mainly girls) feel more comfortable in this environment. The stronger the left-hemisphere preference, the more successful these learners can be. Conversely, right-hemisphere preferred learners (mainly boys) are not comfortable; the stronger the right-hemisphere preference, the more hostile the learning environment seems. This could explain why most teachers admit that they have many more discipline problems with boys than with girls. Maybe what this research is saying is that

> *Most K–12 public schooling inadvertently favors left hemisphere preferred learners.*

boys (more accurately, right-hemisphere-preferred learners) are not born with a "mean gene," but are too often placed in uncomfortable learning environments where they react rebelliously. This might also partially explain why over twice as many boys as girls are in remedial and special education programs nationally.[17]

Impact on Mathematics and Science Programs. As mentioned earlier, male and female brains deal differently with numbers and computation. When I was writing the first edition of this book, considerable agreement suggested that these differences were significant and could account for the fact that girls in secondary schools were much more likely to have difficulty in mathematics classes. As they lost confidence in their mathematics ability, girls took fewer courses and scored lower on tests. The same reasoning applied to girls' difficulties in science courses, especially those requiring more mathematics, such as chemistry and physics.

But more recent scanning studies indicate that gender differences in computational processing are minor and become even less important when the brain encounters higher mathematics.[18] In other words, the genetic (nature) component is less significant than we once thought. It seems more likely that social and cultural forces have had greater influence. Boys in secondary schools are encouraged by their parents and teachers to take more mathematics and science, their experiences in such classes are more compatible with their hemispheric preferences, and they thus score better on tests in these areas. Girls, on the other hand, often encounter a stereotype that presumes females are poor performers in mathematics. One recent study showed that female performance on mathematics tests was lower than males just because of the existence of this stereotype, and that female performance improved once the stereotype threat was removed.[19]

The good news is that the gender gap is narrowing. The percentage of girls taking various mathematics and science courses is close to or exceeds that of boys, and their test scores on a national average are only about one percent lower.[20] This is an encouraging trend. In part, the explanation for this outcome may be the introduction of computers into the classroom. Both boys and girls are on a level playing field. Computer lessons are not closely linked with past successes or failures, representing a new experience—with a new set of skills. Moreover, computers are patient and fun, contributing to novelty and the fulfillment of expectations of success.

Our job now is to ensure that educators and parents recognize that boys may have some different learning preferences from girls, but that both genders have similar *capabilities* to succeed in mathematics and science. To that end, we need to curb the cultural and social forces that would feed past stereotypes about whether students of a certain gender should take only certain subjects.

Spoken Language Specialization

Many animals have developed ways to communicate with other members of their species. Birds and apes bow and wave appendages; honeybees dance to map out the location of food; and even one-celled animals can signal neighbors by emitting an array of different chemicals. By

Some Specialized Areas of the Brain

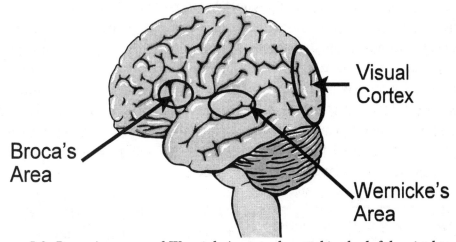

Figure 5.2 Broca's area and Wernicke's area, located in the left hemisphere, are the two major language processing centers of the brain. The visual cortex, across the back of both hemispheres, processes visual stimuli.

contrast, human beings have developed an elaborate and complex means of spoken communication that many say is largely responsible for our place as the dominant species on this planet. Spoken language is truly a marvelous accomplishment for many reasons. At the very least, it gives form to our memories and words to express our thoughts. The human voice can pronounce about 200 vowel and 600 consonant sounds that allow it to speak any of the estimated 6,500 languages that exist today. With practice, the voice becomes so fine-tuned that it makes only about one sound error per million sounds and one word error per million words.

Before the advent of scanning technologies, we explained how the brain produced spoken language on the basis of evidence from injured brains. A person with damage to Broca's[21] area (Figure 5.2) could understand language but could not speak fluently. Those with damage to Wernicke's[22] area could speak fluently, but what they said was quite meaningless. The inferences, then, were that Broca's area stored vocabulary, grammar, and probably syntax of one's native language, while Wernicke's area was the site of native language sense and meaning.

But more recent research, using scanners, indicates that spoken language production is a far more complex process than previously thought. When preparing to produce a spoken sentence, the brain uses not only Broca's and Wernicke's areas, but also calls on several other neural networks scattered throughout the left hemisphere. Nouns are processed through one set of patterns; verbs are processed by separate neural networks. The more complex the sentence structure, the more areas that are activated, including the right hemisphere.

Learning Spoken Language

Is Language Pre-Wired in the Brain? In the 1950s, MIT linguist Noam Chomsky theorized that young children could not possibly learn the rules of language grammar and syntax merely by imitating adults. He proposed that nature endowed humans with the ability to acquire their native language by attaching what they hear to a language template that is pre-wired in the brain by birth—just as baby tigers are pre-wired to learn how to hunt. Other linguists now suggest that language acquisition may be the result of some genetic predisposition coupled with the baby brain's incredible ability to sort through the enormous amount of information it takes in—including language—and to find regular patterns within it.[23] Although the debate over how much language is pre-wired into the brain is far from over, researchers are gaining some remarkable insights into how the young brain masters language (Figure 5.3).

> *The neurons in a baby's brain are capable of responding to the sounds of all the languages on this planet.*

Learning Sounds Called Phonemes. The neurons in a baby's brain are capable of responding to the sounds of all the languages on this planet. At birth (some say even before birth) babies respond first to the *prosody*—the rhythm, cadence, and pitch—of their mothers' voice, not the words. Spoken language consists of minimal units of sound, called *phonemes*, which combine to form syllables. For example, in English, the consonant sound "t" and the vowel sound "o" are both phonemes that combine to form the syllable *to-* as in *tomato*.

Although the infant's brain can perceive the entire range of phonemes, only those that are repeated get attention, as the neurons reacting to the unique sound patterns are continually stimulated and reinforced. By the age of 10 to 12 months, the toddler's brain has begun to distinguish and remember phonemes of the native language and to ignore foreign sounds. For example, one study showed that at the age of 6 months, American and Japanese babies are equally good at discriminating between the "l" and "r" sounds, even though Japanese has no "l" sound. However, by age 10 months, Japanese babies have a tougher time making the distinction, while American babies have become much better at it. During this and subsequent periods of growth, the ability to distinguish native sounds improves, while one's ability to distinguish nonnative speech sounds diminishes.[24]

From Phonemes to Words. The next step for the brain is to detect words from the stream of sounds it is processing. This is not an easy task because people don't pause between words when speaking. Yet the brain has to recognize differences between, say, *green house* and *greenhouse*. Remarkably, babies begin to distinguish word boundaries by the age of 8 months even though they don't know what the words mean.[25] They begin to acquire new vocabulary words at the rate of about 10 a day. At the same time, memory and Wernicke's areas are becoming fully functional so the child can now attach meaning to words. Of course, learning words is one skill; putting them together to make sense is another, more complex skill.

Spoken Language Development

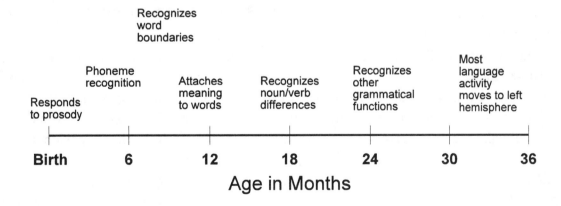

Figure 5.3 An average timeline of spoken language development during the child's first 3 years. There is considerable variation among individual children.

Learning Grammar. Chomsky believed that all languages contain some common rules that dictate how sentences are constructed, and that the brain has preprogrammed circuits that respond to these rules. Modern linguists think that the brain may not be responding so much to basic language rules as to statistical regularities heard in the flow of the native tongue. They soon discern that some words describe objects while others describe actions. Toddlers detect patterns of word order—person, action, object—so they can soon say, "I want cookie." Other grammar features emerge, such as tense, and by the age of 3, over 90 percent of sentences uttered are grammatically correct. Errors are seldom random, but usually result from following perceived rules of grammar. If "I batted the ball" makes sense, why shouldn't "I holded the bat?" Regrettably, the toddler has yet to learn that nearly 200 of the most commonly used verbs in English are irregularly conjugated.

During the following years, practice in speaking and adult correction help the child decode some of the mysteries of grammar's irregularities and a sophisticated language system emerges from what once was babble. No one knows how much grammar a child learns just by listening, or how much is pre-wired. What is certain is that the more children are exposed to spoken language in the early years, the more quickly they can discriminate between phonemes and recognize word boundaries.

Just letting the toddler sit in front of a television does not seem to accomplish this goal, probably because the child's brain needs live human interaction to attach meaning to the words. Moreover, television talk is not the slow, expressive speech that parents use with their infants, which infants like and want to hear.[26] Although toddlers may be attracted to the rapidly changing sounds and images on a television, little or no language development is in progress. There is further evidence that prolonged television watching can impair the growth of young brains. Susan Johnson, a pediatrician at University of California, San

> *Although toddlers may be attracted to the rapidly changing sounds and images on a television, there is little or no language development in progress. Television may actually impair a toddler's brain development.*

Francisco, cites several studies that raise concerns over the effects of television viewing on young minds.[27] These studies point out that the visual system is not stimulated properly by television viewing in that there is no pupil dilation and the eyes stare at the screen and do not move from one point to the next—a skill critical for reading. The images change every 5 to 6 seconds (even faster during commercials) and do not give the higher-thought areas of the brain (in the frontal lobe) time to process the images. The wavelengths of light produced by the television tube's phosphors are very limited compared to the full spectrum of light we receive when viewing objects outdoors. Furthermore, television is replacing the opportunities for the child's brain to create internal images[28] (see Chapter 6 on the importance of imagery).

Language Delay. Most toddlers begin to speak words around the age of 10 to 12 months. In some children, there is a delay and they may not speak coherent words and phrases until nearly 2 years of age. There is evidence that this language delay to 2 years is inherited, and thus represents a distinct disorder not easily remedied by environmental interventions. This revelation diminishes the claim some people make that mainly environmental influences cause language delay.[29]

Language and Cognitive Thought. Several studies are providing strong evidence that language and cognitive thought are separated in the brain. One study involved patients with Williams syndrome, a rare genetic disorder first described in 1961. Children with this disorder have difficulty with simple spatial tasks, and many have IQ scores in the 40 to 50 range and cannot read or write above the first-grade level. Despite these inadequacies, they develop extraordinary spoken language skills. They amass large vocabularies, can speak in complex, grammatically correct sentences, and often have the gift of gab with engaging personalities. Another study showed that deaf people who did not develop any sign language in their early years were still able to express complex thoughts when they learned sign—or in some cases, English—language later.[30]

Implications. Given the evidence that the brain's ability to acquire spoken language is at its peak in the early years, parents should create a rich environment that includes lots of communication activities, such as talking, singing, and reading. In schools, it means addressing any language-learning problems quickly to take advantage of the brain's ability to rewire improper connections during this important period of growth. It also means that parents and teachers should not assume that children with language-learning problems are going to be limited in cognitive thought processes as well.

Learning a Second Language

The power of a young child's brain to learn spoken languages is so immense that it can learn several languages at one time. But by the age of 10 to 12 months, the brain is already beginning to lose its ability to discriminate sounds between its native language and nonnative languages. The implication here is that if we wish children to acquire a second language, it makes sense to start that acquisition during the early years when the brain is actively creating phonemic sound and syntactic networks.

Studies show that proficiency in learning a second language depends not on *how long* nonnatives have been speaking the

> *Proficiency in learning a second language depends not on how long nonnatives have been speaking the language, but on how early in life they began learning it.*

181

language, but on *how early in life* they began learning it. Researchers Jacqueline Johnson and Elissa Newport found that immigrants who started speaking English at ages 3 to 7 spoke like natives and with no discernible accent. Those who started speaking between ages of 8 and 10 had about 80 percent of the proficiency of native speakers; those who started between ages 11 and 15 spoke with only half the proficiency, and those who started after age 17 had only about 15 percent of the proficiency of the average person born in America.[31] This indicates that the window of opportunity (see Chapter 1) for language acquisition slides down in the preteen years so that learning a second language later is possible but more difficult.

Why Is It More Difficult to Learn a Second Language Later? For most people, the brain areas primarily involved in language acquisition are no longer responsive to foreign sounds after the preteen years. Thus, other areas of the brain must be programmed to recognize, distinguish, and respond to foreign phonemes. Furthermore, scanning studies using fMRIs show that second languages acquired in adulthood are spatially separated in the brain from native languages. However, when acquired in the preteen years, native and second languages are represented in the same frontal areas (Broca's area).[32] Hence, younger and older brains react to second language learning very differently.

Although it seems that younger brains are more adept at language learning, this research should not be interpreted to discourage adolescents and adults from pursuing second language study. Nor should it be assumed that youngsters will become fluent solely by studying a second language a few hours a week in the primary grades. Further, the difficulties facing adults learning a second language are very different from those of children. If these difficulties are properly addressed, then learning a second language as an adult can be a rewarding experience, although it may require more focus, more effort, and greater motivation (See the **Practitioner's Corner** on p. 201 at the end of this chapter on acquiring a second language).

> *Although young brains are naturally adept at language learning, this research should not be interpreted to discourage adolescents and adults from pursuing second language study.*

Learning to Read

Is Reading a Natural Ability? Not really. The brain's ability to acquire spoken language with amazing speed and accuracy is the result of genetic hard-wiring and specialized cerebral areas that focus on this task. But there are no areas of the brain that specialize in reading. In fact, reading is probably the most difficult task we ask the brain to undertake. Reading is a relatively new phenomenon in the development of humans. As far as we know, the genes have not incorporated reading into their coded structure, probably because reading—unlike spoken language —has not emerged over time as a survival skill.

Many cultures (but not all) do emphasize reading as an important form of communication and insist it be taught to their children. And so the struggle begins. To get that brain to read, here's what we are saying, for example, to the English-speaking child: "That language you have been speaking quite correctly for the past few years can be represented by abstract symbols called the *alphabet*. We are going to disrupt that sophisticated spoken language

> **There are no areas of the brain that specialize in reading. Reading is probably the most difficult task we ask the brain to undertake.**

protocol you have already developed and ask you to reorganize it to accommodate these symbols, which, by the way, are not very reliable. There are lots of exceptions, but you'll just have to adjust."

How Does the Brain Read? To read, the brain must first learn the alphabet, whose letter names do not always represent their sounds in words. When are *f* or *l* ever pronounced as "ef" or "el" in English? Then the brain must connect those letters to phonemes that the child has been using successfully for years. Just as the brain thinks it knows what letter represents a phoneme sound, it discovers that the same symbol can have *different* sounds, such as the *a* in *cat* and in *father*. Next it learns that a group of letters makes a syllable, but that the same group of letters, say -*ough* can have *multiple* sounds, as in *cough*, *bough*, *dough*, and *through*. Simple, isn't it?

Researchers using fMRIs are getting a clearer picture of the cerebral processes involved in reading: The word (for example, *dog*) is first recorded in the visual cortex (Figure 5.4), then decoded by a structure on the left side of the brain called the *angular gyrus*, which separates it into its basic sounds, or phonemes (e.g., the letters d-o-g are pronounced "duh, awh, guh"). This process activates Broca's area so that the word can be identified. The brain's vocabulary store and reasoning and concept formation abilities, along with activity in Wernicke's area, combine to provide meaning, producing the thought of a furry animal that barks.[33] All this occurs in a fraction of a second.

Keep in mind that although the process outlined in Figure 5.4 appears linear and singular, it is really bidirectional and parallel, with many phonemes being processed at the same time.

That the brain learns to read at all attests to its remarkable ability to sift through seemingly confusing input and establish patterns and systems. For a few children, this process comes naturally; most have to be taught.

How the Brain Reads

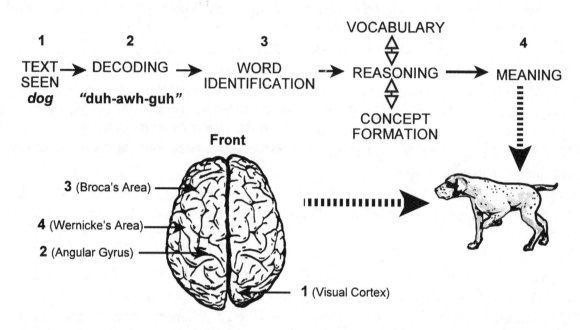

Figure 5.4 *In reading the word* dog *it is first seen (1), then decoded into its phonological elements (2) and identified (3). The higher-level functions of reasoning and concept formation provide the meaning (4) and produce the thought of a furry animal that barks.*

Language and Reading Learning Difficulties

Dysfunction in the Timing of Speech Sounds. Reading is so complex that any small problem along the way can slow or interrupt the process. It is small wonder that children have more problems with reading than any other skill we ask them to learn. Neuroimaging is showing great promise as a tool for diagnosing reading and language difficulties. Recent studies of young children with language-learning difficulties indicate that they may have a dysfunction in brain-timing mechanisms which makes processing of certain speech sounds difficult. Researchers discovered that by using computer-processed language programs that pronounced words more slowly, some children, ages 5 to 10, were able to advance their reading levels by two years after just four weeks of training.[34] This improvement was maintained for at least a year. Another revelation from brain scans is that poor readers' brains show more frontal lobe activity than do good readers' brains. This means that the poor readers are putting forth additional effort—perhaps subvocalizing—to pronounce and interpret the word correctly.[35]

Dyslexia. Newer research is shedding more light on dyslexia. Because dyslexics often confuse *b* and *d*, psychologists thought for many years that dyslexia was merely a vision problem. Researchers now believe that the letters can also be confused because they sound alike. It is the brain's inability to process what it *hears*, not what it *sees*. The problem seems to lie in the decoding process (Figure 5.4). The fMRI scans show an imperfectly functioning system for dividing words into their phonological units—a critical step for accurate reading. Letter reversals can be the result of phonological missteps in the decoding of print to sound and back to print. It is likely that the learner has problems in assigning what he says or hears in his head (the phoneme) to the letters he sees on paper (the grapheme).[36] So maybe dyslexia is really *dysphonia*—an incorrect association between phoneme and grapheme. If so, then remedial strategies should focus on reestablishing correct phonemic connections with intense practice.

> *Some forms of dyslexia may be the brain's inability to process what it hears, not what it sees.*

There is convincing evidence that dyslexia is largely inherited. Thus, it is a chronic problem and not just a "phase." The stereotype that nearly all dyslexics are boys is not true, although it probably persists because boys are more likely to show their frustration with reading by acting out. Studies indicate that many girls are affected as well, and are not getting help.

Dysfunction in the Timing of Visual Processing (Irlen Syndrome). Some reading difficulties may be caused by *problems in visual processing*. Reading calls for the visual system to process the visual stimuli of text and transfer it to other cognitive areas for word recognition and meaning. This procedure requires a specific time sequence to move the text stimuli along, clear the visual field, and redirect the eyes to the next fixation point on the page. If the timing is sluggish, letters and words can overlap, causing confusion, and the eye movements become inefficient. The result is that the reader sees text that is distorted in some way. The text may be blurry or shaky, form a swirl, or look washed out. Conscientious students may continue to struggle with the reading but will eventually get migraine headaches. This disorder, identified in the early1980s by Helen Irlen, was originally called scotopic sensitivity syndrome, but is more commonly referred to as Irlen Syndrome.[37]

After working first with adults who complained of these symptoms, Irlen discovered that using color filters corrected the distorted text for many readers. Later researchers found that changing and removing certain colors of light reset and improved the visual timing sequence. They also found that fluorescent lights cause a high contrast between the text and the background of the reading material that can aggravate the distortion.[38] Irlen syndrome appears to have a genetic connection. One major study showed that either or both parents of 84 percent of children with the disorder had similar symptoms.[39] Irlen estimates that about 12 to 14 percent of the general population has the disorder (from slight to severe), but that this number rises to 33 percent in children who may otherwise have been misdiagnosed as having dyslexia, ADD, or ADHD. Training is now available to classroom teachers to help them identify the syndrome and learn how to use the inexpensive color filters that have been shown to be effective for most readers with this condition.[40]

Implications for Teaching Reading. The battle between the phonics and the whole language approaches to reading continues to rage in many school districts as it has for the past 20 years. Science may seem to be no match for this debate, which is often fueled by politics and religion. Nevertheless, based on the research described above, the teaching of reading should begin with a recognition that spoken words must be broken into sounds represented by letters, and then flow to vocabulary, meaning, context, and syntax. The key is the right mix of phonemic awareness and interesting, developmentally appropriate literature (see the **Practitioner's Corner** on p. 205 for suggestions on teaching reading).

PRACTITIONER'S CORNER

Testing Your Hemispheric Preference

There are many instruments available to help individuals assess their hemispheric preference. The one below takes just a few minutes. The results are only an indication of your preference and are not conclusive. You should use additional instruments to collect more data before reaching any firm conclusion about your hemispheric preference.

Directions: From each pair below, circle A or B corresponding to the sentence that **best describes you.** Answer all questions. There are no right or wrong answers.

1. A. I prefer to find my own way of doing a new task.
   B. I prefer to be told the best way to do a new task.

2. A. I have to make my own plans.
   B. I can follow anyone's plans.

3. A. I am a very flexible and occasionally unpredictable person.
   B. I am a very stable and consistent person.

4. A. I keep everything in a particular place.
   B. Where I keep things depends on what I am doing.

5. A. I spread my work evenly over the time I have.
   B. I prefer to do my work at the last minute.

6. A. I know I am right because I have good reasons.
   B. I know when I am right, even without reasons.

7. A. I need a lot of variety and change in my life.
   B. I need a well-planned and orderly life.

8. A. I sometimes have too many ideas in a new situation.
   B. I sometimes don't have any ideas in a new situation.

– Continued –

Testing Your Hemispheric Preference—Continued

9.   A.   I do easy things first and the important things last.
       B.   I do the important things first and the easy things last.

10.   A.   I choose what I **know** is right when making a hard decision.
       B.   I choose what I **feel** is right when making a hard decision.

11.   A.   I plan my time for doing my work.
       B.   I don't think about the time when I work.

12.   A.   I usually have good self-discipline.
       B.   I usually act on my feelings.

13.   A.   Other people don't understand how I organize things.
       B.   Other people think I organize things well.

14.   A.   I agree with new ideas before other people do.
       B.   I question new ideas more than other people do.

15.   A.   I tend to think more in **pictures.**
       B.   I tend to think more in **words.**

16.   A.   I try to find the one best way to solve a problem.
       B.   I try to find different ways to solve a problem.

17.   A.   I can usually **analyze** what is going to happen next.
       B.   I can usually **sense** what is going to happen next.

18.   A.   I am not very imaginative in my work.
       B.   I use my imagination in nearly everything I do.

19.   A.   I begin many jobs that I never finish.
       B.   I finish a job before starting a new one.

– Continued –

Testing Your Hemispheric Preference—Continued

20. A. I look for new ways to do old jobs.
    B. When one way works well, I don't change it.

21. A. It is fun to take risks.
    B. I have fun without taking risks.

Scoring:

Count the number of "A" responses to questions 1, 3, 7, 8, 9, 13, 14, 15, 19, 20, and 21. Place that number on the line to the right.   A._____

Count the number of "B" responses to the remaining questions. Place that number on the line to the right.   B._____

Total the "A" and "B" responses you counted.   Total_____

The total indicates your hemispheric preference according to the following scale:

0–5   Strong left hemisphere preference
6–8   Moderate left hemisphere preference
9–12   Bilateral hemisphere balance (little or no preference)
13–15   Moderate right hemisphere preference
16–21   Strong right hemisphere preference

Reflection:

A. Did your score surprise you? Why or why not?

B. Describe here what your score may tell you about your teaching.

C. What implications do your answers in B above have for your students?

PRACTITIONER'S CORNER

Teaching to the Whole Brain: General Guidelines

Although the two hemispheres process information differently, we learn best when both are engaged in learning. Just as we would catch more balls with both hands, we catch more information with both hemispheres processing and integrating the learning. Teachers should design lessons that include activities directed at both hemispheres so that students can integrate the new learning into a meaningful whole. Here are some ways to do that in daily planning:

- **Deal With Concepts Verbally *and* Visually.** When teaching new concepts, alternate discussion with visual models. Write key words on the board that represent the attributes of the concept, then use a simple diagram to show relationships among the key ideas within and between concepts. This helps students attach both auditory and visual cues to the information, increasing the likelihood that sense and meaning will emerge. When showing a film or videotape, show the *smallest* segment with *maximum* meaning, then stop the tape and have students discuss what was shown.

- **Design Effective Visual Aids.** How we position information on a visual aid (overhead transparency, board, easel pad) indicates the relationships of concepts and ideas, which are processed by the right hemisphere. Vertical positioning implies a step or time sequence, or hierarchy. Thus, writing

    Delaware
    Pennsylvania
    New Jersey

is appropriate to indicate the order of these states' admission into the Union (chronology). Writing them horizontally

    Delaware, Pennsylvania, New Jersey

implies a parallel relationship that is appropriate to identify any three populous eastern states. Avoid writing information in visual aids in a haphazard way whenever a parallel or hierarchical relationship between or among the elements is important for students to remember.

– Continued –

190

Teaching to the Whole Brain: General Guidelines—Continued

- **Discuss Concepts Logically *and* Intuitively.** Concepts should be presented to students from different perspectives that encourage the use of both hemispheres. For example, if you are teaching about the Civil War, talk about the factual (logical) events, such as major causes, battles, and the economic and political impacts. When the students understand these, move on to more thought-provoking (intuitive) activities, such as asking what might have happened if Lincoln had not been assassinated, or what our country might be like now if the Confederate states had won the war.

  After teaching basic concepts in arithmetic, ask students to design a number system to a base other than 10. This is a simple and interesting process that helps students understand the scheme of our decimal number system. In literature, after reading part of a story or play, ask students to write a plausible ending using the facts already presented. In science, after giving some facts about the structure of the periodic table of the elements, ask students to explain how they would experiment with a new element to determine its place in the table.

- **Avoid Conflicting Messages.** Make sure that your words, tone, and pacing match your gestures, facial expressions, and body language. The left hemisphere interprets words literally, but the right hemisphere evaluates body language, tone, and content. If the two hemispheric interpretations are inconsistent, a conflicting message is generated. The student withdraws internally to resolve the conflict and is no longer focused on the learning.

- **Design Activities and Assessments for Both Hemispheres.** Students of different hemispheric preference express themselves in different ways. Give students options in testing and in completing assignments so they can select the option best suited to their learning styles. For example, after completing a major unit on the U.S. Civil War, students could write term papers on particular aspects of the war, draw pictures, create and present plays or write songs of important events, or construct models that represent battles, the surrender at Appomattox, and so on.

PRACTITIONER'S CORNER

Strategies for Teaching to the Whole Brain

Students learn best when teachers use strategies that engage the whole brain. Although newer research is showing that both hemispheres work together in many more processing activities than previously thought, it is still useful to know teaching strategies that involve the skills inherent in—but not necessarily limited to—each hemisphere. *Remember that we cannot educate just one hemisphere*. Rather, we are ensuring that our daily instruction includes activities that stimulate the whole brain. Here are some teaching strategies to consider.[41]

Teaching Strategies That Activate Left-Hemisphere Functions

- **Efficient Classroom Organization.** Have an efficient work area. Distribute the talkers around the room; they will spark discussions when needed.

- **Relevant Bulletin Boards.** Organize bulletin boards to be relevant to the current content and easily understood.

- **Clean the Board.** Make clean erasures on the board. This reduces the chance that previous and unrelated word cues will become associated with the new topic under discussion.

- **Use a Multisensory Approach.** Let students read, write, draw, and compute often in all subject areas.

- **Use Metaphors.** Create and analyze metaphors to enhance meaning and encourage higher-order thinking.

- **Encourage Punctuality.** Stress the importance of being on time. Encourage students to carry agendas.

- **Encourage Goal Setting.** Teach students to set study goals for themselves, stick to their goals, and reward themselves when they achieve them.

– Continued –

Strategies for Teaching to the Whole Brain—Continued

- **Stimulate Logical Thinking.** Ask "what if?" questions to encourage logical thinking as students consider all possibilities for solving problems.

Teaching Strategies That Activate Right-Hemisphere Functions

- **Give Students Some Options.** For example, allow them to do oral or written reports. Oral reports help students piece concepts together while requiring fewer mechanics than written work.

- **Use Visual Representations.** Use the board and overhead projector to show illustrations, cartoons, charts, timelines, and graphs that encourage students to visually organize information and relationships. Have students create or collect their own visual representations of the new concepts.

- **Help Students Make Connections.** Tying lessons together and using proper closure (Chapter 3) allow the brain to compare new information to what has already been learned.

- **Encourage Direct Experiences.** Facilitate direct experiences with new learning through role-playing, simulations, and involvement in real-world situations.

- **Allow for Student-to-Student Interaction.** Students need time to interact with each other as they discuss the new learnings. Remember, whoever explains, learns.

- **Teach for Transfer.** Teach students to use generalities and perceptions. Have them use metaphors and similes to make connections between unlike items. This is an important function for future transfer of learning.

- **Incorporate Hands-On Learning.** Provide frequent opportunities for experiential and hands-on learning. Students need to realize that they must discover and order relationships in the real world.

– Continued –

Strategies for Teaching to the Whole Brain—Continued

Use the chart below to decide what types of classroom strategies would work best with students whose hemisphere and sensory preferences are as indicated. Use the **bridging** and **hugging** strategies you learned in Chapter 4 to help you with this.

Modality	Left-Hemisphere Preference	Right-Hemisphere Preference
Visually Preferred		
Kinesthetically Preferred		
Auditorily Preferred		

– Continued –

194

Strategies for Teaching to the Whole Brain—Continued

A. What are your hemispheric and sensory preferences?

Hemispheric Preference:_____

Sensory Preference(s):_____

B. How did your preferences in A influence the strategies you designed in the chart for this activity? Jot down the results of your analysis here. Were there any surprises?

_____

_____

_____

_____

_____

_____

_____

_____

_____

_____

PRACTITIONER'S CORNER

Concept Mapping—General Guidelines

Concept mapping consists of extracting ideas and terms from curriculum content and plotting them visually to show and name the relationships among them. The learner establishes a visual representation of relations between concepts that might have been presented only verbally. Integrating visual and verbal activities enhances understanding of concepts whether they be abstract, concrete, verbal, or nonverbal. The key to concept mapping is the clear indication of the relationship that one item has to another. West, Farmer, and Wolff (1991) summarize nine types of cognitive relationships:

Name	Relationship	Example
1. Classification	A is an example of B	A cat is a mammal.
2. Defining/subsuming	A is a property of B	All mammals have hair.
3. Equivalence	A is identical to B	$2(a + b) = 2(b + a)$
4. Similarity	A is similar to B	A donkey is like a mule.
5. Difference	A is unlike B	A spider is not an insect.
6. Quantity	A is greater/less than B	A right angle is greater than an acute angle.
7. Time sequence	A occurs before/after B	In mitosis, prophase occurs before metaphase.
8. Causal	A causes B	Combustion produces heat.
9. Enabling	A enables/allows B	A person must be at least 18 years old to vote.

– Continued –

Concept Mapping—General Guidelines—Continued

Concept mapping uses graphic diagrams to organize and represent the relationships between and among the components. These diagrams are also called *graphic* and *visual organizers*. Students should discuss these different types of relationships and give their own examples before attempting to select a concept map. There are dozens of possible organizers.[42] Below are three common types. In each, the relationship between items is written as a legend (for a few examples) or next to the line connecting the items (when there are many examples).

- **Spider maps** best illustrate classification, similarity, and difference relationships.

- **Hierarchy maps** illustrate defining and/or subsuming, equivalence, and quantity relationships.

- **Chain maps** illustrate time sequence, casual, and enabling relationships.

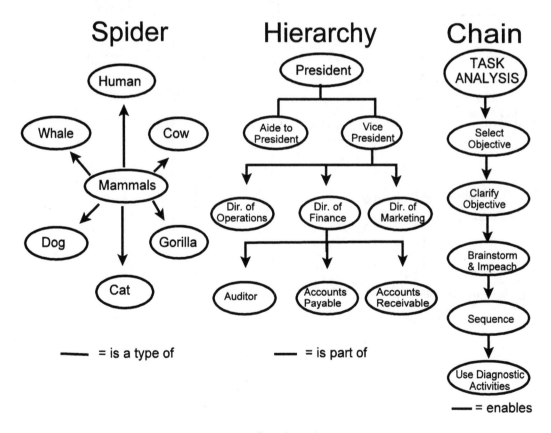

– Continued –

197

Concept Mapping—General Guidelines—Continued

Below are three more types of concept maps.

- **Story maps** are useful for classifying main ideas with supporting events and information from the story.

- **Analogy maps** illustrate similarities and differences between new and familiar concepts.

- **K-W-L maps** illustrate the degree of new learning that will be needed. The "K" is for what we already *know*; "W" is for what we *want* to know; and "L" is for what we *learned*.

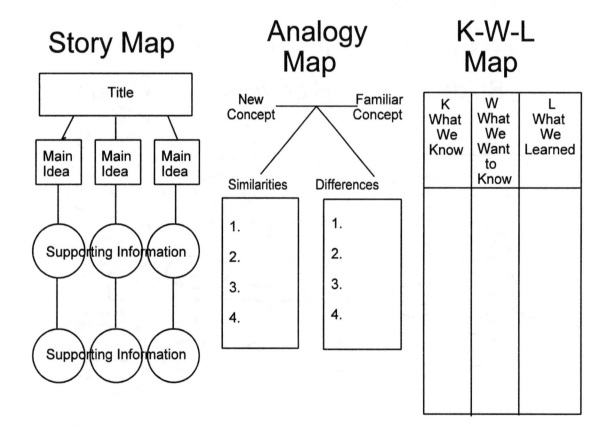

– Continued –

Concept Mapping—General Guidelines—Continued

- **Venn diagrams** map the similarities and differences between two concepts.

- **Plot diagrams** are used to find the major parts of a novel.

- **A brace map** shows subsets of larger items.

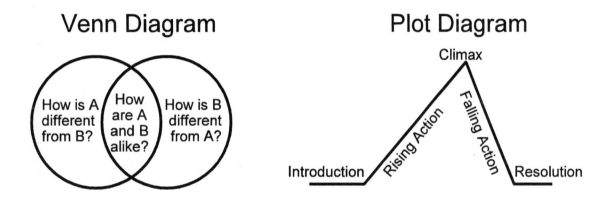

A Brace Map

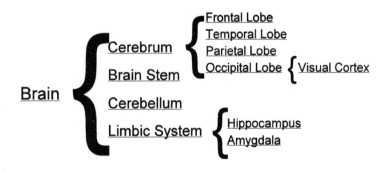

– Continued –

Concept Mapping—General Guidelines—Continued

Directions: Time for practice. Select a broad curriculum concept, such as energy, time, or forms of government. Draw an appropriate graphic organizer in the box below and fill it in with the major parts of the concept. Present your work to other participants.

PRACTITIONER'S CORNER

Acquiring a Second Language

When Should Children Learn a Second Language? Although the brain maintains its ability to learn throughout life, it is quite clear from the research described in this text that language learning occurs most easily during the first ten years or so. We should take advantage of this window of opportunity if we offer second languages in schools.

Why Learn a Second Language? In addition to knowing our native language, we benefit from learning a second language as well. Second language instruction should start as soon as possible. Here are some reasons for learning a second language at an early age:[43]

- Enriches and enhances a child's mental development.

- Gives students more flexibility in thinking, greater sensitivity to language, and a better ear for listening. (The brain learns to respond to phonemes that are different from the native language.)

- Improves understanding of a child's native language. (Unless a language or hearing difficulty exists, research does not support the claim that learning a second language early will interfere with learning the native language.)

- Gives a child the ability to communicate with people he or she would otherwise not have the chance to know.

- Opens the door to other cultures and helps a child understand and appreciate people from other countries. (This is important as our country becomes increasingly heterogeneous.)

- Gives a student a head start in language requirements for college.

- Increases job opportunities in many careers where knowing another language is a considerable asset.

– Continued –

Acquiring a Second Language—Continued

What Are Barriers to Primary-Grade Second Language Programs? The two most common objections are that it is too expensive and that it might interfere with native language development. Primary-grade programs need not cost much at all. Volunteer parents or videotapes can be the source of native speakers, and the materials come at low cost. As for interference, no research evidence supports this contention. Rather, several studies show that strategies used to acquire a second language often help children understand and speak their native language better.

What Are the Characteristics of an Effective K–6 Second Language Program?

- **All students** have access to the program regardless of race/ethnic origin, learning styles, home language, or future academic goals.

- **Program goals** are consistent with the time devoted to second language instruction. In the primary grades, the main goal is to hear the sounds, flow, and syntax of another language. There are different types of K–6 second language programs that achieve different levels of language proficiency and require different time commitments.

- **Sequence** of language instruction should be available through the K–12 school years. Second language acquisition requires consistent practice, so a K–12 sequence is crucial to mastery. For this reason, second language instruction is often exempted from block scheduling formats that limit classes to one semester per year.

- **Systematic curriculum development** in second language content is part of the school plan. Look for ways to include second language experiences across the curriculum.

- **Native speakers** must be used for the primary-grade instruction to ensure that the young brain hears authentic language sounds.

- **Connections between language and culture** are made explicit so that the learners understand the development of the second language in the context of its culture.

– Continued –

Acquiring a Second Language—Continued

Teaching Strategies for Second Language Acquisition

Teaching strategies for second language instruction vary with the age of the learner who is beginning the study. Primary-grade teaching focus is mainly on recognizing, discriminating, and practicing the phonemes of the second language, as spoken by native speakers. Grammar is not taught per se, but implied through extensive student conversation. In the intermediate and later grades (including adult levels), the main goal is to develop communication competencies so that the student feels comfortable speaking, writing, and thinking the second language. Thus, teachers of second languages and of English as a Second Language (ESL) should follow a sequence that begins with young learners. This sequence aims to[44]

- **Develop Communication Competence.** One of the primary goals of learning a second language is to gain competence in communication. This involves acquiring four major competencies, requiring integration of the verbal and nonverbal aspects of language as well as right- and left-hemisphere processing. Teachers should keep these four competencies in mind as they select their instructional strategies:

  Grammatical Competence. The degree to which a student has mastered the formal linguistic code of the language including vocabulary, rules of punctuation, word formation, and sentence structure. This entails the analytic and sequential processing of the left hemisphere.

  Sociolinguistic Competence. The ability to use grammatical forms appropriately in contexts that range from very informal to very formal styles. It includes varying the choice of verbal and nonverbal language to adapt the speech to a specific person or social context, and this requires sensitivity to individual and sociocultural differences. This is essentially the right hemisphere's ability to contextualize language.

  Discourse Competence. The ability to combine form and thought into a coherent expression. It involves knowing how to use conjunctions, adverbs, and transitional phrases to achieve continuity of thought. This requires the integration of both hemispheres; the analytic ability of the left hemisphere

– Continued –

Acquiring a Second Language—Continued

to generate the grammatical features, and the use of the right hemisphere to synthesize them into meaningful, coherent wholes.

Strategic Competence. The ability to use verbal and nonverbal communication strategies, such as body language and circumlocution, to compensate for the user's imperfect knowledge of the language, and to negotiate meaning.

This research points out the need for teachers to ensure that the nonverbal form of intellect is not neglected in second language acquisition. In planning lessons, teachers should:

- Not rely heavily on grammar, vocabulary memorization, and mechanical translations, especially during the early stages of instruction.

- Do more with contextual language, trial and error, brainstorming of meaning, visual activities, and role-playing.

- Give students the opportunity to establish the contextual networking they need to grasp meaning, nuance, and idiomatic expressions.

When these skills are in place, shift to more work on enlarging students' vocabulary and knowledge of grammar.

PRACTITIONER'S CORNER

Considerations for Teaching Reading

Reading is the result of a complex process that relies heavily on previously acquired spoken language, but also requires the learning of specific skills that are not innate to brain functions. Because of the many steps involved in reading, challenges can occur anywhere along the way. Children often devise strategies to overcome problems but may need help in getting to the next step. As with learning any skill, reading requires practice. Here are some points to consider when teaching reading.

- **Phonemic Awareness.** The brain reads by breaking words into sounds. Children first need to be taught the 44 basic sounds in the English language and how these sounds are formed by combinations of the 26 letters of the alphabet. This is known as phonemic-awareness training. The more difficulty a learner has in reading, the more likely the need for concentrated practice on phonemic awareness. Sometimes, learning the names of the letters of the alphabet first can confuse new readers because the names of the letters rarely reveal how they will sound when reading words. (Some reading teachers have found success in teaching the alphabet by each letter's most common phoneme sound, that is, "ah-buh-cuh-duh-eh," etc.)

- **Decoding.** The better that a learner can *sound out* words, the faster the brain processes what it *sees*. Therefore, readers should be taught to discern the individual sounds within words, and to say them aloud. *Dog* is "duh-awh-guh," and *bat* is "bah-ah-tuh." This practice helps the brain remember the decoding process of sight-to-sound so crucial to accurate and fast reading. However, problems develop when the reader's eyes move faster than the sound processing system can decode the phonemes. In this case, slow down the visual speed by having the student move a finger under each grapheme. This also ensures that readers keep their eyes moving across the page, not fixating them into a stare, which also retards the reading process.

– Continued –

Considerations for Teaching Reading—Continued

- **Practice for Comprehension.** Once the code is learned, practice in reading aloud is needed to develop speed and accuracy so that learners can comprehend what they are reading and get a sense of the language's syntax. This also helps teachers hear how accurately the student has matched the visual grapheme with the auditory phoneme.

- **Read With the Learners.** Teachers should read aloud as learners follow along in the text. This helps students with prosody—hearing the flow, rhythm, and tonal changes of the language. Have students move a finger under the words to show that they are correctly matching what they hear the teacher say with what they see on paper.

- **Read to the Learners.** Read literature slightly advanced for the learner while students listen, even with their eyes closed, to absorb the richness, rhythm, imagery, sound, and feeling of language in different contexts.

- **Introduce Literature.** Move on to interesting books and other forms of literature for practice and motivation to read. At this point, it is important to emphasize the contextual nature of the English language. Most meaning and pronunciation comes from *how* words are used in relation to all other words in the sentence (the context). Compare, for example, "The boy picked up the *lead* weight" to "The boy had a *lead* part in the school play."

- **Avoid** asking new readers to guess the sounds of words if they have not had phonemic-awareness training. Without the training, they have no clue how the word should sound, and mispronouncing the word will only reinforce the incorrect association between the grapheme and the phoneme. Remember that practice makes permanent, not necessarily perfect.

The chart on the next page is one possible hierarchy to be considered for teaching reading based on a deeper understanding of the complexity of how the brain reads. In this hierarchy, emphasis is placed on ensuring accurate phonemic awareness at the very beginning of reading instruction. More evidence is emerging from brain scans of children reading that problems arise when there is poor phonemic awareness, thus confusing the decoding system.

– Continued –

Considerations for Teaching Reading—Continued

EXAMPLE OF A HIERARCHY
FOR TEACHING READING

Note: This is one suggested procedure for teaching reading that reflects the research on how the brain seems to read. It attempts to balance the early need for solid phonemic awareness with the later introduction of literary samples illustrating the more complex semantic and syntactic elements of language.

Semantics—Recognizing that the meaning of words can change in different contexts. The teacher selects a variety of literature examples to illustrate contextual variations of language.

Syntax—Creating more complex sentences with correct grammatical structure. The teacher reading stories aloud helps learners develop a sense of syntax by listening to the phrasing and word positions in sentences. Having students read aloud allows the teacher to check pronunciation. Then students can move on to silent reading.

Discourse—Constructing and connecting simple sentences in a logical sequence. The student's spoken language has already developed some sentence patterns intuitively, such as subject-predicate-object, as in "I want a cookie" or "He throws the ball."

START HERE:
Phonological—Processing the basic sound elements of language. This requires the student to read aloud to ensure that the correct connections are made between the 44 English phoneme sounds and the 26 letters of the alphabet. Then practice with rhyming, word recognition, and meaning.

PRACTITIONER'S CORNER

Reading Guidelines for All Teachers

To some extent, all teachers are teachers of reading. Beyond the primary grades, students read to learn, and teachers place heavy reliance on their students' ability to acquire information through reading. Because this reliance increases substantially in the upper grades, reading ability is a major determinant of student success in high school. Reading in all subject areas is likely to be more successful when teachers help students use reading skills efficiently and effectively.

- **Have a Reading Plan.** Remember that the brain is always seeking meaning. Good readers approach print strategically looking for general meaning, whereas poor readers often get stuck in details. Good readers scan for key words and phrases that aid in comprehension; they can always go back later if they need details. They ask themselves questions like: How much do I need to read in this sitting? Why am I reading this? What's the main point? Why is it important? What else is this like that I've already learned?

- **Less Is More.** At first, the amount of reading assigned should be just enough to accomplish the task. Don't overwhelm students with non-essential reading, especially in subject areas where they lack confidence.

- **Talk, Talk, and Talk Some More.** You will remember that talk is a very powerful learning and memory tool. When working together, students should ask each other questions about the text they are reading, summarize main points, and clarify anything they did not understand.

- **Use Graphic Organizers.** Have students use or design their own graphic organizers and concept maps to help understand the major points in their reading. This is particularly useful in textbooks and nonfiction reading that is full of detail.

– Continued –

Reading Guidelines for All Teachers—Continued

- **Add Novelty.** Add novelty (Chapter 3) so that students don't see reading as drudgery. For example, get students to speculate on what might happen next in a story, or have them write their own plausible endings. Consider giving them the option to write a song or a poem or a short skit to illustrate some of the story's main events or characters. Let them create their own stories, plays, or publications, which they can read or perform for other students.

Chapter 5—Brain Specialization and Learning

Key Points to Ponder

Jot down on this page key points, ideas, strategies, and resources you want to consider later. This sheet is your personal journal summary and will help to jog your memory.

CHAPTER 5 - NOTES

1. Gazzaniga (1998a).

2. For more detailed explanations of these early experiments, see Gazzaniga (1967).

3. Gazzaniga (1998a, 1998b).

4. Carter (1998), pp. 38–39.

5. Carter (1998), Gazzaniga (1989, 1998b), Springer and Deutsch (1993).

6. Weisman and Banich (2000).

7. Gazzaniga (1998b).

8. Sperry (1966).

9. Knecht et al. (2000).

10. Carter (1998), p. 46.

11. Handedness is established in the fetus by the fifteenth week of gestation. Despite all the sophisticated brain research of modern times, the cause of handedness has still escaped explanation. With nearly 90 percent of people right-handed, this would seem to be the outcome of the logical left hemisphere's control. Is left-handedness, then, pathological? Explanations run from simple genetic determination to some pre-natal disturbance that may have upset the left-brain/right-hand connection, such as unusually high testosterone levels. The mystery continues.

12. Diamond and Hopson (1998); Gur (1995); Kimura (1992); Levy (1985); Shaywitz, Shaywitz, and Gore (1995).

13. Gur et al. (1999).

14. Rabinowicz, Dean, Petetot, and de Courten-Myers (1999).

15. Hedges and Nowell (1995).

16. Kimura (1992).

17. National Center for Education Statistics, *Condition of Education, 1998.*

18. Dehaene, Spelke, Pinel, Stanescu, and Tsivkin (1999).

19. Spencer, Steele, and Quinn (1999).

20. National Center for Education Statistics, *Digest of Education, 1997, 1998.*

21. In 1861, French surgeon Paul Broca noted that damage to the left frontal lobe induced language difficulties generally known as aphasia, wherein patients muttered sounds or lost speech completely. Broca's area (just behind the left temple) is about the size of a quarter.

22. In 1871, German neurologist Carl Wernicke described a different type of aphasia—one in which patients could not make sense out of words they spoke or heard. These patients had damage in the left temporal lobe. Wernicke's area (above the left ear) is about the size of a silver dollar.

23. Bates (1999).

24. Cheour et al. (1998).

25. Van Petten and Bloom (1999).

26. Pinker (1994).

27. Johnson (1999).

28. Buzzell (1998).

29. Dale, et al. (1998).

30. Pinker (1994), p. 53, 293.

31. Johnson and Newport (1991).

32. Kim, Relkin, Lee, and Hirsch (1997).

33. Shaywitz (1996).

34. This result makes sense in light of other studies which show that fast-talking media programs can impair language development in children under 2 years of age.

35. Merzenich et al. (1996) and Tallal et al. (1996).

36. Shaywitz et al. (1998).

37. Irlen and Robinson (1996).

38. Croyle (1998).

39. Robinson, Foreman, and Dear (1996).

40. For more information on Irlen Syndrome, including training opportunities, visit the website at www.irlen.com.

41. Some of these are adapted from Key (1991).

42. See Bromley, Irwin-DeVitis, and Modlo (1995) and Hyerle (1996).

43. The suggestions on these pages are offered by the Center for Applied Linguistics which has numerous resources for early foreign language learning. Their website is www.cal.org.

44. Danesi (1990).

CHAPTER 6

THE BRAIN AND THE ARTS

The quality of civilization can be measured through its music, dance, drama, architecture, visual art, and literature. We must give our children knowledge and understanding of civilization's most profound works.

— Ernest L. Boyer

Chapter Highlights: This chapter discusses how recent brain imaging studies are helping us understand the role and importance of music, the visual arts, and movement in brain growth and cognitive function. It suggests ways to incorporate artistic activities into lessons at all grade levels and in all subject areas.

We have never discovered a culture on this planet, past or present, that doesn't have art. Yet there have been a number of cultures—even today—that don't have reading and writing. Why is that? One possible explanation is that the activities represented by the arts—dance, music, drama, and visual arts—are basic to the human experience and necessary for survival. If they weren't, why would they have been part of every civilization from the Cro-Magnon cave dwellers to the urban citizens of the 21st century?

The Arts Are Basic to the Human Experience

The Arts Are Part of Human Development. As we learn more about the brain, we continue to find clues as to why the activities required for the arts are so fundamental to the brain's activities. Music: It seems that certain structures in the auditory cortex respond only to musical tones. Dance: A portion of the cerebrum and most of the cerebellum are devoted to initiating and coordinating all kinds of movement, from intense running to the delicate sway of the arms. Drama:

214

Specialized areas of the cerebrum focus on spoken language acquisition and call on the limbic system to provide the emotional component. Visual arts: The internal visual processing system can recall reality or create fantasy with the same ease.

Contrary to Oscar Wilde's comment that "All art is quite useless," these cerebral talents did not develop by accident. They are the result of many centuries of interaction between humans and their environment, and the continued existence of these talents must indicate they contribute in some way to our survival. In those cultures that do not have reading and writing, the arts are the media through which that culture's history, mores, and values are transmitted to the younger generations. They also transmit more basic information necessary for the culture's survival, such as how and what to hunt for food and how to defend the village from predators. Consequently, art is an important force behind group survival. For example, about 1,000 of the 6,000 or so languages on this planet are spoken in just one place—New Guinea! Each language is totally unrelated to any other known language in New Guinea (or elsewhere) and is spoken by a tribe of just a few thousand people living within a ten-mile radius. Even more astonishing is that each tribe has its own music, visual arts, and dance.[1]

> **We have never discovered a culture on this planet—past or present—that doesn't have music, art, and dance.**

In modern cultures, the arts are rarely thought of as survival skills, but rather as frills—the esthetic product of a wealthy society with lots of time to spare. In fact, people pay high ticket prices to see the arts performed professionally, leading to the belief that the arts are highly valued. This cultural support is often seen in high schools, which have their choruses, bands, drama classes, and an occasional dance troupe. Yet seldom do elementary schools enjoy this support, precisely when the young brain is most adept at refining the skills needed to develop artistic talent.[2] Just as financial and intellectual commitment for teaching second languages in elementary schools is weak at best, so is the support for elementary music, visual arts, and dance instruction. Furthermore, when school budgets get tight, these elementary grade programs are among the first to be reduced or eliminated.

The Arts and the Young Brain. In Chapter 1, we discuss the explosive growth of dendrites and synaptic connections during the brain's early years. Much of what young children do as play—singing, drawing, dancing—are natural forms of art. These activities engage all the senses and help wire the brain for successful learning. When children enter school, these art activities need to be continued. The cognitive areas are developed as the child learns songs and rhymes, and creates drawings and finger paintings. The dancing and movements during play develop gross motor skills, and the sum of these activities enhances emotional well-being. Of course, whatever we offer children in arts education should be developmentally appropriate, and not represent just an extrapolation of an adult approach.

Why Teach the Arts?

The basic arguments I make here are these:

- The arts play an important role in human development, enhancing the growth of cognitive, emotional, and psychomotor pathways.

- Schools have an obligation to expose children to the arts at the earliest possible time and to consider the arts as fundamental—not optional—curriculum areas.

- Learning the arts provides a higher quality of human experience throughout a person's lifetime.

The Sciences Need the Arts

Few people will argue against studying the natural sciences in the elementary and middle schools, and support remains strong for the sciences—including Advanced Placement courses—in high schools. When budgets get tight, some people even view music and other arts courses as a drain on the funds needed to preserve science and mathematics courses.

Others often see science and the arts as polar opposites. The sciences are thought of as objective, logical, analytical, reproducible, and useful; the arts are supposed to be subjective, intuitive, sensual, unique, and frivolous. In the competition between the arts and sciences in U.S. society, the arts have frequently lost. Typically, more public and private funds are given to any single technical or scientific discipline than all the arts combined.[3]

But scientists and mathematicians know that the arts are vital to their success and use skills borrowed from the arts as scientific tools. These include the ability to observe accurately, to think spatially (how does an object appear when I rotate it in my head?) and perceive kinesthetically (how does it move?). These skills are not usually taught as part of the science curriculum but are at home in writing, drama, painting, and music.

Indeed, the arts often inform the sciences. For example:

- Buckminster Fuller's geodesic domes can describe soccer balls and architectural buildings, as well as the structure of viruses and some recently discovered complex and enormous molecules.

How Education in the Arts Develops Cognitive Growth

Although the arts are often thought of as separate subjects, like chemistry or algebra, they really are a collection of skills and thought processes that transcend all areas of human engagement. When taught well, the arts develop cognitive competencies that benefit learners in every aspect of their education and prepare them for the demands of the 21st century. Elliot Eisner (1998) of Stanford University identifies these eight competencies:

■ **The perception of relationships.** Creating a work in music, words, or any other art discipline helps students recognize how parts of a work influence each other and interact. For example, this is the kind of skill that enables an executive to appreciate the way a particular system affects every other subsystem in an organization.

■ **An attention to nuance.** The arts teach students that small differences can have large effects. Great amounts of visual reasoning go into decisions about nuance, form, and color to make an art work satisfying. In writing, similarly, great attention to detail in use of language is needed to employ allusion, innuendo, and metaphor.

■ **The perspective that problems can have multiple solutions, and questions can have multiple answers.** Good things can be done in different ways. Schools often emphasize learning focused on a single correct answer. In business and in life, most difficult problems require looking at multiple options with differing priorities.

■ **The ability to shift goals in process.** Work in the arts helps students recognize and pursue goals that were not thought of at the beginning. Too often in schools, the relationship of means to ends is oversimplified. Arts help us see that ends can shift in process.

How Education in the Arts Develops Cognitive Growth – Continued

■ **The permission to make decisions in the absence of a rule.** Arithmetic has rules and measurable results, but many other things lack that kind of rule-governed specificity. In the absence of rules, it is personal judgment that allows one to assess what feels right and to decide when a task is well done.

■ **The use of imagination as the source of content.** Arts enhance the ability to visualize situations and use the mind's eye to determine the rightness of planned action.

■ **The acceptance of operating within constraints.** No system, whether linguistic, numerical, visual, or auditory covers every purpose. Arts give students a chance to use the constraints of a medium to invent ways to exploit those constraints productively.

■ **The ability to see the world from an aesthetic perspective.** Arts help students frame the world in fresh ways – like seeing the Golden Gate Bridge from a design or poetic angle.

▸ NASA employs artists to design displays that present satellite data so that it is accurate, yet understandable.

▸ A biochemist looks at the fiber folds in her weaving cloth as another way of explaining protein folding.

▸ Computer engineers code messages to the frequencies of a specific song to prevent interception or blocking of the message, unless the decoder knows the song.

▸ Genetic researchers convert complex data into musical notation to facilitate analysis of the data, as for example, decoding the sequence of genes in a chromosome.

Thus, playing piano, writing a poem, or creating a painting sharpen observations, hone details, and put things into context. These are the same tools needed by a good scientist. The study of the arts not only allows students to develop skills that will improve the quality of their lives but also sustains the same creative base from which scientists and engineers seek to develop their innovations and breakthroughs of the future.

Impact of the Arts on Student Learning

Although learning in most other disciplines often develops only a single talent or skill, the arts engage many skills and abilities. In 1999, the Arts Education Partnership and the President's Committee on the Arts and the Humanities issued a report that contained the findings of seven independent studies looking at the impact of the arts on student learning. There is a remarkable agreement among the findings of these studies:[4]

> *Although learning in other disciplines often develops a single talent or skill, the arts engage many skills and abilities.*

Disaffected Students. The arts reach students who are not otherwise being reached. Arts sometimes provide the only reason that certain students stay in touch with school. Without the arts, these young people would be left with no access to a community of learners. Studies done recently in the Chicago public schools showed that in 1998, sixth-grade students in schools with an arts-based curriculum scored about 14 percentage points higher on the Iowa Test of Basic Skills (ITBS) reading section than a matched population (for neighborhood, family income, and academic performance) of sixth graders in the regular schools. On the ITBS mathematics section, 60 percent of the arts-based students averaged at or above grade level, whereas the remainder of the students averaged just over 40 percent. This significant jump in mathematics scores is of particular research interest and is discussed in more detail later in this chapter.

Ninth graders in the arts-based schools averaged ninth grade–fifth month performance in reading on the Test of Achievement and Proficiency, whereas all other ninth graders averaged eighth grade–fifth month. Furthermore, in both the sixth and ninth grade tests, the improved performance has continued to grow since the inception of the arts-based program in 1993. Results like those in Chicago and other places have convinced many students to remain in school.

Different Learning Styles. The arts reach students in ways they are not otherwise being reached. Ample research evidence indicates that students learn in many different ways. This research also notes that some students can become behavior problems if conventional classroom practices are not engaging them. Success in the arts is often a bridge to successful learning in other areas, thereby raising a student's self-concept.

Table 6.1 shows how students involved in arts-based youth organizations have a better self-concept than a standard student population. These numbers are particularly significant when we consider that students in the arts organizations are twice as likely to have stressful home situations involving parents getting a divorce, going on and off welfare, or losing a job. The students in this sample noted how the arts allowed them to express pent-up feelings and to gain some distance from these problems by talking about them, thinking, and listening.

Table 6.1 Percentage of Students in Standard School Population and in Arts-Based Youth Organizations Reporting a Positive Perception of Self [5]		
	Standard School Population	Arts-Based Youth Organizations
Student feels good about him/herself.	76.2	92.3
Student feels s/he is a person of worth.	75.9	90.9
Student is able to do things as well as others.	76.2	88.8
Student, on the whole, is satisfied with self.	70.0	84.6

Personal and Interpersonal Connections. The arts connect students to themselves and each other. Creating art is a personal experience, as students draw upon their own resources to produce the result. This is a much deeper involvement than just reading text to get an answer. Studies show that the attitudes of young people toward one another improve through their arts learning experiences.

School and Classroom Climate. The arts transform the environment for learning. Schools become places of discovery when the arts are the focus of the learning environment. Arts change the school culture, break down barriers between curriculum areas, and can even improve the school's physical appearance. Because administrators and teachers determine a school's climate, a study of 29 arts-rich New York City schools compared some indicators of school climate to the remaining, non-arts schools. In the arts-rich schools administrators encouraged teachers to take risks, broaden the curriculum, and learn new skills. The teachers had a significantly higher degree of innovation in their instruction, were more supportive of students, and had greater interest in their own professional development. Once again, the arts-rich program had a much greater impact on these results than did the students' socioeconomic status.

Gifted Students. The arts provide new challenges for those students already considered successful. Students who outgrow their learning environment usually get bored and complacent. The arts can offer a chance for unlimited challenge. For instance, older students may teach and mentor younger ones, and some students may work with professional artists.

The World of Work. The arts connect learning experiences to the world of everyday work. The adult workplace has changed. The ability to generate ideas, bring ideas to life, and communicate them to others are keys to workplace success. Whether in a classroom or in a studio as an artist, the student is learning and practicing future workplace behaviors.

Let's take a look at the three major forms of artistic expression—music, visual arts, and dance and drama—and observe what brain research is telling us. What impact will these studies have on student learning and success?

Music

No one area has gained more notoriety in recent years than the impact of music on the brain. Numerous books are on the market touting the so-called "Mozart Effect" and promising that music can do all sorts of things from relieving pain, to increasing a child's IQ, to improving mathematics skills. To what degree are these claims backed by credible scientific evidence? As with most claims of this nature, there is an emerging body of scientific data, followed by media attention and a lot of hype. Let's try to sort out what the research in music is saying so that we can reap its benefits while making informed decisions about the validity of the assertions.

Effects of Listening to Music Versus Creating Instrumental Music

Research on the effects of music on the brain and body can be divided into the effects of *listening* to music, and the effects of *creating* or *producing* music on an instrument, especially an acoustic rather than an electronic one. The brain and body respond very differently in these two situations. Unfortunately, laypersons and, to some extent, the media have not recognized this crucial distinction. Consequently, they have

> *How the brain responds when creating music is very different from how it responds when listening to music.*

mistakenly assumed that the results of studies that involved creating music would be repeated when listening to music. If educators want to use the research on the effects of music to benefit students, then it is important that they differentiate the studies on listening from those on creating music.

How the Brain Listens to Music

The sounds of music are transmitted to the inner ear and are broken down according to the specific frequencies that make up the sounds (Figure 6.1). Different cells in the *cochlea* respond to different frequencies, and their signals are mapped out in the auditory cortex, especially in the right hemisphere in which perceptions of pitch, melody, and harmony emerge. This processing information is then transmitted to the frontal lobe where the music can be linked to emotion, thoughts, and past experiences. Each hemisphere of the brain contains areas that respond to both music and language. But, as mentioned in Chapter 5, the left hemisphere also contains regions of specialization that respond only to language, and the right has areas devoted exclusively to music perception. This explains why some people can be extraordinarily talented in language skills but have difficulty humming a melody. The reverse situation occurs in the brains of idiot savants, individuals who are talented musicians despite severe language retardation.[6]

Music can also be imagined because people have stored representations of songs and the sounds of musical instruments in their long-term memory. When a song is imagined, the brain cells that are activated are identical to those used when a person actually hears music from the outside world. But when a song is imagined, brain scans show that the visual cortex is also stimulated so that visual patterns are imaged as well. The mechanism that triggers musical imagery is not yet understood, but it is not uncommon for people to have songs running through their heads when they get up in the morning.

How the Brain Hears Music

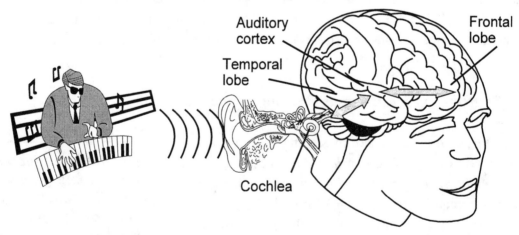

Figure 6.1 *Sound entering the ear is converted into nerve impulses in the cochlea. These impulses are transmitted to the auditory cortex in the temporal lobe in which specialized regions, especially in the right hemisphere, analyze pitch and timbre. Information from the auditory cortex is transmitted to the frontal lobe, which associates the sound of music with thought and stimulates emotions and past experiences.*

Is Music Inborn? Many researchers now believe that the ability to perceive and enjoy music is an inborn human trait. But is there any credible evidence to support the biological basis of music? First of all, any behavior thought to have a biological foundation must be universal. Even though the uses of music may vary across past and current cultures, all cultures do sing and associate certain meanings and emotions with music.

Second, biologically based behaviors should reveal themselves early in life. Researchers have shown that infants of just three months old can learn and remember to move an overhead crib mobile when a certain song is played. Thus, infants can use music as a retrieval cue. In addition, the memory of the specific song lasted more than seven days.[7] Moreover, preschool children spontaneously use music in their communication and play.

Third, if music has a strong biological component, then it should exist in other animals. Monkeys can form musical abstractions, such as determining harmonic patterns. Although many animals use musical sounds to attract mates and signal danger, only humans have developed a sophisticated and unlimited musical repertoire.

> **Compelling evidence suggests that the brain's response to music has strong biological roots.**

Fourth, if music has biological roots, we might expect the brain to have specialized areas for music—and it does. For example, areas in the auditory cortex are organized to process pitch. Furthermore, the brain's ability to respond emotionally to music is connected to biology and culture. The biological aspect is supported by the fact that the brain has specialized areas that respond only to music, and these areas are able to stimulate the limbic system, provoking an emotional response. PET scans show that the neural areas stimulated depend on the type of music—melodic tunes stimulate areas that evoke pleasant feelings, whereas dissonant sounds activate other limbic areas that produce unpleasant emotions.[8]

The Benefits of Listening to Music

Therapeutic Benefits. For many years, medical researchers and practitioners have reported on the therapeutic effects of music to relieve stress, diminish pain, and treat other more severe disabilities, such as mental retardation, Parkinson's disease, Alzheimer's disease, and visual and hearing impairments. Other studies have shown that listening to music can boost immune function in children and that premature babies exposed to lullabies in the hospital went home earlier. The sheer volume of studies and positive results attest to music's therapeutic benefits.

How does music work this magic? It's still a mystery, but there are some important hints. Researchers have known for a long time that music can directly influence blood pressure, pulse, and the electric activity of muscles. Newer evidence shows that music may even help build and strengthen connections between brain cells in the cortex. This effect is important, and some doctors are already using music to help rehabilitate stroke patients. Some stroke patients who have lost their ability to speak retain their ability to sing. By getting patients to sing what they want to say, their fluency improves, and therapists can use existing pathways to retrain the speech centers of the brain.

Educational Benefits. The notion that music could affect cognitive performance catapulted from the research laboratory to the television talk shows in 1993 when Frances Rauscher and Gordon Shaw conducted a study using 84 college students. They reported that the students' spatial-temporal reasoning—the ability to form mental images from physical objects, or to see patterns in time and space—improved after listening to Mozart's Sonata for Two Pianos in D Major (K.448) for 10 minutes.[9] But the students' improved abilities faded within an hour.

The results of this study, promptly dubbed "The Mozart Effect," were widely publicized and soon reinterpreted to incorrectly imply that listening to a Mozart sonata would enhance intelligence by raising IQ. In fact, the study reported that the music improved only spatial-temporal reasoning (one of many components of total IQ) and that the effect quickly faded. But the results did encourage the researchers to go further and test whether *creating* music would have a longer-lasting effect.

Shaw was convinced that listening to the complex melodic variations in Mozart's sonata (K.448) stimulated the frontal cortex more than simpler music. He and several colleagues tested this idea by having subjects take turns listening to Mozart's sonata (K.448), Beethoven's *Für Elise*, and popular piano music. The fMRIs showed that both the popular and the Beethoven piano music activated only the auditory cortex in all subjects. The Mozart sonata, however, activated the auditory as well as the frontal cortex in all of the subjects, leading Shaw to suggest that there *is* a neurological basis for the "Mozart Effect."[10]

Several studies have shown that listening to music can stimulate the parts of the brain that are responsible for memory recall and visual imagery.[11] This may explain why background music in the classroom helps many students stay focused while completing certain learning tasks.

The Benefits of Creating Music

Although passive listening to music does have some therapeutic and short-term educational benefits, the making of music seems to provide many more cerebral advantages. One major study involved 78 preschoolers from three California preschools, including one serving mostly poor, inner-city families. The children were divided into four groups. One group (Keyboard) took individual, 12- to 15-minute piano lessons twice a week along with singing instruction. Another group (Singing) took 30-minute singing lessons five days a week, and a third group (Computer) trained on computers. The fourth group received no special instruction. All students took tests before the lessons began to measure different types of spatial-reasoning skills.

After six months, the children who received six months of piano keyboard training had improved their scores by 34 percent on tests measuring spatial-temporal reasoning (Figure 6.2). On other tasks, there was no difference in scores. Furthermore, the enhancement lasted for days, indicating a substantial change in spatial-temporal function. The other three groups, in comparison, had only slight improvement on all tasks.[12]

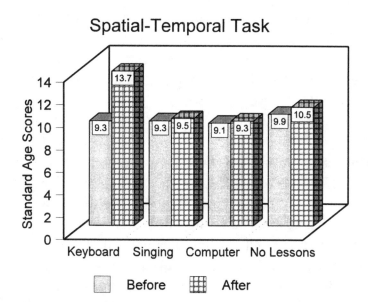

Spatial-Temporal Task

Keyboard: Before 9.3, After 13.7
Singing: Before 9.3, After 9.5
Computer: Before 9.1, After 9.3
No Lessons: Before 9.9, After 10.5

Standard Age Scores

Before | After

Figure 6.2 The graph shows the results of a spatial-temporal task performed by the preschool students before and after piano keyboard training, group singing, training on the computer, and no lessons. National standard age scores for all ages are 10, showing that these were average children before training.

Piano Keyboard Versus the Computer Keyboard. Why did piano keyboard training improve test performance by 34 percent while the computer keyboard training didn't? Remember that the study measured spatial-temporal improvements only. As this and other studies show, music training seems to specifically influence neural pathways responsible for spatial-temporal reasoning, and that effect is more noticeable in the young brain. This may be due to the combination of tactile input from striking the piano keys, auditory input from the sounds of the notes, and the visual information of where one's hand is on the keyboard. This is a much more complex interaction than from the computer keyboard. Computers, of course, are very valuable teaching tools, but when it comes to developing the neural pathways responsible for spatial abilities, the piano keyboard is much more effective.

Can Music Make You Smarter in Mathematics?

Of all the academic subjects, mathematics seems to be most closely connected to music. Music relies on fractions for tempo and on time divisions for pacing, octaves, and chord intervals.

Here are some mathematical concepts that are basic to music.[13]

▸ **Patterns.** Music is full of patterns of chords, notes, and key changes. Musicians learn to recognize these patterns and use them to vary melodies. Inverting patterns, called counterpoint, helps form different kinds of harmonies.

▸ **Counting.** Counting is fundamental to music because one must count beats, count rests, and count how long to hold notes.

▸ **Geometry.** Music students use geometry to remember the correct finger positions for notes or chords. Guitar players' fingers, for example, form triangular shapes on the neck of the guitar.

▸ **Ratios and Proportions, and Equivalent Fractions.** Reading music requires an understanding of ratios and proportions, that is, a whole note needs to be played twice as long as a half note, and four times as long as a quarter note. Because the amount of time allotted to one beat is a mathematical constant, the duration of all the notes in a musical piece are relative to one another on the basis of that constant. It is also important to understand the rhythmic difference between 3/4 and 4/4 time signatures.

▸ **Sequences.** Music and mathematics are related through sequences called intervals. A mathematical interval is the difference between two numbers; a musical interval is the ratio of their frequencies. Here's another sequence: Arithmetic progressions in music correspond to geometric progressions in mathematics.

Motivated by the studies showing that music improved spatial-temporal reasoning, Gordon Shaw set out to determine whether this enhancement would help young students learn specific mathematics skills. He focused on proportional mathematics, which is particularly difficult for many elementary students, and which is usually taught with ratios, fractions, and comparative ratios. Shaw and his colleagues worked with 136 second-grade students from a low socioeconomic neighborhood in Los Angeles. One group (Piano-ST) was given four months of piano keyboard training, as well as computer training and time to play with a newly designed computer software to teach

> *The making of music seems to provide the greatest cerebral advantages.*

proportional mathematics. The second group (English-ST) was given computer training in English and time to play with the software; the third group (No Lessons) had neither music nor specific computer lessons, but did play with the computer software.

The Piano-ST group scored 27 percent higher on proportional math and fractions subtests than the English-ST students, and 166 percent higher than the No Lessons group (Figure 6.3). These findings are significant because proportional mathematics is not usually introduced until fifth or sixth grade, and because a grasp of proportional mathematics is essential to understanding science and mathematics at higher levels.[14]

A 1998 study showed how making music can make a difference for students from low socioeconomic status. The low socioeconomic students who took music lessons from eighth through twelfth grade increased their test scores in mathematics and scored significantly higher than those low socioeconomic students who were not involved in music. Mathematics scores more than doubled, and history and geography scores increased by 40 percent.[15]

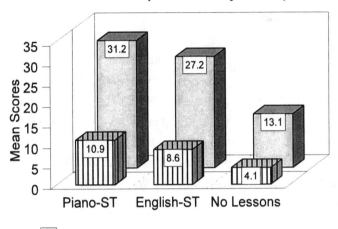

Piano and Computer Study Groups

Overall Score

||| Fractions and Proportions Sub-test

Figure 6.3 *The mean overall, and fraction and proportions sub-test scores of the group that had piano and computer training with special software (Piano-ST), the group with computer and software (English-ST), and the group with no lessons.*

School Districts Take Steps to Change Practice. The results of these studies are sufficiently convincing that some public school districts are now taking steps to require music training of all primary grade students. Here are just a few that have started this innovation:

▶ The Kettle Moraine district in Wales, Wisconsin, is now requiring piano lessons for all K–5 students after a pilot study showed that kindergartners who had piano lessons scored a remarkable 43 to 53 percent higher on tests of problem-solving abilities.

▶ The Daviess County school district in Owensboro, Kentucky, also has adopted a long-range program, dubbed "Graduation 2010," that eventually will require all students to learn the piano (or another musical instrument), chess, and a second language.

▸ The Lancaster County, South Carolina, public schools now require piano keyboarding in all elementary schools.

The Visual Arts

The human brain has the incredible ability to form images and representations of the real world or sheer fantasy within its mind's eye. Solving the mystery of DNA's structure, for example, required Watson and Crick in the early 1950s to imagine numerous three-dimensional models until they hit on the only image that explained the molecule's peculiar behavior—the spiral helix. This was an incredible marriage of visual art and biology that changed the scientific world forever. Exactly how the brain performs the functions of imagination and meditation may be uncertain, but no one doubts the importance of these valuable talents, which have allowed human beings to develop advanced and sophisticated cultures.

Imagery

For most people, the left hemisphere specializes in coding information verbally whereas the right hemisphere codes information visually. Although teachers spend much time talking (and sometimes have their students talk) about the learning objective, little time is given to developing visual cues. This process, called *imagery*, is the mental visualization of objects, events, and arrays related to the new learning and represents a major way of storing information in the brain. Imagery can take place in two ways: *imaging* is the visualization in the mind's eye of something that the person has actually experienced; *imagining* depicts something the person has not yet experienced and, therefore, has no limits.

A mental image is a pictorial representation of something physical or of an experience. The more information an image contains, the richer it is. Some people are more capable of forming rich images than others, but the research evidence is clear: Individuals can be taught to search their minds for images and be guided through the process to select appropriate images that, through hemispheric integration, enhance learning and increase retention. When the brain creates images, the same parts of the visual cortex are activated as when the eyes process real world input.[16] Thus, the powerful visual processing system is available even when the brain is creating internal pictures in the mind's eye.

The human brain's ability to do imagery with such efficiency is likely due to the importance of imagery in survival. When confronted with a potentially life-threatening event—say, a car speeding toward you in the wrong traffic lane—the brain's visual processing system and the frontal lobes process several potential scenarios in a fraction of a second and initiate a reflex reaction that is most likely to keep you alive. I am concerned that as students engage more passively with today's electronic media, they are not giving adequate practice in imaging and imagining, a skill that not only affects survival but also increases retention and, through creativity, improves the quality of life.

> *Imagery not only affects survival, but increases retention and improves the quality of life.*

Training students in imagery encourages them to search long-term storage for appropriate images and to use them more like a movie than a photograph. For example, one recalls the house one lived in for many years. From the center hall with its gleaming chandelier, one mentally turns left and "walks" through the living room to the sun room beyond. To the right of the hall is the paneled dining room and then the kitchen with the avocado green appliances and oak cabinets. In the back, one sees the flagstone patio, the manicured lawn, and the garden with its variety of flowers. The richness of the image allows one to focus on just a portion of it and generate additional amounts of detail. In this image, one could mentally stop in any room and visualize the furniture and other decor. Imagery should become a regular part of classroom strategies as early as kindergarten. In the primary grades, the teacher should supply the images to ensure accuracy.

Imagery can be used in many classroom activities, including notetaking, cooperative learning groups, and alternative assessment options. Mindmapping is a specialized form of imagery that originated when the left-brain/right-brain research emerged in the 1970s. The process combines language with images to help show relationships between and among concepts, and how they connect to a key idea. Buzan (1989) and Hyerle (1996) illustrate different ways in which mind maps can be drawn.

Movement

The mainstream educational community has often regarded thinking and movement as separate functions, assigning them different priorities. Activities involving movement, such as dance, theater, and occasionally sports, are often reduced or eliminated when school budgets get tight. But as brain studies probe deeper into the relationship between body and mind, the importance of movement to cognitive learning becomes very apparent.

Movement and the Brain

Discovering a New Role for the Cerebellum? In earlier chapters, we discussed the long-known role of the cerebellum in coordinating motor functions. For several decades, neuroscientists assumed that the cerebellum carried out its coordinating role by communicating exclusively with the cerebrum's motor cortex. But this view didn't explain why some patients with damage to the cerebellum also showed impaired cognitive function. Recent research centered on the cerebellum shows that its nerve fibers communicate with other areas of the cerebrum as well.

> *The more we study the role of the cerebellum, the more we realize that movement and learning are inescapably linked.*

The body's movement is first detected by the sensory systems in the inner ear (see Figure 6.1). Impulses in the inner ear travel to the cerebellum, and from there to the rest of the brain, including the sensory areas and the visual cortex. The inner ear also stimulates the reticular activating system (see Chapter 2), which you may recall regulates incoming data and, thus, is critical for getting our attention.[17] This interaction among these various brain areas helps us keep our balance and convert thought into action.

Studies have found that signals from the cerebellum go to multiple areas in the cerebrum, arousing attention, memory, spatial perception, and the frontal lobe's cognitive functions—the same areas that are stimulated during learning.[18] It seems that the more we study the cerebellum, the more we realize that movement is inescapably linked to learning (Figure 6.4)!

Autism. Further evidence of the link between the cerebellum and cognitive function has come from some studies of autism. Brain images show that many autistic children have smaller cerebellums and fewer cerebellar neurons. This cerebellar deficit may explain the impaired cognitive and motor functions seen in autism.[19, 20]

Using movement and other intense sensory experiences, therapy centers working with autistic and ADHD children are reporting remarkable improvement in their ability to focus their attention to complete a task, as well as an increased ability to listen quietly when others share ideas.

Physical Exercise Increases Oxygen in the Brain. Even short, moderate physical exercise can increase the amount of oxygen in the blood, which the brain needs for fuel. The concentration of oxygen affects the brain's ability to carry out its tasks. A recent study confirmed that higher concentrations of oxygen in the blood significantly enhanced cognitive performance in healthy young adults. They were able to recall more words from a list and had faster reaction times. Moreover, their cognitive abilities varied directly with the amount of oxygen in the brain.[21]

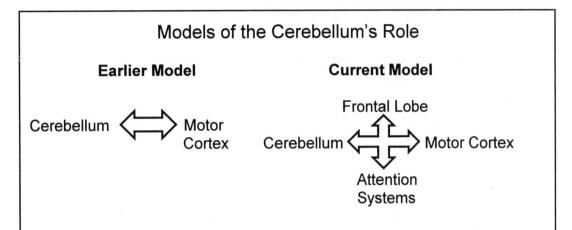

Figure 6.4 *There now is evidence that the cerebellum stimulates many more areas of the brain than previously thought, including those associated with cognitive function. Movement and learning have constant interplay.*

Despite the realization that physical activity enhances brain function and learning, secondary students spend most of their classroom time sitting. Furthermore, enrollment in high school daily physical education classes dropped from 42 percent in 1991 to near 20 percent in 1998, and female adolescents are much less physically active than male adolescents.

Implications for Schools

Armed with the new knowledge that movement is connected to cognitive learning, teachers and administrators need to encourage more movement in all classrooms at all grade levels. At some point in every lesson, students should be up and moving about, preferably talking about their new learning. Not only does the movement increase cognitive function, but it also helps students get rid of kinesthetic energy—the "wiggles," if you will—so they can settle down and concentrate better later. Mild exercise before a test also makes sense. So does teaching dance to all students in K–8 classrooms. Dance techniques help students become more aware of their physical presence, spatial relationships, breathing, and of timing and rhythm in movement.

> *At some point in most lessons, students should be up and moving around, talking about the new learning.*

231

Summarizing the research on the interplay of motion and the cognitive functions of the brain, we should consider using movement activities because they[22]

- ► Involve more sensory input, which is likely to hold the students' attention for a longer period of time.

- ► More closely resemble what students would be doing outside of school. Many students are involved with interesting kinesthetic activities after school. Doing these types of activities in school awakens and maintains that interest.

- ► Engage other cerebral aptitudes, such as music or visual-spatial skills, thus enhancing integration of sensory perception. This process will help students make connections between new and past learnings.

- ► Are more likely to lead to long-term recall. You can easily recall that time you participated in the school play or other public performance. Your memory is clear because this experience activated your kinesthetic sensory system.

- ► Stimulate the right hemisphere and help the student perceive concepts in their totality, rather than in the traditional language patterns (left hemisphere) that are so common.

Teachers can find many ways to weave movement into all lessons: act out a social studies lesson; walk through a map of the world or plot out a geometric formula on the gymnasium floor; use a dance to show the motion of molecules in the different states of matter or the planets in the solar system (See **Practitioner's Corner** on p. 240 for some additional suggestions).

PRACTITIONER'S CORNER

Including the Arts in All Lessons

Including arts activities in any subject and at any grade level can be simple and fun. It doesn't need to be additional work and may substitute for some other activity you usually do.

❏ **Visual Arts.** Are there components of the lesson that students can draw, sketch, color, or paint? Would a visual arts project be acceptable as an alternative assessment to measure student understanding?

> *Example:* A science teacher has a student draw a chart to illustrate the important steps in an experiment.

❏ **Music.** Is there an appropriate song or other musical composition that could be incorporated into the lesson or unit? Remember that music is a very effective memory device. Is there a familiar tune that would help students remember important facts about the unit?

> *Example:* A social studies teacher has students put important facts about the Revolutionary War to a familiar melody.

❏ **Literary Device.** Could students write a poem, limerick, or play to illustrate major points in the unit? Rhyming is also an excellent memory tool: "In fourteen hundred ninety-two, Columbus sailed the ocean blue ..."

> *Example:* A mathematics teachers has students devise limericks to help them remember the mathematical order of operations.

❏ **Dance and Theater.** Is there a dance that could help students remember some critical events or information? Can students act out a play that other students wrote?

> *Example:* An English teacher has students write and act out a different but plausible ending to Shakespeare's *Romeo and Juliet*.

❏ **Community Artists.** Are there community artists who can demonstrate their skills in the classroom? Teachers working with artists receive on-the-job training, and learn techniques that they can use later on their own.

PRACTITIONER'S CORNER

Using Music in the Classroom

Listening to music in the classroom can promote student focus and productivity at all grade levels. Remember that no one musical selection, nor the volume at which it is played, will please *everyone*. Just ensure that the music played enhances rather than interferes with the situation or task. Here are a few guidelines to consider when planning to use music:

- **When to Play the Music.** Music can be played at different times during the learning episode. Be sure to choose the appropriate music for the particular activity. Music can be played

     – before class begins (choose music that sets the emotional mood)
     – when students are up and moving about (choose an upbeat tune)
     – when the students are busy doing seat work, either alone or in groups (choose music that facilitates the learning task)
     – at the end of the class (students leave on a positive note, looking forward to returning)

  It is not advisable to play music when you are doing direct instruction (unless the music is part of the lesson) because it can be a distraction.

- **Be Aware of Beats Per Minute.** Because music can affect a person's heart rate, blood pressure, and emotional mood, the number of beats per minute in the music is very important. If you are using the music as background to facilitate student work, choose music that plays at about 60 beats per minute (the average heartbeat rate). If the music is accompanying a fast-paced activity, then choose 80 to 90 beats per minute. To calm down a noisy group as, say, in the school cafeteria or commons area, choose music at 40 to 50 beats per minute.

- **With or Without Lyrics?** Using music with or without lyrics depends on the purpose of playing the music. Music played at the beginning or end of

– Continued –

Using Music in the Classroom—Continued

class can contain lyrics because the main purpose is to set a mood, not get focus. But if students are working on a learning task, lyrics become a distraction. Some students will try to listen to the lyrics, and others may discuss them—in both instances, they are off the task.

- **Select Familiar or Unfamiliar Music?** Once again, this depends on the music's purpose. Familiar music is fine when setting a mood. However, when working on a specific assignment, you may wish to use music that is unfamiliar. If the students know the background music, some will sing or hum along, causing a distraction. Choose unfamiliar music, such as classical or new age music, and have enough different selections so that they are each played infrequently. Avoid the nature sounds selections as background music because they can be the source of much discussion and controversy. Of course, nature sounds could be used to stimulate discussion in appropriate lesson contexts.

- **Student Input.** Students may ask to bring in their own selections. To maintain a positive classroom climate, tell them that they *can* bring in their music, *provided the selections meet the above criteria!* Explain to them why this is necessary. Some kinds of student music would be appropriate in certain contexts as, for example, to facilitate a student discussion on interpreting music or another art form. In some cases, music may provide just the amount of meaning needed to enhance learning and retention.

- **Suggestions** (from teachers who have tried these, and reported success):

    - Beginning and end of class:
        Vivaldi – *The Four Seasons*
        Kenny G – Any selection
        Bach – *Brandenburg Concertos*
        Yanni – Most selections
        The Beach Boys
        Chopin – Most selections

        – Continued –

Using Music in the Classroom—Continued

– Fast-paced activity:
Rock
Disco
Reggae
Hits from the '50s and '60s
Marches

– Reflection or processing activity:
Beethoven – *Moonlight Sonata*
Pachebel – *Canon in D major*
Mozart – Piano concertos
Enya (New Age) – Most selections
Ray Lynch (New Age) – Any selection
George Winston – *Seasons*
Gary Lamb (Original) – Any selection

Happy listening!

PRACTITIONER'S CORNER

Using Imagery

Imagery runs the gamut from simple concrete pictures to complex motor learning and multistep procedures. Because imagery is still not a common instructional strategy, it should be implemented early and gradually. These guidelines are adapted from Parrott (1986) and West, Farmer, and Wolff (1991) for using imagery as a powerful aid to understanding and retention.

◆ **Prompting.** Use prompts for telling students to form mental images of the content being learned. They can be as simple as "form a picture in your mind of ..." to more complex directions. Prompts should be specific to the content or task and should be accompanied by relevant photographs, charts, or arrays, especially for younger children.

◆ **Modeling.** Model imagery by describing your own image to the class and explaining how that image helps your recall and use of the current learning. Also, model a procedure and have the students mentally practice the steps.

◆ **Interaction.** Strive for rich, vivid images where items interact. The richer the image, the more information it can include. If there are two or more items in the images, they should be visualized as acting on each other. If the recall is a ball and a bat, for example, imagine the bat hitting the ball.

◆ **Reinforcement.** Have students talk about the images they formed and get feedback from others on their accuracy, vividness, and interaction.

◆ **Add Context.** Whenever possible, add context to the interaction to increase retention and recall. For example, if the task is to recall prefixes and suffixes, the context could be a parade with the prefixes in front urging the suffixes in the rear to catch up.

◆ **Avoid Overloading the Image.** Although good images are complete representations of what is to be remembered, they should not overload the working memory's capacity in older students of about seven items.

237

PRACTITIONER'S CORNER

Visualized Notetaking

Visualized notetaking is a strategy that encourages students to associate language with visual imagery. It combines on paper sequential verbal information with symbols and holistic visual patterns. Teachers should encourage students to link verbal notes with images and symbols that show sequence, patterns, or relationships. Here are a few examples:

✓ **Stickperson.** Use the stickperson symbol to remember information about a person or group of people. The student attaches notes about a person in eight areas to the appropriate spot on the stick figure: ideas to the brain; hopes/vision to the eyes; words to the mouth; actions to the hands; feelings to the heart; movement to the feet; weaknesses to the Achilles tendon; and strengths to the arm muscle.

✓ **Expository Visuals.** These take many forms. Use a set of flow boxes to help students collect and visualize the cause-effect interrelationships for an event. Causes are written in the boxes on the left, the event in the center box, and effects in the boxes on the right. Creating different designs to visualize other topics is a valuable imaging activity.

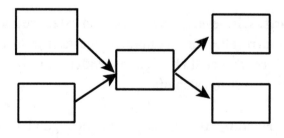

– Continued –

Visualized Notetaking—Continued

✓ **Notebook Design.** Even the design of the notebook page can call imagery into play to enhance learning and retention. One variation involves dividing the notebook page into sections for topics, vocabulary, important questions, things to remember, next homework assignment, and next test (see example below). Positioning each area on the page acts as a visual organizer that promotes the use of appropriate symbols.

Topics:	Things to Remember:
Vocabulary:	Next Homework Assignment:
Important Questions:	Next Test:

Notebook Pages

✓ **Mindmapping.** Mind maps are powerful visual tools for remembering relationships between and among parts of a key idea. Using a mind map for notes helps the student see relationships unfolding during the notetaking process. The maps also allow students to look beyond the obvious, make inferences, and discover new knowledge not otherwise possible in the traditional lecture notetaking format. See Buzan (1989) and Hyerle (1996) for lots of ideas on different ways to draw and use mind maps.

PRACTITIONER'S CORNER

Strategies for Using Movement

Incorporating movement activities into lessons is interesting and fun for the teacher and the students. Although moving around in class is common in the primary grades, it drops dramatically at the secondary level. Middle and high school teachers are understandably concerned about having adequate time to cover the enormous amount of material in the curriculum. But because trading a few minutes of teacher talk for a movement activity can actually increase the amount of learning retained, it could be a very worthwhile investment of time.

Remember that students are participating less in the physical education program. Yet physical activity is essential to promoting the normal growth of mental function, to generating positive emotions, and in learning and remembering cognitive material. Some suggestions are as follows:

- **Energizers.** Use movement activities to energize students who are at low points in their energy levels (e.g., during early morning periods for high school students or during that downtime just past the middle of the day). For example,

    "Measure the room's length in hand spans."
    "Touch seven objects in the room that are the same color."
    "Go to four different sources of information in this room."
    "In your group, make a poster-sized mind map of this unit."

    Use ball toss games for review, storytelling, and vocabulary building.

- **Acting Out Key Concepts.**[23] This strategy uses the body in a physical way to learn and remember a difficult concept. If the lesson objective is to learn the continents, try this: Stand in front of a world map. Say the continent and point to the assigned body part.

North America = left hand	Europe = forehead
Asia = right hand	Africa = waist
South America = left knee	Australia = right knee
Antarctica = a point on the floor between the feet	

– Continued –

Strategies for Using Movement—Continued

Allow time for practice, then remove the map and repeat the activity.
Is there a difficult concept that you teach that could be acted out?

■ **Role-Playing.** Do role-plays on a regular basis. For example, students can organize extemporaneous pantomime or play charades to dramatize major points in a unit. Have them develop and act out short commercials advertizing upcoming units or to review previously learned material.

■ **Vocabulary Building: Act Out the Word.**[24] Look for vocabulary words that lend themselves to a physical movement. Then,
   a. Say the word
   b. Read the meaning
   c. Do the movement (the movement acts out the meaning of the word).

For example,
   a. *oppugn*
   b. "to oppose or attack"
   c. make body gestures that indicate "opposing" or "attacking."

Do the three parts (a, b, and c) three times. This places the information in working memory. Now continue rehearsing the word, and use it in context so that it transfers to long-term memory.

■ **Verbal to Physical Tug-of-War.** In this activity, students choose a partner and a topic from the unit they have been learning. Each student forms an opinion about the topic and has 30 seconds to convince a partner why his or her own topic is more important (the verbal tug-of-war). After this debate, the partners separate to opposite sides for a physical tug-of-war with a rope.

Chapter 6—The Brain and the Arts

Key Points to Ponder

Jot down on this page key points, ideas, strategies, and resources you want to consider later. This sheet is your personal journal summary and will help to jog your memory.

CHAPTER 6 – NOTES

1. Diamond, J. (1992).

2. Several private school initiatives have been the exception, most notably the Montessori schools and the Waldorf schools.

3. Many of the science examples in this section are taken from Root-Bernstein (1997).

4. Fiske (1999).

5. Fiske (1999), p. 30.

6. The discovery that the auditory cortex (located in the temporal lobes) in the right hemisphere has regions that respond only to music came from studies comparing patients who have damage to their left or right temporal lobes. Patients with right temporal lobe damage have lost the ability to recognize familiar songs, a condition known as *amusia*. However, only the response to music is affected. The patients can still recognize human voices, traffic sounds, and other auditory information.

7. Fagan et al. (1997).

8. Blood, Zatorre, Bermudez, and Evans (1999).

9. Rauscher, Shaw, and Ky (1993).

10. Muftuler, Bodner, Shaw, and Nalcioglu (1999).

11. Nakamura et al. (1999).

12. Rauscher et al. (1997).

13. Some of this information comes from an Internet source that deals with issues involving music education. See www.WhyMusicEd@aol.com.

14. Graziano, Peterson, and Shaw (1999).

15. Catterall, Chapleau, and Iwanga (1999).

16. Kosslyn et al. (1999).

17. Hannaford (1995).

18. Middleton and Strick (1998).

19. Courchesne (1999).

20. The brainstem in many autistic children also is smaller, apparently due to a genetic defect in the early stages of gestation. For more information on this aspect of autism, see Rodier (2000).

21. Scholey et al. (1999).

22. Patterson (1997).

23. Chapman and King (2000).

24. Chapman (1995).

CHAPTER 7

THINKING SKILLS AND LEARNING

In general, however, teaching devoted to memorization does not facilitate the transfer of learning and probably interferes with the subsequent development of understanding. By ignoring the personal world of the learner, educators actually inhibit the effective functioning of the brain.

– Renate Caine and Geoffrey Caine,
Making Connections:
Teaching and the Human Brain

Chapter Highlights. This chapter discusses some of the characteristics and dimensions of human thinking. It reviews Bloom's Taxonomy, notes its continuing compatibility with current research on higher-order thinking, and explains its relationship to difficulty, complexity, and intelligence.

How can something as tangible as the human brain create such phantom things as ideas? How does it create Beethoven's symphonies, Michelangelo's sculptures, and Einstein's universe? What processes translate the countless neuron firings into thoughts and then into products of magnificent beauty or weapons of destruction? The human brain collects information about the world and organizes it to form a representation of that world. This representation, or mental model, describes *thinking,* a process that an individual human uses to function in that world.

The Thinking Brain

Characteristics of Human Thinking

Thinking is easier to describe than to define. Its characteristics include the daily routine of reasoning where one is at the moment, where one's destination is, and how to get there. It includes developing concepts, using words, solving problems, abstracting, intuiting, and anticipating the future. Other aspects of thinking include learning, memory, creativity, communication, logic, and generalization. How and when we use these aspects often determine the success or failure of our many interactions with our environment. This chapter discusses thinking, explores strategies that attempt to describe the characteristics of various types of thinking, and suggests how they can be used in the classroom to promote higher-order thinking and learning.

Types of Thinking

Can you answer these questions?

Who was the second president of the United States?

What are the similarities and differences between the post-Civil War and post-Vietnam War periods?

Defend why we should or should not have capital punishment.

Each of these questions requires you to think, but the type of thinking involved is not the same. The first question requires you to simply refer to a listing you have in long-term storage that recalls the sequence of presidents. Dealing with the second question is quite different. You must first recall what you have stored about both wars, separate these items into lists, then analyze them to determine which events were similar and which were different. The third question requires the retrieval and

> **Brain scans show that different parts of the brain are involved as the problem-solving task becomes more complicated.**

processing of large amounts of information about capital punishment, its impact on society, and its effectiveness as a deterrent to crime. Then you need to form a judgment about whether you believe criminals will be influenced by a capital punishment penalty. These three questions require different and increasingly complex thought processes to arrive at acceptable answers. Thus, some thinking is more complex than other thinking. Brain scans indicate that different parts of the brain, particularly in the frontal cortex, are involved as the problem-solving task becomes more complicated.[1]

The brain has evolved different mechanisms for dealing with various situations. Logic is one of those. It recognizes, for example, that if A is equal to B, and B is equal to C, then A must be equal to C. There are other mechanisms, too. Rationality, pattern identification, image making, and approximation are all forms of thinking that serve to help the individual deal with a concept, a problem, or a decision.

Thinking as a Representational System

Although the file cabinets and their ordered system are useful metaphors for explaining the operation of long-term storage in the information processing model (Chapter 2), they do not explain all the situations one encounters when the brain behaves as a representational system. Sometimes we cannot recognize a person's face, but we remember the name and the events that surrounded our first meeting with this person. And just thinking of the word *beach* evokes a complex series of mental events that corresponds to the internal representation we have of all the beaches we have ever encountered. Beaches gleam in the sun, are often hot, create a shoreline, merge with water, are dotted with umbrellas, and recall memories of holiday fun. The word itself is not actually a beach, but it brings forth many associations having to do with beaches. This is an example of a representational system, and it illustrates the diversity of patterns in human thinking.[2] It is this recognition of diversity that has led to the notion of multiple intelligences. That is, an individual's thinking patterns vary when encountering different challenges, and these semiautonomous variations in thinking result in different degrees of success in learning.

Thinking and Emotion

Emotions play an important role in the thinking process. In Chapter 2, we discussed the amygdala that encodes emotional messages to long-term storage. We also noted that emotions often take precedence during cerebral processing and can impede or assist cognitive learning. If we like what we are learning, we are more likely to maintain interest and move to higher-level thinking. We tend to probe and ask those "what if?" kinds of questions. When we dislike the learning, we usually spend the least amount of time with it and stay at minimal levels of processing.

Can Thinking Be Taught?

The ordinary experience of thinking about a beach raises intriguing questions about how the brain is organized to think with increasing complexity. What skills does the human brain need to maneuver through simple and complex thoughts? Can these skills be learned and, if so, how and when should they be taught?

Perhaps a more basic question is: Can we teach people to think? Some educators believe the answer to this question is a resounding *yes*, and they have published programs to teach thinking. These programs grew out of the realization during the past decade that students still do not think as critically as they should to be successful in a world that is constantly changing and increasingly complex. Even though I agree with this premise and admire the initiative, I believe the approach is somewhat misleading in light of what we know about the development and operations of the human brain. Educators' efforts to "teach thinking" promote the notion that young human beings do not think and thus must be taught. On the contrary, there is growing evidence that humans are born with a brain that has all the sensory components and neural organization necessary to survive successfully in its environment. The neural organization changes dramatically, of course, as the child grows and learns, resulting in the expansion of some networks and the elimination of others.

Even the most superficial look at human information processing reveals a vast system of magnificent neural networks that can learn language, recognize one face among thousands, and infer an outcome by rapidly analyzing data. Every bit of evidence available suggests that the human brain is *designed* for thinking. To imply that we must teach it to think demeans its structure and functions, ignores the current research, insults the natural curiosity of our students, and arrogantly suggests that if we did not do so, the individual would flounder in a "thoughtless" environment where survival would be the primary worry. So if the brain is capable of higher-order thinking, why do we see so little of it in the normal course of student discussion and performance?

Test Question No. 10: People must be taught to do higher-order thinking.

Answer: False. We begin thinking from birth (if not before). We can teach learners how to organize content (such as using critical attributes, and mnemonics) and apply skills to promote more efficient thinking.

Schools Demand Little Complex Thinking

I suggest that the reason our students are not thinking critically is that we have not exposed them consistently to models or situations in school that require them to do so. Schooling, for the most part, demands little more than convergent thinking. Its practices and testing focus on content acquisition through rote rehearsal, rather than the processes of thinking for analysis and synthesis. Too often, merely repeating the answer is considered more important than the process used to get the answer. Consequently, students and teachers have become accustomed to dealing with learning at the lowest levels of complexity. What

> **We do not teach the brain to think. We can, however, help learners to organize content to facilitate more complex processing.**

we are trying to do now is recognize these limitations, rewrite curriculum, retrain teachers, and encourage students to use their innate thinking abilities to process learning at higher levels of complexity. In other words, we are teaching them *how to organize content in such a way that it facilitates and promotes higher-order thinking*. We are *not* teaching them to *how to think*.

This distinction does not "split hairs" or "play with words." On the contrary, it is a very important distinction that determines the perspective we have when dealing with learners. Teachers who believe they are teaching students *how to think* perpetuate the teaching-learning scheme that treats students as "vessels to be filled." However, accepting that we are *sharpening skills to facilitate thinking* places the teacher in the proper position of guiding students through the more effective use of their innate processes and abilities. The teacher's role shifts, as a current saying goes, from being the "sage on stage" to the "guide on the side."

The Dimensions of Human Thinking

Designing Models

Cognitive psychologists have been designing models for decades in an effort to describe the dimensions of thinking and the levels of complexity of human thought. The models have generally divided thought into two categories, *convergent* or lower-order thinking and *divergent* or higher-order thinking. Other multidimensional frameworks have appeared that attempt to describe all aspects of thinking in detail. Of course, a model is only as good as its potential for achieving a desired goal (in this case, encouraging higher-order thinking) and the likelihood that teachers feel sufficiently comfortable with the model to make it a regular part of their classroom practice. In examining the models that describe the dimensions of thinking, most include the following four major areas:

1. Basic Processes. The tools we use to transform and evaluate information are:

Observing – includes recognizing and recalling.

Finding Patterns and Generalizing – includes classifying, comparing and contrasting, and identifying relevant and irrelevant information.

Forming Conclusions Based on Patterns – includes hypothesizing, predicting, inferring, and applying.

Assessing Conclusions Based on Observations – includes checking consistency, identifying biases and stereotypes, identifying unstated assumptions, recognizing over- and undergeneralizations, and confirming conclusions with facts.

The consistency with which these basic processes appear in most models results from the recognition that they allow us to make sense of our world by pulling together bits of information into understandable and coherent patterns. Further, these processes support the notion that conclusions should be based on evidence. From these conclusions, we form patterns that help us to hypothesize, infer, and predict.

2. Domain-Specific Knowledge. This refers to the knowledge in a particular content area that one must possess in order to carry out the basic processes described above.

3. Metacognition. This is the awareness one has of one's own thinking processes. It means that students should know when and why they are using the basic processes, and how these functions relate to the content they are learning.

4. Affective Domain. As mentioned earlier, researchers are more aware than ever of the role the affective domain (emotions and feelings) plays in learning—in this case, in the development and use of thinking skills. When students recognize the power of their own thinking, they use their skills more and solve problems for themselves rather than just waiting to be told the answers.

What model can teachers use that, when properly implemented, promotes thinking, has been successful in the past, and holds the promise of success for the future? My response is to revisit the taxonomy of the cognitive domain developed over 40 years ago by Benjamin Bloom.

Revisiting Bloom's Taxonomy of the Cognitive Domain

Why This Model?

"What's old is new again" goes the old saying. In education, it seems often we are looking for the quick fix to solve problems. I propose that a thinking skills model that has been around for decades may be, like that old saying, our answer to raising student thinking to higher levels.

One of the more enduring and useful models for enhancing thinking was developed by Benjamin Bloom in the 1950s. Bloom's system of classification, or taxonomy, identifies six levels of complexity of human thought (Bloom 1956). I believe that reintroducing this in classes can upgrade the quality of teacher instruction and student learning for the following reasons:

- It is familiar to many prospective and practicing teachers.

- It is user-friendly and simple when compared to other models.

- It requires only modest retraining for teachers to understand the relationship between the difficulty and complexity components.

- It helps teachers recognize the difference between difficulty and complexity, so they can help slower learners improve their thinking and achievement significantly.

- It can be implemented in every classroom immediately without waiting for major reform or restructuring.

- It is inexpensive in that teachers need only a few supplementary materials to use with the current curriculum.

- It motivates teachers because they see their students learning better, thinking more profoundly, and showing more interest.

- It is consistent with the latest research on brain functions.

I am very much aware that Bloom's Taxonomy has been standard fare in preservice and inservice teacher training for many years.[3] Yet I suspect, as Bloom himself had conjectured, that the taxonomy's value as a model for moving all students to higher levels of thinking has barely been explored. In fact, my experience has been that most teachers remember this model with little enthusiasm and with even less understanding of its use to promote thinking and learning. More important, as we will discuss later, its connection to student ability has been largely misunderstood and misapplied. This situation is regrettable because the model is easy to understand and, when used correctly, can accelerate learning and elevate student interest and achievement, especially for slower learners.

The Model's Structure

Let's look at the model to understand how it organizes complexity and to appreciate its value in aiding less able students to experience the excitement of higher-order thinking and the exhilaration of greater achievement.

> **Bloom's Taxonomy remains one of the most useful tools for moving students, especially slower learners, to higher levels of thinking.**

The six levels of Bloom's Taxonomy (see Table 7.1), from the least to the most complex, are as follows: knowledge, comprehension, application, analysis, synthesis, and evaluation. Although there are six separate levels, the hierarchy of complexity is not rigid, and the individual may move easily among the levels during extended processing.

Below is a review of each level using the story of *Goldilocks* and the bombing of Pearl Harbor as examples of how two differing concepts can be taken through the taxonomy.

Knowledge. Knowledge is defined as the mere rote recall of previously learned material, from specific facts to a definition or a complete theory. All that is required is bringing it forth in the form in which it was learned. This is recall of semantic memory. It represents the lowest level of learning in the cognitive domain because there is no presumption that the learner understands what is being recalled. Students in first grade recite the Pledge of Allegiance daily. Do they comprehend what they are saying? (If so, would one fine, patriotic boy have started his pledge with, *I led the pigeons to the flag of the United States of America ... ?*)

> *Examples*: What did Goldilocks do in the three bears' house?
> What was the date of the bombing of Pearl Harbor?

Comprehension. This level describes the ability to make sense of the material. This may occur by converting the material from one form to another (words to numbers), by interpreting the material (summarizing a story), or by estimating future trends (predicting the consequences or effects). This learning goes beyond mere rote recall and represents the lowest level of under-

Table 7.1 Bloom's Taxonomy of the Cognitive Domain[4]

Below are the levels in decreasing order of complexity with terms and sample activities that illustrate the thought processes at each level.

LEVEL	TERMS	SAMPLE ACTIVITIES
Evaluation	appraise assess judge	Which of the two main characters in the story would you rather have as a friend? Why? Is violence ever justified in correcting injustices? Why or why not? Which of the environments we've studied seems like the best place for you to live? Defend your answer.
Synthesis	imagine compose design infer	Pretend you were a participant in the Boston Tea Party and write a diary entry that tells what happened. Rewrite *Little Red Riding Hood* as a news story. Design a different way of solving this problem. Formulate a hypothesis that might explain the results of these three experiments.
Analysis	analyze contrast distinguish deduce	Which events in the story are fantasy and which really happened? Compare and contrast the post–Civil War period with the post–Vietnam War period. Sort this collection of rocks into three categories. Which of these words are Latin derivatives and which are Greek?
Application	practice calculate apply	Use each vocabulary word in a sentence. Calculate the area of your classroom. Think of three situations in which we would use this mathematics operation.
Comprehension	summarize discuss explain	Summarize the paragraph in your own words. Why are symbols used on maps? Write a paragraph explaining the duties of the mayor.
Knowledge	define label recall	What is the definition of a verb? Label the three symbols on this map. What are the three branches of government?

standing. When a student understands the material, rather than merely recalling it, the material becomes available for future use to solve problems and to make decisions. Comprehension questions attempt to determine if the students understand the information in a sensible way. When this happens, students may say, "Now I get it."

Examples: Why did Goldilocks like the baby bear's things best?
Why did the Japanese bomb Pearl Harbor?

Application. Application refers to the ability to use learned material in new situations with a minimum of direction. It includes the application of such things as rules, concepts, methods, and theories to solve problems. The learner activates procedural memory and uses convergent thinking to select, transfer, and apply data to complete a new task. Practice is essential at this level.

Examples: If Goldilocks came to your house today, what things might she do?
If you had been responsible for the defense of the Hawaiian Islands, what preparation would you have made against an attack?

Analysis. Analysis is the ability to break material into its component parts so that its structure may be understood. It includes identifying parts, examining the relationships of the parts to each other and to the whole, and recognizing the organizational principles involved. The learner must be able to organize and reorganize information into categories. The brain's frontal lobes are working hard at this level. This stage is more complex because the learner is aware of the thought process in use (metacognition) and understands both the content and structure of the material.

Examples: What things in the Goldilocks story could have really happened?
What lesson did our country learn from Pearl Harbor?

Synthesis. Synthesis refers to the ability to put parts together to form a plan that is new to the learner. It may involve the production of a unique communication (essay or speech), a plan of operations (research proposal), or a scheme for classifying information. This level stresses creativity, with major emphasis on forming *new* patterns or structures. This is the level where learners use divergent thinking to get an *Aha!* experience. It indicates that being creative requires a great deal of information, understanding, and application to produce a tangible product. Michelangelo could never have created the *David* or the *Pietà* without a thorough comprehension of human anatomy and types of marble, as well as the ability to use polishing compounds and tools with accuracy. His artistry comes from the mastery with which he used his knowledge and skill to carve magnificent pieces. Although most often associated with the arts, synthesis can occur in all areas of the curriculum (see Chapter 6).

Examples: Retell the story as *Goldilocks and the Three Fishes*.
Retell the story of Pearl Harbor assuming the U.S. armed forces had been ready for the attack.

Evaluation. Evaluation[5] is concerned with the ability to judge the value of material based on specific criteria. The learner may determine the criteria or be given them. The learner examines criteria from several categories and selects those that are the most relevant to the situation. Activities at this level almost always have multiple and equally acceptable solutions. This is the highest level of cognitive thought in this model because it contains elements of all the other levels, plus conscious judgments based on definite criteria. At this level, learners tend to consolidate their thinking and become more receptive to other points of view.

Examples: Do you think it was right for Goldilocks to go into the bears' house without having been invited? Why or why not?
Do you feel that the bombing of Pearl Harbor has any effect on Japanese-American relations today? Why or why not?

Important Characteristics of the Model

Two points need to be made here. First, these levels are cumulative, that is, each level above "knowledge" includes all those of lesser complexity. A learner cannot comprehend material without knowing it. Similarly, one cannot correctly apply a learning without comprehending it. Second, the lower three levels (knowledge, comprehension, and application) describe a *convergent* thinking process whereby the learner recalls and focuses what is known and comprehended to solve a problem through application. The upper three levels (analysis, synthesis, and evaluation) describe a *divergent* thinking process, because the learner's processing results in new insights and discoveries that were not part of the original information. When the learner is thinking at these upper levels, thought flows naturally from one to the other and the boundaries disappear.

Testing Your Comprehension of the Taxonomy

To determine if you comprehend the taxonomy's six different levels, complete the activity below. Then, look at the answers and explanation following the activity.

Directions. Identify the highest level (remember, the levels are cumulative) of the taxonomy indicated in these learning objectives.

1.   Given a ruler to measure the room, find how long the room is.

2.   What is the Sixth Amendment to the U.S. Constitution?

3.   Given copies of the Articles of Confederation and the Bill of Rights, the learner will write a comparison of the two documents and discuss similarities and differences.

4.   Identify and write a question for each level of the taxonomy.

5.   Use your own words to explain the moral at the end of the fable.

6.   Given two ways to solve the problem, the learner will make a choice of which to use and give reasons.

7.   Create your own fairy tale including all the characteristics of a fairy tale.

Answers:

1.   *Application.* The learner must know the measuring system, comprehend the meaning of length, and use the ruler correctly.

2.   *Knowledge.* The learner simply recalls that the Sixth Amendment deals with the rights of the accused.

3.   *Analysis.* The learner must separate both documents into their component parts and compare and contrast them for relationships that describe their similarities and differences.

4.   *Application.* The learner knows each level, comprehends its definition, then uses this information to write the question for each level.

5.   *Comprehension.* The learner shows comprehension by explaining the fable's moral.

6.   *Evaluation.* The learner chooses between two feasible options and explains the reasons for the choice.

7.   *Synthesis.* Using the general characteristics of fairy tales, the learner creates a new one.

The Taxonomy and the Dimensions of Thinking

To what extent does Bloom's Taxonomy meet the four areas mentioned earlier that are included within most of the newer models describing the dimensions of thinking?

Basic Processes. The six levels of the taxonomy cover all the skills included under these processes. *Observing* is contained in the levels of knowledge and comprehension. *Finding patterns* and *generalizing* are skills in the levels of knowledge, comprehension, and analysis. Forming conclusions based on patterns is in analysis and synthesis. Finally, *assessing conclusions* is a characteristic of the taxonomy's evaluation level.

Domain-Specific Knowledge. This is the equivalent of Bloom's knowledge level.

Metacognition. This is the one area that is not explicitly cited in any one of the six levels. Nonetheless, when analyzing or discussing the rationale for selecting from among equally viable choices at the evaluation level, the learner has to reflect on the processes used to arrive at the selection and gather data to defend the choice. This self-awareness of the thinking process used is the essence of metacognition. The other components, such as having a respect for self-monitoring as a valued skill, a positive and personal attitude toward learning, and an attention to learning through introspection and practice, are very likely to result from the accurate, frequent, and systematic use of the taxonomy's upper levels.

The Affective Domain. Because we are making comparisons to Bloom's Taxonomy of the Cognitive Domain, it is apparent that there is no reference to affective processes. Thus, we need to look at the Taxonomy of the Affective Domain, developed by Krathwohl, Bloom and Masia (1964) recognized the power of this domain of learning long before neuroscience revealed the importance of emotions in attention and learning. Not only do we want students to learn cognitive information and skills and how to apply them but we also want them to appreciate and value their use. Developing positive attitudes in students toward learning enhances interest, increases retention, and should be a major goal of every teacher.

As with the cognitive domain, each of the five levels of the affective domain taxonomy is a prerequisite to the successful performance of the next higher level. Within each level there is a range of attributes. The five levels are

Receipt. At this level, the range of receiving occurs when learners progress from merely being aware of cognitive information, to receiving it, then to directing their attention to it even when they could be distracted.

Response. This level deals with the degree of the learner's willingness to respond to the cognitive strategies, ranging from acquiescence, to cooperation, to enthusiasm for learning the skill.

Value. This level ranges from the learner's believing in the worth of the skill, to choosing the new skill over a previous skill, to developing a strong commitment to it.

Organization. This level ranges from learners identifying the characteristics of the cognitive skill to their bringing together elements, characteristics, and other attributes into a coherent whole.

Characterization. The learners' use of the strategies has become habitual and they have incorporated this systematically into their philosophies of learning.

Pairing cognitive and affective taxonomies provides a strong foundation to move students toward higher-level thinking as a regular part of learning practice.

The Critical Difference Between Complexity and Difficulty

Complexity and difficulty describe completely different mental operations, but are often used synonymously. This error, resulting in the two factors being treated as one, limits the use of the taxonomy to enhance the thinking of all students. By recognizing how these concepts are different, the teacher can gain valuable insight into

> *Regrettably, teachers are more likely to increase difficulty, rather than complexity, when attempting to raise student thinking.*

the connection between the taxonomy and student ability. *Complexity* describes the *thought process* that the brain uses to deal with information. In Bloom's Taxonomy (Table 7.1), it can be described by any of the six words representing the six levels. The question *What is the capital of Rhode Island?* is at the knowledge level, while the question *Tell me in your own words what is meant by a state capital* is at the comprehension level. The second question is more *complex* than the first because it is at a higher level in Bloom's Taxonomy.

Difficulty, on the other hand, refers to the *amount of effort* that the learner must expend *within* a level of complexity to accomplish a learning objective. It is possible for a learning activity to become increasingly difficult without becoming more complex. For example, the question *Name the states of the Union* is at the knowledge level of complexity because it involves simple recall (semantic memory) for most students. The question *Name the states of the Union and their capitals* is also at the knowledge level but is more difficult than the prior question because it involves more effort to recall more information. Similarly, the question *Name the states and their capitals in order of their admission to the Union* is still at the knowledge level, but it is considerably more difficult than the first two. It requires gathering more information and then sequencing it by chronological order.

Levels of Bloom's Taxonomy

Difficulty and Complexity

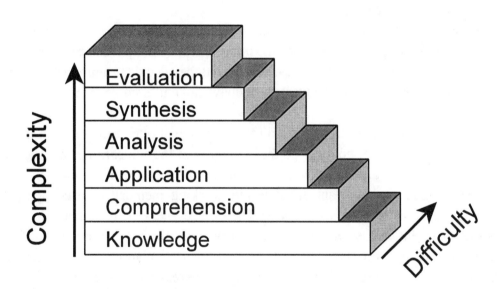

Figure 7.1 Complexity and difficulty are different. Complexity establishes the level of thought; difficulty determines the amount of effort within each level.

These are examples of how a student can exert great effort to achieve a learning task while processing at the lowest level of thinking. When seeking to challenge students, classroom teachers are more likely (perhaps unwittingly) to increase difficulty rather than complexity as the challenge mode. This may be because they do not recognize the difference between these concepts or that they believe that difficulty is the method for achieving higher-order thinking (Figure 7.1).

Connecting Complexity and Difficulty to Ability

When teachers are asked whether complexity or difficulty is more closely linked to student ability, they more often choose complexity. Some explain their belief that only students of higher ability can carry out the processes indicated in analysis, synthesis, and evaluation. Others say that whenever they have tried to bring slower students up the taxonomy, the lesson got bogged down. Yet I will argue, along with Bloom, that the real connection to ability is difficulty, not complexity.

The mistaken link between complexity and ability is the result of an unintended but very real self-fulfilling prophesy. Here's how it works. Teachers allot a certain amount of *time* for the class to learn a concept, usually based on how long they think it will take the *average* student to learn it (Figure 7.2). The

> **With guidance and practice, slower learners can regularly reach the higher levels of Bloom's Taxonomy.**

fast learners learn the concept in less than the allotted time. During the remaining time, their brains often sort the concept's sublearnings into important and unimportant categories, that is, they select the critical attributes for storage and discard what they decide is unimportant. This explains why fast learners are usually fast retrievers: They have not cluttered their memory networks with trivia.

Meanwhile, the slower learners need more than the allotted time to learn the concept. If that time is not given to them, not only do they lose part of the sublearnings but they also do not have time to do any sorting. If the teacher attempts to move up the taxonomy, the fast learners have the concept's more important attributes in working memory to use appropriately and successfully at the higher levels of complexity. The slow learners, on the other hand, have not had time to sort, have cluttered their working memory with all the sublearnings (important and unimportant), and do not recognize the parts needed for more complex processing. For them, it is like taking five big suitcases on an overnight trip, whereas the fast learners have taken just a small bag packed with the essentials. As a result, teachers become convinced that higher-order thinking is for the fast learners and that ability is linked to complexity.

Bloom reported on studies that included slower students for whom the unimportant material was not even taught.[6] The curriculum was sorted from the start, and the focus was on critical attributes and other vital information. When the teacher moved up the taxonomy, these students in some cases demonstrated better achievement than the control groups! When teachers differentiate between complexity and difficulty, a new view of Bloom's Taxonomy emerges, one which promises more success for more students.

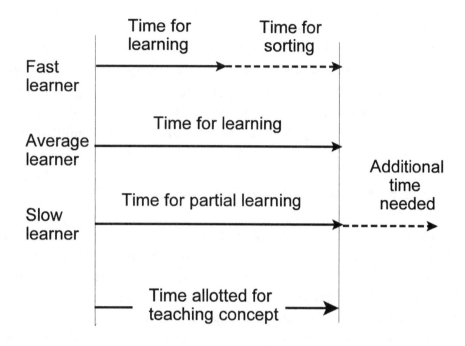

Figure 7.2 *The time allotted to learn a concept is usually fixed even though students learn at different rates.*

The Taxonomy and Constructivism

In their description of the characteristics of constructivist teachers, Brooks and Brooks (1993) noted that these teachers ask open-ended questions and continually encourage students to analyze, synthesize, and evaluate. From this description, it seems evident that teachers who constantly use the upper levels of Bloom's Taxonomy are demonstrating, among other things, constructivist behaviors.

Curriculum Changes to Accommodate the Taxonomy

The implications from these studies are very significant in that they tell us two important things about using the taxonomy.

- If teachers avoid the self-fulfilling prophecy snare, they can get slower learners to do higher-order thinking successfully and often.

- One way to accomplish this is to review the curriculum and remove the topics of least importance to gain the time needed for practice at the higher levels. An effective method for doing this is to set priorities among all the concepts in a curriculum, delete the least important bottom 20 to 25 percent, and use the time gained by this sorting and paring to move all students **up the taxonomy.** Finally, take advantage of the power of positive transfer by integrating these concepts with previously taught material and connecting them to appropriate concepts in other curriculum areas.

Higher-Order Thinking Increases Understanding and Retention

The number of neurons in our brains declines as we age, but our ability to learn, remember, and recall is dependent largely on the number of connections between neurons. The stability and permanency of these connections reflect the nature of the thinking process and the type and degree of rehearsal that occurred during the learning episode.

As mentioned earlier, PET scans show that elaborative rehearsal, involving higher-order thinking skills, engages the brain's frontal lobe. This engagement helps learners make connections between past and new learning, creates new pathways, strengthens existing pathways, and increases the likelihood that the new learning will be consolidated and stored for future retrieval.

Many teachers recognize the need to do more activities that require elaborate thinking rather than just rote rehearsal. They admit that when they move up through higher levels of Bloom's Taxonomy (or any other thinking skills framework) students demonstrate a much greater depth of understanding. However, they also admit that there are barriers to using this approach regularly because it takes more time. Examples of the barriers they cite are the pressures to cover an ever-expanding curriculum and the tyranny of quick-answer testing of all types. These obstacles will not be overcome easily, but teachers can work toward a compromise—finding ways to engage the novel brain with challenging activities and developing alternative assessment strategies.

> *Our students would make a quantum leap to higher-order thinking if every teacher in every classroom correctly and regularly used Bloom's Taxonomy.*

Other Thinking Skills Programs

There are other thinking skills programs and models available, and new ones are appearing regularly. My analysis of them is that they may be very useful after extensive teacher training, substantial curricular reform, and sizable investments for new materials. Until that happens, I urge that we implement the programs needed to train teachers now to use Bloom's Taxonomy correctly and successfully. I am convinced that if every teacher correctly implemented the taxonomy in every classroom and in every subject area, our students would make a quantum leap forward in their ability to do higher-order thinking. And they can do this now while waiting for more comprehensive reform efforts to become reality.

UP THE TAXONOMY!

PRACTITIONER'S CORNER

Understanding Bloom's Taxonomy

Directions: With a partner, explain verbally what the pictorial view below is all about. Then fill in the chart on the next page, using the explanation of the pictures to describe your thought processing at each level of the taxonomy.

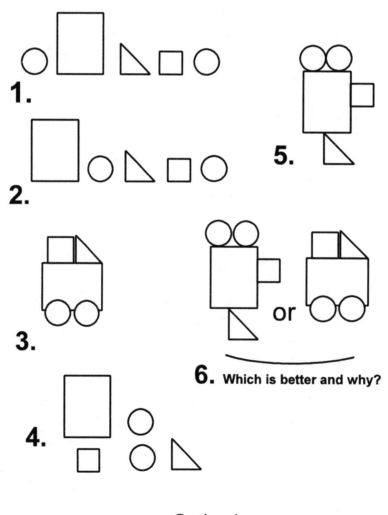

6. Which is better and why?

– Continued –

Understanding Bloom's Taxonomy—Continued

Directions: Write on the lines below the six levels of Bloom's Taxonomy, starting with the least complex at the bottom. Then write a few words next to each level that explain the type of processing that occurs when describing the various pictures on the previous page.

LEVEL	DESCRIPTION of PROCESSING
6.	
5.	
4.	
3.	
2.	
1.	

PRACTITIONER'S CORNER

Take a Concept/Situation Up the Taxonomy!

 **Directions:** Think of a task that you need to accomplish with your own child, parent, colleague, or spouse (e.g., how to use the washing machine with different types of clothes, planning a vacation) and describe questions or activities that move the task up Bloom's Taxonomy.

CONCEPT/SITUATION:_____

Evaluation (judging material using certain criteria):

Synthesis (putting ideas together to form a new whole):

Analysis (breaking down a concept and looking for relationships):

Application (using a concept or principle in a new situation):

Comprehension (translating the material to achieve understanding):

START HERE: Knowledge (rote remembering of information):

PRACTITIONER'S CORNER

Some Tips on Using Bloom's Taxonomy

- **Watch the Behavior of the Learner.** The learner's behavior reveals the level of complexity where processing is taking place. Whenever the brain has the option of solving a problem at two levels of complexity, it generally chooses the less complex level. Teachers can inadvertently design activities that they believe are at one level of complexity that students actually accomplish at a different (usually lower) level.

- **Remember That the Levels Are Cumulative.** Each level includes the levels of lesser complexity. Students must deal with the new learnings thoroughly and successfully at lower levels before moving to upper levels. It is very difficult to create a product (synthesis) without a solid knowledge base and sufficient practice in applying the learnings.

- **Beware of Mimicry.** Sometimes students seem to be applying their learning to a new situation (application level) when they are just mimicking the teacher's behavior. Mimicry is knowledge level. For students to be really at the application level, they must understand why they are using a particular process to solve *new* problems.

- **Discuss Core Concepts at the Higher Levels.** Not all topics are suitable for processing at the upper levels. There are some areas in which creativity is not desired (e.g., basic arithmetic, spelling, the rules of grammar), but consider taking to the upper levels every concept that is identified as a core learning. This helps students to attach meaning and make connections to past learnings, thereby significantly increasing retention.

- **Choose Complexity Over Difficulty.** Give novel, multisensory tasks to move students progressively up the taxonomy. Limit the exposure to trivial information and discourage students from memorizing it, a process that many find monotonous and meaningless. Instead, give them divergent activities in analysis, synthesis, and evaluation that are more interesting and more likely to result in a deeper understanding of the learning objectives.

PRACTITIONER'S CORNER

Bloom's Taxonomy: Increasing Complexity

Examples become more complex from bottom to top, and more difficult from left to right.

BLOOM'S LEVEL		INCREASING LEVEL OF DIFFICULTY ⟶	
I N C R E A S I N G C O M P L E X I T Y	EVALUATION	Compare the *two* main characters in the story. Which would you rather have as a friend and why?	Compare the *four* main characters in the story. Which would you rather have as a friend and why?
	SYNTHESIS	Rewrite the story from the point of view of the dog.	Rewrite the story from the points of view of the dog *and of the cat.*
	ANALYSIS	What were the similarities and differences between this story and the one we read about the Civil War hero?	What were the similarities and differences between this story, the one we read about the Civil War hero, *and the one about the Great Depression*?
	APPLICATION	Think of another situation that could have caused the main character to behave that way.	Think of at least *three* other situations that could have caused the main character to behave that way.
	COMPREHENSION	Write a paragraph that describes the childhood of any one of the main characters.	Write a paragraph that describes the childhood of each of the *four* main characters.
	KNOWLEDGE	Name the major characters in this story.	Name the major characters and the *four locations* in this story.

PRACTITIONER'S CORNER

Understanding the Difference
Between Complexity and Difficulty

First, let's try a real-life application.

1. Select a partner and decide who is Partner A and who is Partner B.

2. Each partner performs, in turn, the activities for each situation in Table 7.2 below.

3. When both partners have completed the three situations, discuss whether complexity or difficulty was changed **in each situation** when moving from A's to B's activity.

Table 7.2 Deciding Whether Complexity or Difficulty Is Increased			
Situation	Partner A's Activity	Partner B's Activity	Complexity or Difficulty Changed? How?
1	Tell your partner the month of your birth and the city and state where you were born.	Tell your partner the make of your current automobile.	
2	Roll a piece of paper into a ball. Stand 10 feet from your partner. Ask your partner to stand and to form his/her arms into a ring in front (as though to hug someone). Now toss the ball five times and try to get all five tosses through the ring formed by your partner's arms.	Repeat what your partner just did, except stand facing away from your partner and toss the paper ball over your head five times, still aiming for your partner's ringed arms.	
3	Fanfold a piece of paper. Then explain to your partner three uses for the folded paper.	After listening to your partner's explanation of the uses, choose one you think is best and explain why.	

– Continued –

Understanding the Difference Between Complexity and Difficulty—Continued

Now, let's try a school situation.

Examine how each teacher in Table 7.3 below changes Activity A to Activity B. Then decide if the teacher has increased that activity's level of complexity or difficulty.

Table 7.3 Deciding Whether Complexity or Difficulty Is Increased			
Teacher	Activity A	Activity B	Increased Complexity or Difficulty?
1	Make an outline of the story you just read.	Make an outline of the last two stories you read.	
2	Compare and contrast the personalities of Julius Caesar and Macbeth.	After reading three acts of *Macbeth*, write a plausible ending.	
3	Choose one character in the story you would like to be and explain your choice.	Choose two characters in the story you would like to be and explain why.	
4	Name the three most common chemical elements on Earth.	Describe in your own words what is meant by a chemical element.	

Reflections:

Is complexity or difficulty more closely related to intelligence?

How will understanding that difference affect my teaching?

– Continued –

Understanding the Difference Between Complexity and Difficulty—Continued

Summary: Increasing the *difficulty* of a task adds to the students' efforts without increasing the level of their thinking processes. Think of it as moving *horizontally* within a level of Bloom's Taxonomy. Strategies such as repetition and drill tend to increase difficulty. Jot down below some other strategies that increase difficulty. For what types of learning would it be important to use strategies to increase difficulty?

_____

_____

_____

_____

_____

Increasing the *complexity* of a task causes the students to change the way they mentally process the task. Think of it as moving *vertically* up Bloom's Taxonomy from one level to a higher one. Strategies that cause students to compare and contrast, or to choose among options and defend their choice, are examples of increasing complexity. Jot down below some other strategies that increase complexity. For what types of learning would it be important to use strategies to increase complexity?

_____

_____

_____

_____

PRACTITIONER'S CORNER

Questions to Stimulate Higher-Order Thinking

Incorporate these questions into lesson plans to stimulate higher-order thinking. Be sure to read the guidelines for using Bloom's Taxonomy to ensure the maximum effectiveness of these questions. Remember to provide adequate wait time. Students should become accustomed to this type of questioning in every study assignment.

What would you have done? Why do think this is the best choice?

What are some of the things you wondered about while this was happening?

Could this ever really happen? What might happen next?

What do you think might happen if … ? What do you think caused this?

How is it different from …? Can you give an example?

Where do we go next? Where could we go for help on this?

Have we left out anything important?

Can we trust the source of this material?

In what other ways could this be done? How can you test this theory?

How many ways can you think of to use …?

Do you agree with this author/speaker? Why or why not?

Can you isolate the most important idea?

How could you modify this? How would changing the sequence affect the outcome?

How can you tell the difference between … and …?

Chapter 7—Thinking Skills and Learning

Key Points to Ponder

Jot down on this page key points, ideas, strategies, and resources you want to consider later. This sheet is your personal journal summary and will help to jog your memory.

CHAPTER 7 – NOTES

1. Jausovec and Jausovec (2000).

2. Restak (1988).

3. I realize that much of what I write here in the Second Edition is not very different from that in the first. Why no change, you ask? In the intervening years, I have seen the emergence of state-adopted curriculum standards, a greater emphasis on state and national testing, and an intense public insistence that school and teacher accountability be measured in test scores. Consequently, with little progress towards looking at other, more recent-vintage thinking skills programs, I am perfectly comfortable reiterating my plea to look again at the aging, yet timelessly effective taxonomy of Benjamin Bloom.

4. Bloom (1956).

5. The name of this level often creates confusion because one immediately thinks of testing. Bloom intended for *evaluation* to mean a judgement or assessment of different individual options within a group, and the selection of one option supported by a defensible rationale.

6. Bloom (1976).

CHAPTER 8

PUTTING IT ALL TOGETHER:
PLANNING FOR
TODAY AND TOMORROW

The human memory is different from that of a computer's in that it is selective. Items of interest—those that ultimately have some bearing on survival—are retained better than those that are not. So personal and meaningful memories can be held in their billions while dry facts learnt at school may soon fade away.

— Rita Carter,
Mapping the Mind

Chapter Highlights. This chapter focuses on how to use the research presented in this book to plan daily lessons. It suggests guidelines and a format for lesson design, and it mentions support systems to maintain expertise in the techniques and move toward continuous growth.

The preceding chapters discussed some of the major strides that research is making in exploring how the brain processes information and learns. There are suggestions on how to translate these new discoveries into practical classroom strategies that can improve the efficacy of teaching and learning. But this information is of value to students only if teachers can incorporate it into their classroom practice so that it becomes part of their daily instructional behavior. The question now is: How do we use this large amount of information when planning our daily lessons?

Considerations for Daily Planning

General Guidelines

Start by keeping the following general thoughts in mind while planning:

- Learning engages the entire person (cognitive, affective, and psychomotor domains).

- The human brain seeks patterns in its search for meaning.

- Emotions are an integral part of learning, retention, and recall.

- Past experience always affects new learning.

- The brain's working memory has a limited capacity.

- Lecture usually results in the lowest degree of retention.

- Rehearsal is essential for retention.

- The brain is a parallel processor performing many functions simultaneously.

- Practice does not make perfect.

- Each brain is unique.

Lesson Design

To use this research in daily planning, we need a lesson plan model as a framework. The model of lesson components that evolved from Madeline Hunter's (1982) work at UCLA since the 1970s continues to serve that purpose well. I have made minor modifications to Hunter's original model to include some of the more recent strategies.[1] The nine components of the design are:

1.   *Anticipatory Set*. This strategy captures the students' focus. Almost any technique to get their initial attention can be valuable. Vary the initial attention-getter to provide novelty, and remember the power of humor in getting attention and setting a positive emotional climate for the lesson to follow. Once you get their initial attention, the rest of the set is most effective when it

     (a)   allows students to remember an experience that will help them acquire the new learning (positive transfer)

     (b)   involves active student participation (while avoiding "guessing" games during prime-time-1),

     (c)   is relevant to the learning objective

2.   *Learning Objective*. This is a clear statement of what the students are expected to accomplish during the learning episode,[2] including the levels of difficulty and complexity, and should include

     (a)   a specific statement of the learning

     (b)   the overt behavior that demonstrates whether the learning has occurred and whether the appropriate level of complexity has been attained

3.   *Purpose*. This states *why* the students should accomplish the learning objective. Whenever possible, it should refer to how the new learning is related to the students' prior and future learnings to facilitate positive transfer and meaning.

4.   *Input*. This is the information and the procedures (skills) that students will need to acquire in order to achieve the learning objective. It can take many forms, including reading, lecture, cooperative learning groups, audiovisual presentations, the Internet, and so on.

5.   *Modeling*. Clear and correct models help students make sense of the new learning and establish meaning. Models must be given first by the teacher and be accurate, unambiguous, and noncontroversial. Nonexemplars might be included later to show contrast.

6.   *Check for Understanding*. This refers to the strategies the teacher will use during the learning episode to verify that the students are accomplishing the learning objective. The check could be in the form of oral discussion, written quiz, think-pair-share, or any other overt format that yields the necessary data. Depending on the results of these checks, the teacher may provide more opportunities for input, reteach, or move on.

7. *Guided Practice.* During this time, the student is applying the new learning in the presence of the teacher who provides immediate and specific feedback on the accuracy of the learner's practice.

8. *Closure.* This is the time when the mind of the learner can summarize for itself its perception of what has been learned. The teacher gives specific directions for what the learner should mentally process and provides adequate time to accomplish it. This is usually the last opportunity the learner has to attach sense and meaning to the new learning, both of which are critical requirements for retention. Daily closure activities can take many forms, such as using synergy strategies or journal writing. Closure activities for the end of a unit might include writing plays, singing songs, reciting poetry, playing quiz games, and so on.

> *Closure is usually the last opportunity the learner has to attach sense and meaning to new learning.*

9. *Independent Practice.* After the teacher believes that the learners have accomplished the objective at the correct level of difficulty and complexity, students try the new learning on their own to enhance retention and develop fluency.

Important Note. Not every lesson needs to include every component. However, the teacher should consider each component and choose those that are relevant to the learning objective. For example, when introducing a new major unit of study, the lesson may focus primarily on *objectives* (What do we hope to accomplish?) and *purpose* (Why are we studying this?). On the other hand, a review lesson before a major test might include more ways of *checking for understanding* and for *guided practice*.

> *Not every lesson needs every component. The teacher should consider each component and choose those that are relevant to the learning objective.*

Table 8.1 shows the lesson components, their purpose, their relationship to the research, and an example from a lesson on teaching the characteristics of suffixes.

Table 8.1 Components to Consider in Designing Lessons

LESSON COMPONENT	PURPOSE	RELATIONSHIP TO RESEARCH	EXAMPLE
Anticipatory Set	Focuses students on the learning objective.	Establishes relevance and fosters positive transfer during prime-time-1.	"Think of what we learned yesterday about prefixes and be prepared to discuss them."
Learning Objective	Identifies what is to be learned by the end of the lesson.	Students know what they should learn and how they will know they have learned it.	"Today we will learn about suffixes, and you will make up words with them."
Purpose	Explains why it is important to accomplish this objective.	Knowing the purpose for learning something builds interest and establishes meaning.	"Learning about suffixes will help us understand more vocabulary and give us greater creativity in our writing."
Input	Gives students the information, sources, and skills they will need to accomplish the objective.	Bloom's **knowledge** level. Helps identify critical attributes.	"Suffixes are letters placed after words to change their meanings."
Modeling	Shows the process or product of what students are learning.	Modeling enhances sense and meaning to help retention.	"Examples are: *-less*, as in helpless; *-able*, as in drinkable; and *-ful*, as in doubtful."
Check for Understanding	Allows instructor to verify if students understand what they are learning.	Bloom's **comprehension** level.	"I'll ask some of you to tell me what you learned so far about the meaning and use of suffixes."
Guided Practice	Allows the students to try the new learning under teacher guidance.	Bloom's **application** level. Practice provides for fast learning.	"Here are 10 words. Add an appropriate suffix to each and explain their new meanings."
Closure	Allows students time to mentally summarize and internalize the new learning.	Last chance to attach sense and meaning, thus improving retention.	"I'll be quiet now while you think about the attributes and uses of suffixes."
Independent Practice	Students try new learning on their own to develop fluency.	This practice helps make the new learning permanent.	"For homework, add suffixes to the words on page 121 to change their meanings."

Twenty-One Questions to Ask During Planning

Table 8.2 contains some important questions that teachers should ask while planning lessons. The questions relate, of course, to information and strategies included in previous chapters. Following each question is the rationale for considering it and the chapter number where its main reference can be found.

Table 8.2 Questions to Ask When Planning Lessons		
QUESTION	**RATIONALE**	**CHAPTER**
1. What tactics am I using to help students attach meaning to the learning?	Meaning helps retention.	2
2. How will I use humor in this lesson?	Humor is an excellent focus device and adds novelty.	2
3. Have I divided the learning episode into mini-lessons of about 20 minutes each?	Short lesson segments have proportionally less down-time than longer ones.	3
4. What motivation and novelty strategies am I using?	Motivation and novelty increase interest and accountability.	1 & 2
5. Which type of rehearsal should be used with this learning, and when?	Rote and elaborative rehearsal serve different purposes.	3
6. Am I using the prime-times to the best advantage?	Maximum retention occurs during the prime-times.	3
7. What will the students be doing during down-time?	Minimum retention occurs during down-time.	3
8. Does my plan allow for enough wait time when asking questions?	Wait time is critical to allow for student recall to occur.	3
9. What chunking strategies are appropriate for this objective?	Chunking increases the number of items working memory can handle at one time.	3
10. What related prior learning should be included for distributed practice?	Distributed practice increases long-term retention.	3
11. How will I maximize positive transfer and minimize negative transfer?	Positive transfer assists learning; negative transfer interferes.	4
12. Have I identified the critical attributes of this concept?	Critical attributes help distinguish one concept from all others.	4

Table 8.2 Questions to Ask When Planning Lessons		
13. Are the concepts or skills too similar to each other?	Concepts and skills that are too similar should not be taught together.	4
14. How will I show students how they can use (transfer) this learning in the future?	The prospect of future transfer increases motivation and meaning.	4
15. Is it appropriate to use a metaphor with this objective?	Metaphors enhance transfer, hemispheric integration, and retention.	4
16. Have I included activities that are multisensory?	Using many senses increases retention.	5
17. Would a concept map help here?	Concept maps help hemispheric integration and retention.	5
18. Am I using strategies that promote imaging and imagining?	Imaging and imagining help establish meaning, promote novelty, and increase retention.	6
19. Would some music be appropriate? If so, what kind and when?	Some music assists processing and cooperative learning activities.	6
20. How will I move this objective up Bloom's Taxonomy?	The taxonomy's upper levels involve higher-order thinking and are more interesting.	7
21. What emotions (affective domain) need to be considered or avoided in learning this objective?	Emotions play a key role in student acceptance and retention of learning.	7

Maintaining Skills for the Future

This book suggests many strategies that teachers can try to enhance the effectiveness of the teaching-learning process. The strategies have been derived from the current research on how we learn. Teachers who try these strategies for the first time may need support and feedback on the effectiveness of their implementation. The school-based support system is very important to maintaining teacher interest and commitment, especially if the new strategies don't produce the desired results in the classroom right away.

The Building Principal's Role

Building principals play a vital role in establishing a school climate and culture that are receptive to new instructional strategies and in maintaining the support systems necessary for continuing teacher development. Providing opportunities for teachers to master an expanded repertoire of research-based instructional techniques is an effective way for principals to foster collaboration, establish their role as an instructional leader, and enhance the teaching staff's pursuit of professional inquiry.

Types of Support Systems

Peer Coaching. This structure pairs two teachers who periodically observe each other in class. During the lesson, the observing teacher is looking for the use of a particular strategy or technique that was identified in a preobservation conference. After the lesson, the observing teacher provides feedback on the results of the implementation of the strategy. The non-threatening and supportive nature of this peer relationship encourages teachers to take risks and try new techniques that they might otherwise avoid for fear of failure or administrative

> **The quality of learning rarely exceeds the quality of teaching.**

scrutiny. Peer coaches undergo initial training in how to set the observation goal at the preconference and on different methods for collecting information during the observation.

Study Groups. Forming small groups of teachers and administrators to study a particular topic further is an effective means of expanding understanding and methods of applying new strategies. The group members seek out new research on the topic and exchange and discuss information, data, and experiences in the group setting. Each group focuses on one or two topics, such as wait time, transfer, and retention techniques. Groups within a school or district can use cooperative learning techniques as a means of sharing information across groups.

Action Research. Conducting small research studies in a class or school can provide teachers with the validation they may need to incorporate new strategies permanently into their repertoire. For example, deliberately changing the length of the wait time after posing questions yields data on how the amount and quality of student responses vary with the wait time. If several teachers carry out this research and exchange data, they will have the evidence to support the continued use of longer wait time as an effective strategy. Action research on the use of humor and music in the classroom can help teachers determine the value of these strategies on student performance. Teachers can then share their results with colleagues at faculty meetings or study group sessions. This format also advances the notion that teachers should be involved in research projects as part of their professional growth.

Workshops on New Research. Periodic workshops that focus on new research findings in the teaching and learning process are valuable for updating teachers' knowledge base. Areas such as the transfer and transformation of learnings, reflection, memory, and concept development are the targets of extensive research at this time and should be monitored to determine if new findings are appropriate for district and school workshops.

When educators encourage ongoing staff development activities, such as study groups and action research, they are recognizing that our understanding of the teaching-learning process is in continual change as the research yields more data on how the amazing brain learns. True professionals are committed to updating their knowledge base constantly, and they recognize individual professional development as a personal and lifelong responsibility that will enhance their effectiveness.

Conclusion

Although the "Decade of the Brain" has come and gone, the potential contributions of neuroscience to educational practice continue. The very fact that neuroscientists and educators are meeting and talking to each other is evidence that we have crossed a new frontier in our profession. There are, of course, no magic answers that make the complex processes of teaching and learning successful all the time. Educators recognize that numerous variables affect this dynamic interaction, many of which are beyond the teacher's influence or control. What teachers *can* control is their own behavior. My hope is that this book provides teachers with some new information, strategies, and insights that will increase their chances of success with more students.

PRACTITIONER'S CORNER

Reflections on Lesson Design

Here's a sample lesson design using the information processing model in Chapter 2.

Objective: The learner will be able to describe verbally the major parts of the brain processing model in the text *How the Brain Learns*.

Anticipatory Set: "Take a moment to think about whether it is important for teachers to know how we believe the brain selects and processes information. Then discuss your thoughts with your partner."

Purpose: "The purpose of this lesson is to give you some of the latest research we have on how we think the brain processes information so that you can be more successful in choosing those teacher actions that are more likely to result in learning."

Input: The teacher describes major steps in the process, including uptake by senses, interplay of the perceptual register and short-term memory, working memory, long-term storage, the cognitive belief system, and self-concept. Emphasizes the importance of sense and meaning, as well as of past experiences, throughout the entire process.

Modeling: Teacher explains the four metaphors (venetian blinds, clipboard, work table, and filing cabinets). Uses examples of working memory capacity, uses hands as model, and shows the model brain.

Check for Understanding: Teacher has students fill in the function sheet after several parts of the model are covered, and has them use the synergy strategy to discuss with their partners.

Guided Practice: Teacher gives examples of sense and meaning differences, and of positive and negative self-concept differences, to determine the extent of application of the model.

Closure: "Take a few minutes to quietly summarize in your mind the major parts of the brain processing model, and be prepared to explain them."

Independent Practice: Visit teachers' classrooms to determine the extent to which they use the model in presenting their lessons.

Chapter 8—Putting It All Together

Key Points to Ponder

Jot down on this page key points, ideas, strategies, and resources you want to consider later. This sheet is your personal journal summary and will help to jog your memory.

CHAPTER 8 – NOTES

1. Hunter's original design had seven components. I have taken the *purpose of the lesson* from the *lesson objective* where Hunter placed it and made it a separate component to emphasize its importance in establishing the lesson's relevance for students. I have also added *closure* as a separate component because of the high impact this strategy has on improving retention of learning.

2. When the teacher states the learning objective explicitly at the beginning of the lesson, we call that an *expository* lesson—that is, the objective is now "exposed." Sometimes, we prefer to have the students discover the lesson objective on their own. This is obviously called a *discovery* lesson. Discovery lessons require more careful planning and guidance to ensure that the students actually get to the intended objective. If the learner doesn't know where the lesson is supposed to be going, *any* place will do.

GLOSSARY

Action research. A systematic process for evaluating the effectiveness of classroom practices using the techniques of research.

Amygdala. The almond-shaped structure in the brain's limbic system that encodes emotional messages to long-term storage.

Angular gyrus. A brain structure that decodes visual information about words so they can be matched to their meanings.

Apoptosis. The genetically programmed process in which unneeded or unhealthy brain cells are destroyed.

Axon. The neuron's long and unbranched fiber that carries impulses away from the cell to the next neuron.

Bloom's Taxonomy of the Cognitive Domain. A model developed by Benjamin Bloom in the 1950s for classifying the complexity of human thought into six levels.

Brain stem. One of the major parts of the brain, it receives sensory input and monitors vital functions such as heartbeat, body temperature, and digestion.

Cerebellum. One of the major parts of the brain, it coordinates muscle movement.

Cerebrum. The largest of the major parts of the brain, it controls sensory interpretation, thinking, and memory.

Chunking. The ability of the brain to perceive a coherent group of items as a single item or chunk.

Circadian rhythm. The daily cycle of numerous body functions, such as breathing and body temperature.

Closure. The teaching strategy that allows learners quiet time in class to mentally reprocess what they have learned during a lesson.

Cognitive belief system. The unique construct one uses to interpret how the world works, on the basis of experience.

Computerized tomography (CT, formerly CAT) scanner. An instrument that uses X-rays and computer processing to produce a detailed cross-section of brain structure.

Confabulation. The brain's replacement of a gap in long-term memory by a falsification which the individual believes to be correct.

Constructivism. This theory of learning states that active learners use past experiences and chunking to construct sense and meaning from new learning, thereby building larger conceptual schemes.

Corpus callosum. The bridge of nerve fibers that connects the left and right cerebral hemispheres and allows communication between them.

Cortex. The thin but tough layer of cells covering the cerebrum that contains all the neurons used for cognitive and motor processing.

Critical attribute. A characteristic that makes one concept different from all others.

Delayed sleep phase disorder. A chronic condition caused mainly by a shift in an adolescent's sleep cycle that results in difficulty falling asleep at night and waking up in the morning.

Dendrite. The branched extension from the cell body of a neuron that receives impulses from nearby neurons through synaptic contacts.

Electroencephalograph (EEG). An instrument that charts fluctuations in the brain's electrical activity via electrodes attached to the scalp.

Endorphins. Opiate-like chemicals in the body that lessens pain and produces pleasant and euphoric feelings.

Engram. The permanent memory trace that results when brain tissue is anatomically altered by an experience.

Frontal lobe. The front part of the brain that monitors higher-order thinking, directs problem solving, and regulates the excesses of the emotional (limbic) system.

Functional magnetic resonance imaging (fMRI). An instrument that measures blood flow to the brain to record areas of high and low neuronal activity.

Glial cells. Special "glue" cells in the brain that surround each neuron providing support, protection, and nourishment.

Gray matter. The thin but tough covering of the brain's cerebrum also known as the cerebral cortex.

Hemisphericity. The notion that the two cerebral hemispheres are specialized and process information differently.

Hippocampus. A brain structure that compares new learning to past learning and encodes information from working memory to long-term storage.

Imagery. The mental visualization of objects, events, and arrays.

Immediate memory. A temporary memory where information is processed briefly (in seconds) and subconsciously, then either blocked or passed on to working memory.

Limbic system. The structures at the base of the cerebrum that control emotions.

Long-term potentiation. The increase in synaptic strength and sensitivity that endures as a result of repeated, frequent firings across a synapse between two associated neurons. As of now, it is the accepted mechanism for explaining long-term storage.

Long-term storage. The areas of the cerebrum where memories are stored permanently.

Magnetic resonance imaging (MRI). An instrument that uses radio waves to disturb the alignment of the body's atoms in a magnetic field to produce computer-processed, high-contrast images of internal structures.

Mnemonic. A word or phrase used as a device for remembering unrelated information, patterns, or rules.

Motor cortex. The narrow band across the top of the brain from ear to ear that controls movement.

Myelin. A fatty substance that surrounds and insulates a neuron's axon.

Neuron. The basic cell making up the brain and nervous system, consisting of a globular cell body, a long fiber called an axon which transmits impulses, and many shorter fibers called dendrites which receive them.

Neuroplasticity. The lifelong ability of the brain to reorganize neural networks based on new experiences.

Neurotransmitter. One of nearly 100 chemicals stored in axon sacs that transmit impulses from neuron to neuron across the synaptic gap.

Phonemes. The minimal units of sound in a language that combine to make syllables.

Positron emission tomography (PET) scanner. An instrument that traces the metabolism of radioactively tagged sugar in brain tissue producing a color image of cell activity.

Primacy-recency effect. The phenomenon whereby one tends to remember best that which comes first in a learning episode and second best that which comes last.

Prime-time. The time in a learning episode when information or a skill is more likely to be remembered.

Prosody. The rhythm, cadence, accent patterns, and pitch of a language.

Rehearsal. The reprocessing of information in working memory.

Retention. The preservation of a learning in long-term storage in such a way that it can be identified and recalled quickly and accurately.

Reticular activating system (RAS). The dense formation of neurons in the brain stem that controls major body functions and maintains the brain's alertness.

Self-concept. Our perception of who we are and how we fit into the world.

Synapse. The microscopic gap between the axon of one neuron and the dendrite of another.

Thalamus. A part of the limbic system that receives all incoming sensory information, except smell, and shunts it to other areas of the cortex for additional processing.

Transfer. The influence that past learning has on new learning, and the degree to which the new learning will be useful in the learner's future.

Wait time. The period of teacher silence that follows the posing of a question before the first student is called to respond.

White matter. The support tissue that lies beneath the cerebrum's gray matter (cortex).

Windows of opportunity. Important periods in which the young brain responds to certain types of input to create or consolidate neural networks.

Working memory. The temporary memory wherein information is processed consciously.

BIBLIOGRAPHY

Acebo, C., Wolfson, A., & Carskadon, M. (1997). Relations among self-reported sleep patterns, health, and injuries in adolescents. *Sleep Research*, *27*, 149.

American Association of School Administrators. (1998, January). *The School Administrator*.

Amunts, K., Schlaug, G., Jancke, L., Steinmetz, H., Schleicher, A., Dabringhaus, A., & Zilles, K. (1997). Motor cortex and hand motor skills: Structural compliance in the human brain. *Human Brain Mapping*, *5*, 206–215.

Association for Supervision and Curriculum Development. (1998, November). *Educational Leadership*.

Banich, M. (1997). *Neuropsychology: The neural bases of mental function*. New York: Houghton Mifflin.

Bates, E. (1999, July-August). Language and the infant brain. *Journal of Communication Disorders*, *32*, 195–205.

Begley, S. (2000, January 1). Rewiring your gray matter. *Newsweek,* 63-65.

Blood, A. J., Zatorre, R. J., Bermudez, P., & Evans, A. C. (1999, April). Emotional responses to pleasant and unpleasant music correlate with activity in paralimbic brain regions. *Nature Neuroscience*, *2*, 382–387.

Bloom, B. S. (1956). *Taxonomy of educational objectives (cognitive domain)*. New York: Longman.

Bloom, B. S. (1976). *Human characteristics and school learning*. New York: McGraw-Hill.

Bromley, K., Irwin-DeVitis, L., & Modlo, M. (1995). *Graphic organizers*. New York: Scholastic.

Brooks, J., & Brooks, M. (1993). *In search of understanding: The case for constructivist classrooms*. Alexandria, VA: Association for Supervision and Curriculum Development.

Buckner, R. L., Kelley, W. M., & Petersen, S. E. (1999, April). Frontal cortex contributions to human memory formation. *Nature Neuroscience, 2*, 311–314.

Butterworth, B. (1999). *What counts: How every brain is hardwired for math*. New York: Free Press.

Buzan, T. (1989). *Use both sides of your brain* (3rd ed.). New York: Penguin.

Buzzell, K. (1998). *The children of Cyclops: The influence of television viewing on the developing human brain*. San Francisco: Association of Waldorf Schools of North America.

Cahill, L., & McGaugh, J. (1998). Mechanisms of emotional arousal and lasting declarative memory. *Trends in Neuroscience, 21*, 294–299.

Caine, R., & Caine, G. (1991). *Making connections: Teaching and the human brain*. Alexandria, VA: Association for Supervision and Curriculum Development.

Calvin, W., & Ojemann, G. (1994). *Conversations with Neil's brain: The neural nature of thought and language*. Menlo Park, CA: Addison-Wesley.

Carskadon, M. A., Acebo, C., Wolfson, A. R., Tzischinsky, O., & Darley, C. (1997). REM sleep on MSLTS in high school students is related to circadian phase. *Sleep Research, 26*, 705.

Carter, R. (1998). *Mapping the mind*. Los Angeles: University of California Press.

Catterall, J., Chapleau, R., & Iwanga, J. (1999, Fall). Involvement in the arts and human development: Extending an analysis of general associations and introducing the special cases of intense involvement in music and in theater arts. *Monograph Series No. 11*. Washington, DC: Americans for the Arts.

Chapman, C. (1995). *If the shoe fits: Developing the multiple intelligences classroom*. Arlington Heights, IL: Skylight.

Chapman, C., & King, R. (2000). *Test success in the brain compatible classroom.* Tucson, AZ: Zephyr.

Cheour, M., Ceponiene, R., Lehtokoski, A., Luuk, A., Allik, J., Alho, K., & Näätänen, R. (1998, September). Development of language-specific phoneme representations in the infant brain. *Nature Neuroscience, 1*, 351–353.

Courchesne, E. (1999, March 23). An MRI study of autism: The cerebellum revisited. Letter in *Neurology, 52*, 1106–1107.

Croyle, L. (1998, September). Rate of reading, visual processing, colour and contrast. *Australian Journal of Learning Disabilities, 3*, 13–20.

Dale, P. S., Simonoff, E., Bishop, D.V.M., Eley, T. C., Oliver, B., Price, T. S., Purcell, S., Stevenson, J., & Plomin, R. (1998, August). Genetic influence on language delay in two-year-old children. *Nature Neuroscience, 1*, 324–328.

Damasio, A. (1999). *The feeling of what happens: Body and emotion in the making of consciousness.* New York: Harcourt Brace.

Danesi, M. (1990). The contribution of neurolinguistics to second and foreign language theory and practice. *System, 3*, 373–396.

Davis, J. (1997). *Mapping the mind: The secrets of the human brain and how it works.* Secaucus, NJ: Birch Lane Press.

Dehaene, S. (1997). *The number sense: How the mind creates mathematics.* New York: Oxford University Press.

Dehaene, S., Spelke, E., Pinel, P., Stanescu, R., & Tsivkin, S. (1999, May 7). Sources of mathematical thinking: Behavioral and brain-imaging evidence. *Science, 284*, 970-974.

Diamond, J. (1992). *The third chimpanzee: The evolution and future of the human animal.* New York: Harper Perennial.

Diamond, M., & Hopson, J. (1998). *Magic trees of the mind: How to nurture your child's intelligence, creativity, and healthy emotions from birth through adolescence.* New York: Dutton.

Droz, M., & Ellis, L. (1996). *Laughing while learning: Using humor in the classroom.* Longmont, CO: Sopris West.

Eisner, E. (1998, January). Does experience in the arts boost academic achievement? *Art Education*, 51.

Fagan, J., Prigot, J., Carroll, M., Pioli, L., Stein, A., & Franco, A. (1997, December). Auditory context and memory retrieval in young infants. *Child Development, 68,* 1057–1066.

Fiske, E. B. (Ed.). (1999). *Champions of change: The impact of the arts on learning.* Washington, DC: President's Committee on the Arts and the Humanities.

Gardner, H. (1983). *Frames of mind: The theory of multiple intelligences.* New York: Basic Books.

Gazzaniga, M. S. (1967, August). The split brain in man. *Scientific American,* 24–29.

Gazzaniga, M. S. (1989). Organization of the human brain. *Science, 245,* 947–952.

Gazzaniga, M. S. (1998a). *The mind's past.* Berkeley: University of California Press.

Gazzaniga, M. S. (1998b, July). The split brain revisited. *Scientific American,* 48–55.

Goleman, D. (1995). *Emotional intelligence: Why it can matter more than I.Q.* New York: Bantam.

Graziano, A. B., Peterson, M., & Shaw, G. L. (1999, March 15). Enhanced learning of proportional math through music training and spatial-temporal training. *Neurological Research, 21,* 139–152.

Gur, R. (1995). Sex differences in regional cerebral glucose metabolism during a resting state. *Science, 267,* 528–531.

Gur, R., Turetsky, B., Matsui, M., Yan, M., Bilker, W., Hughett, P., & Gur, R.E. (1999, May 15). Sex differences in brain gray and white matter in healthy young adults: Correlations with cognitive performance. *The Journal of Neuroscience, 19,* 4065–4072.

Hannaford, C. (1995). *Smart moves: Why learning is not all in your head.* Arlington, VA: Great Ocean.

Hart, L. (1983). *Human brain and human learning.* New York: Longman.

Hedges, L., & Nowell, A. (1995). Sex differences in mental test scores: Variability and numbers of high scoring individuals. *Science, 269,* 41–45.

Hunter, M. (1982). *Mastery teaching.* El Segundo, CA: T.I.P. Publications.

Hyerle, D. (1996). *Visual tools for constructing knowledge.* Alexandria, VA: Association for Supervision and Curriculum Development.

Irlen, H., & Robinson, G. L. (1996, December). The effect of Irlen coloured filters on adult perception of workplace performance. *Australian Journal of Learning Disabilities, 1,* 7–15.

Jausovec, N., & Jausovec, K. (2000, April 3). EEG activity during the performance of complex mental problems. *International Journal of Psychophysiology, 36,* 73–88.

Johnson, J., & Newport, E. (1991). Critical period effects on universal properties of language: The status of subjacency in the acquisition of a second language. *Cognition, 39,* 215–258.

Johnson, S. (1999, May). *Strangers in our homes: TV and our children's minds.* Paper presented at the Waldorf School, San Francisco.

Kagan, S., & Kagan, M. (1998). *Multiple intelligences: The complete MI book.* San Clemente, CA: Kagan Cooperative Learning.

Kempermann, G., & Gage, F. (1999, May). New nerve cells for the adult brain. *Scientific American,* 48–53.

Key, N. (1991). *Research methodologies for whole-brained integration at the secondary level.* Report No. SP 037894. Pueblo, CO: U.S. Government Document Service.

Kim, K., Relkin, N., Lee, K., & Hirsch, J. (1997). Distinct cortical areas associated with native and second languages. Letter to *Nature, 388*, 171–174.

Kimura, D. (1992, September). Sex differences in the brain. *Scientific American*, 119–124.

Knecht, S., Deppe, M., Drager, B., Bobe, L., Lohmann, H., Ringelstein, E., & Henningsen, H. (2000, January). Language lateralization in healthy right-handers. *Brain, 123*, 74–81.

Korol, D. L., & Gold, P. E. (1998). Glucose, memory, and aging. *American Journal of Clinical Nutrition, 67*, 764S–771S.

Kosslyn, S. M., Pascual-Leone, A., Felician, O., Camposano, S., Keenan, J. P., Thompson, W. L., Ganis, G., Sukel, K. E., & Alpert, N. M. (1999, April 2). The role of Area 17 in visual imagery: Convergent evidence from PET and rTMS. *Science, 284*, 167–170.

Kotulak, R. (1996). *Inside the brain: Revolutionary discoveries of how the mind works.* Kansas City, MO: Andrews McMeel.

Krathwohl, D. R., Bloom, B. S., & Masia, B. B. (1964). *Taxonomy of educational objectives—The classification of educational goals: Handbook II: Affective domain.* New York: McKay.

Kripke, D. F., Youngstedt, S. D., & Elliot, J. A. (1997). Light brightness effects on melatonin duration. *Sleep Research, 26*, 726.

Laviola, G., Adriani, W., Terranova, M. L., & Gerra, G. (1999). Psychobiological risk factors for vulnerability to psychostimulants in human adolescents and animal models. *Neuroscience Biobehavior Review, 23*(7), 993–1010.

Leonard, J. (1999, May-June). The sorcerer's apprentice: Unlocking the secrets of the brain's basement. *Harvard Magazine*, 56–62.

Levy, J. (1985, May). Right brain, left brain: Fact and fiction. *Psychology Today*.

Loftus, E. (1997, September). Creating false memories. *Scientific American*, 51–55.

Loomans, D., & Kolberg, K. (1993). *The laughing classroom: Everyone's guide to teaching with humor and play*. New York: H. J. Kramer.

Maquire, E. A., Frith, C. D., & Morris, R.G.M. (1999, October). The functional neuroanatomy of comprehension and memory: The importance of prior knowledge. *Brain, 122*, 1839–1850.

Merzenich, M. M., Jenkins, W. M., Johnston, P., Schreiner, C., Miller, S. L., & Tallal, P. (1996, January 5). Temporal processing deficits of language-learning impaired children ameliorated by training. *Science*, 271.

Middleton, F. A., & Strick, P. L. (1998, September). Cerebellar output: Motor and cognitive channels. *Trends in Cognitive Sciences, 2*, 348–354.

Miller, G. A. (1956). The magical number seven, plus or minus two: Some limits in our capacity for processing information. *Psychological Review, 63*, 81–97.

Muftuler, L. T., Bodner, M., Shaw, G. L., & Nalcioglu, O. (1999). *fMRI of Mozart effect using auditory stimuli*. Abstract presented at the 7th meeting of the International Society for Magnetic Resonance in Medicine, Philadelphia.

Nakamura, S., Sadato, N., Oohashi, T., Nishina, E., Fuwamoto, Y., & Yonekura, Y. (1999, November 19). Analysis of music-brain interaction with simultaneous measurement of regional cerebral blood flow and electroencephalogram beta rhythm in human subjects. *Neuroscience Letters, 275*, 222–226.

National Association of Secondary School Principals. (1998, May). *NASSP Bulletin*.

National Center for Education Statistics. (1999). *Condition of Education, 1998*. Washington, DC: Author.

National Center for Education Statistics. (1999). *Digest of Education, 1997, 1998*. Washington, DC: Author.

Ornstein, R., & Thompson, R. (1984). *The amazing brain.* Boston: Houghton Mifflin.

Parrott, C. A. (1986). Visual imagery training: Stimulating utilization of imaginal processes. *Journal of Mental Imagery, 10,* 47–64.

Patterson, M. N. (1997). *Every body can learn.* Tucson, AZ: Zephyr.

Perkins, D., & Salomon, G. (1988, September). Teaching for transfer. *Educational Leadership, 46,* 22–32.

Pinker, S. (1994). *The language instinct: How the mind creates language.* New York: Harper Perennial.

Rabinowicz, T., Dean, D., Petetot, J., & de Courten-Myers, G. (1999, February). Gender differences in the human cerebral cortex: More neurons in males; more processes in females. *Journal of Child Neurology, 14,* 98–107.

Rauscher, F. H., Shaw, G. L., & Ky, K. N. (1993). Music and spatial task performance. *Nature, 365,* 611.

Rauscher, F. H., Shaw, G. L., Levine, L. J., Wright, E. L., Dennis, W. R., & Newcomb, R. L. (1997). Music training causes long-term enhancement of preschool children's spatial-temporal reasoning. *Neurological Research, 19,* 2–8.

Reiss, D., Neiderheiser, J., Hetherington, E. M., & Plomin, R. (2000). *The relationship code: Deciphering genetic and social influences on adolescent development.* Cambridge, MA: Harvard University Press.

Restak, R. M. (1988). *The mind.* New York: Bantam.

Robinson, G. L., Foreman, P. J., & Dear, K.B.G. (1996). The familial incidence of symptoms of scotopic sensitivity/Irlen syndrome. *Perceptual and Motor Skills, 83,* 1043–1055.

Rodier, P. (2000, February). The early origins of autism. *Scientific American, 282,* 56–63.

Roediger, H. L., III, & McDermott, K. B. (1995). Creating false memories: Remembering words not presented in lists. *Journal of Experimental Psychology: Learning, Memory, and Cognition, 21*, 803–814.

Root-Bernstein, R. S. (1997, July 11). Art for science's sake. *Chronicle of Higher Education*, B6.

Rose, S. (1992). *The making of memory*. New York: Doubleday.

Rowe, M. B. (1974). Wait-time and rewards as instructional variables: Their influence on language, logic, and fate control. *Journal of Research on Science Teaching, 2*, 81–94.

Russell, P. (1979). *The brain book*. New York: E. P. Dutton.

Schacter, D. (1996). *Searching for memory: The brain, mind, and the past*. New York: Basic Books.

Schlaug, G., Jancke, L., Huang, Y. X., & Steinmetz, H. (1995). In-vivo evidence of structural brain asymmetry in musicians. *Science, 267*, 699–701.

Scholey, A. B., Moss, M. C., Neave, N., & Wesnes, K. (1999, November). Cognitive performance, hyperoxia, and heart rate following oxygen administration in healthy young adults. *Physiological Behavior, 67*, 783–789.

Shadmehr, R., & Holcomb, H. H. (1997, August 8). Neural correlates of motor memory consolidation. *Science, 277*, 821–825.

Shallice, T. (1999, July). The origin of confabulations. *Nature Neuroscience, 2*, 588–590.

Shaywitz, S. E. (1996, November). Dyslexia. *Scientific American*, 98–104.

Shaywitz, B. A., Shaywitz, S. E., & Gore, J. (1995). Sex differences in the functional organization of the brain for language. *Nature, 373*, 607–609.

Shaywitz, S. E., Shaywitz, B. A., Pugh, K. R., Fulbright, R. K., Constable, R. T., Mencl, W. E., Shankweiler, D. P., Liberman, A. M., Skudlarski, P., Fletcher, J. M., Katz, L., Marchione, K. E., Lacadie, C., Gatenby, C., & Gore, J. C. (1998,

March 3). Functional disruption in the organization of the brain for reading in dyslexia. *Neurobiology, 5*, 2636–2641.

Smith, E. E., & Jonides, J. (1999, March 12). Storage and executive processes in the frontal lobes. *Science, 283*, 1657–1661.

Sousa, D. A. (1998, May). Brain research can help principals reform secondary schools. *NASSP Bulletin, 82*, 21–28.

Sousa, D. A. (1998, December 16). Is the fuss about brain research justified? *Education Week*, p. 52.

Sowell, E. R., Thompson, P. M., Holmes, C. J., Jernigan, T. L., & Toga, A. W. (1999). In-vivo evidence for post-adolescent brain maturation in frontal and striatal regions. *Nature: Neuroscience, 2*, 859–861.

Spencer, S. J., Steele, C. M., & Quinn, D. M. (1999, January). Stereotype threat and women's math performance. *Journal of Experimental Social Psychology, 35*, 4-28.

Sperry, R. (1966). Brain bisection and consciousness. In Eccles, J. (Ed.), *How the self controls its brain*. New York: Springer-Verlag.

Springer, S., & Deutsch, G. (Eds.). (1993). *Left brain/right brain* (4th ed.). New York: W. H. Freeman.

Squire, L. R., & Kandel, E. R. (1999). *Memory: From mind to molecules*. New York: W. H. Freeman.

Stahl, R. J. (1985). *Cognitive information processes and processing within a uniprocess superstructure/microstructure framework: A practical information-based model.* Unpublished manuscript, University of Arizona, Tucson.

Stein, H. (1987, July-August). Visualized notetaking: Left-right brain theory applied in the classroom. *The Social Studies*.

Tallal, P., Miller, S. L., Bedi, G., Byma, G., Wang, X., Nagarajan, S., Schreiner, C., Jenkins, W. M., & Merzenich, M. M. (1996, January 5). Fast-element enhanced speech improves language comprehension in language-learning impaired children. *Science, 271*, 81–84.

Thomas, E. (1972, April). The variation of memory with time for information appearing during a lecture. *Studies in Adult Education*, 57–62.

Thomas, L. (1979). *The Medusa and the snail*. New York: Viking Press.

Van Petten, C., & Bloom, P. (1999, February). Speech boundaries, syntax, and the brain. *Nature Neuroscience, 2*, 103–104.

Wagner, A. D., Schacter, D. L., Rotte, M., Koutstaal, W., Maril, A., Dale, A. M., Rosen, B. R., & Buckner, R. L. (1998, August 21). Building memories: Remembering and forgetting of verbal experiences as predicted by brain activity. *Science, 281*, 1188–1191.

Weisman, D. H., & Banich, M. T. (2000). The cerebral hemispheres cooperate to perform complex but not simple tasks. *Neuropsychology, 14*, 41–59.

West, C. K., Farmer, J. A., & Wolff, P. M. (1991). *Instructional design: Implications from cognitive science*. Englewood, Cliffs, NJ: Prentice-Hall.

Wlodkowski, R., & Jaynes, J. (1990). *Eager to learn*. San Francisco: Jossey-Bass.

Wolfson, A., & Carskadon, M. (1998). Sleep schedules and daytime functioning in adolescents. *Child Development, 69*, 875–887.

Wynn, K. (1995). Origins of numerical knowledge. *Mathematical Cognition, 1*, 54–63.

Internet Sites

Dana Alliance for Brain Initiatives: www.dana.org
Information on the Child's Brain: www.iamyourchild.org
National Institutes of Health: www.nih.gov
Neuroscience for Kids: www.weber.u.washington.edu/~chudler/neurok.html
U.S. Department of Education: www.ed.gov

INDEX

Page numbers in **boldface** are **Practitioner's Corners**.

Action research, 6–7, **10–12**, 282
Affective domain:
    taxonomy of, 257–258
Amygdala, 17, 18–19
Angular gyrus, 183
Apoptosis, 23
Astrocytes, 20
Arts:
    gifted students and, 221
    human development and, 214
    including in all lessons, **233**
    sciences and, 216
    student learning and, 219–221
    young brain and, 215
Attention deficit hyperactivity disorder (ADHD), 230
Autism, 230

Bloom, B., 250, 251
Bloom's Taxonomy of the Cognitive Domain, 251–263, **264–271**
    See also Complexity; Difficulty
Bogen, J., 167
Boyer, E., 214
Brain fuel, 22–23
Brain scans, types of, 2
Brain specialization:
    hemisphere, 167–177
    spoken language, 177–186
    See also Gender differences; Hemisphericity;
    Language acquisition; Reading
Brain stem, 17–18
Bridging, 147, **157–158**
Broca's area, 177–178, 182
Buzan, T., 93, 229

Caine, G., 245
Caine, R., 245
Carter, R., 275
Cerebellum, 16, 17, 20, 230, 231
Cerebrum, 17, 19–20

Chomsky, N., 178, 180
Chugani, H., 4
Chunking, 109–110, **129–130**
Circadian rhythms, 101–104, **126–127**
Climate, classroom, **61–62**, 220
Closure, **70**
Cochlea, 222
Cognitive belief system, 51
Complexity, 258–260
Concept mapping, **196–200**
Confabulation, 114–115
Constructivism:
    Bloom's taxonomy and, 261
    information processing model and, 40
    transfer and, 149
Corpus callosum, 17, 19, 167
Cramming, 112
Critical attributes, 144, **153-156**

Declarative memory, 83
Degree of original learning, 145
Delayed sleep phase disorder, 103
Dendrites, 20–21
Difficulty, 258–260
Down-time. *See* Primacy-recency effect
Dyslexia, 185
Dysphonia, 185

Eisner, E., 217
Emotional control, 25
Emotional memory, 83
Engram, 80

Flashbulb memory, 83
Forgetting, 113
Frontal lobe, 16, 17, 19–20
Fuller, B., 216

Gardner, H., 105, 106
Gazzaniga, M., 166, 168
Gender differences, 173–177

Glial cells, 20
Glucose, 22–23
Goleman, D., 43

Hart, L., 15
Hemisphericity, 168–177, **187–189**
Hippocampus, 17, 18
Humor, **63–65**
Hugging, 147, **159–160**
Hunter, M., 4, 100, 136, 142, 146, **153**, 276
Hyerle, D., 229

Imagery, 228–229, **237**
Immediate memory, 41–42
Information Processing Model, 37–54, **55, 56**
    cognitive belief system, 51
    computers and, 39
    convergence zones, 50
    senses, 40
    sensory register, 40–41
    short-term memory, 41–49
Intelligence, 104–106
Irlen syndrome, 185

Johnson, J., 182
Johnson, S., 180
Journal writing, 149, **163**

Kandel, E., 78

Language acquisition, 26, 178–182. *See also* Second
    language acquisition
Learning pyramid, 95–96
Learning style, **57**, 170
Lesson design, 276–281, **284**
Limbic system, 18–19
Logic, 26
Lombardi, V., 99
Long-term potentiation, 80
Long-term storage, 49–50, **71–72**

Mathematics, 26, 225–227
Meaning, 46–49, **69**
Memory:
    drugs to enhance, 80
    stages of, 81–84

threats and emotions affecting, 42–44
    See also Declarative memory; Emotional
    memory; Flashbulb memory; Immediate memory;
    Motor skill memory; Nondeclarative memory;
    Procedural memory; Short-term memory;
    Working memory
Merzenich, M., 4
Metaphors, 148, **161–162**
Mind, 29
Mnemonics, **131–132**
Motivation, **66–68**
Motor cortex, 16, 17
Motor development, 25
Motor skill memory, 83
Motor skills:
    learning, 96–97, **116**
Movement, 229–232, **240–241**
Mozart effect, 221, 224
Music:
    benefits of creating, 224–228
    benefits of listening to, 223–224, **234–236**
    effects of listening versus creating, 221
    how the brain listens to, 222
    instrumental, 26
    mathematics learning and, 225–227
    See also Mozart effect
Myelin sheath, 21

Neurons, 16, 20–23
Neuroplasticity, 3
Neurotransmitters, 21, 22
Newport, E., 182
Nondeclarative memory, 82
Novelty, 27–29, **32**

Occipital lobe, 16, 17

Parietal lobe, 16, 17
Past experiences, 49
    effect on chunking, 110
    self-concept and, 52
Peer coaching, 282
Perkins, D., 146, **157, 159**
Practice, 97–101, **124**
Primacy-recency effect, 88–94, **120–121**
    impact on block scheduling, 92, **122–123**

on-task or off-task activities and, 93–94
Prime-time. *See* Primacy-recency effect
Procedural memory, 82

Rauscher, F., 26, 224
Reading, learning to, 182–186, **205–209**. *See also*
    Dyslexia; Dysphonia; Irlen syndrome
Recall, **125**. *See also* Retrieval
Rehearsal, 85–86, **117–119**
Retention:
    practice and, 101
    varies with teaching method, 95
Retrieval:
    intelligence and, 104–109
Rose, S., 50
Russell, P., 45

Salomon, G., 146, **157**, **159**
Second language acquisition, 181–182, **201–204**
Scotopic sensitivity syndrome, 185. *See also* Irlen
    syndrome
Self-concept, 51–54, 220
Sense, 46–49. *See also* Meaning
Sensory preferences, **57**, **58–60**
Shaw, G., 26, 224
Short-term memory, 41
Sleep cycles, 104. *See also* Delayed sleep phase
    disorder
Specialization, *See* Brain specialization
Sperry, R., 167–168, 170, 171
Spines, 21
Squire, L., 78
Stahl, R., 37
Study groups, 282
Synapse, 21

Synaptic vesicles, 21
Synergy, **73–74**

Temporal lobe, 16, 17
Thalamus, 17, 18
Thinking:
    dimensions of, 249–250
    emotion and, 247
    types of, 246–247
    See also Bloom's Taxonomy of the Cognitive
    Domain
Thomas, L., 1
Transfer:
    association and, 144–145
    defined, 136
    factors affecting, 141–146
    meaning and, 138–139
    similarity and, 142, **151–152**
    teaching for, 146–149
    types, 138
    See also Bridging; Critical attributes; Degree of
    original learning; Hugging; Journal writing;
    Metaphors

Visual arts, 228–229. *See also* Imagery
Visual cortex, 177, 183
Visualized notetaking, **238–239**
Vocabulary development, 25–26
Vogel, P.,167

Wait time, **128**
Water, 23
Wernicke's area, 177, 178
Windows of opportunity, 24–27
Working memory, 44–46

Brain-Compatible Learning from David A. Sousa

How the Brain Learns, Second Edition

David Sousa's practical and powerful best seller enters the 21st century with a valuable new edition, incorporating the previously published main text, the companion learning manual, and the latest discoveries in neuroscience and learning. All the newest information and insights are here, including an updated Information Processing Model, a whole new chapter on the implications of arts in learning, and an expanded list of primary sources.

Brain-Based Learning

The Video Program for *How the Brain Learns*

Join David Sousa for a dynamic 40-minute presentation in which he brings the concept of *How the Brains Learns* to life and gives specific examples of how brain-based learning can be put to use in your classroom. Charts, diagrams, and David Sousa's own clear and engaging style make this unique video a valuable tool for self-learning and an essential part of a larger professional development program for teachers and administrators alike.

Order Form

Corwin Press, Inc.
A Sage Publications Co.
2455 Teller Road
Thousand Oaks, CA 91320-2218

Federal ID Number 77-0260369
(Professional books may be tax-deductible.)

4 Easy Ways to Order

- Call: 805-499-9774
- Toll-Free Fax: 800-4-1-SCHOOL
- E-mail: order@corwinpress.com
- Mail your completed request form

*Note: Domestic shipping and handling charges are $3.50 for the first book and $1.00 for each additional book. All orders are shipped Ground Parcel unless otherwise requested. In Canada, please add 7% GST (12978 6448 RT) and remit in U.S. dollars. Canadian shipping and handling charges are $10.00 for the first book and $2.00 for each additional book. Discounts are available for quantity orders—call Customer Service. Prices are subject to change without notice.

Ship to

Name _____ Title _____
Institution _____
Address _____ No. _____
City _____ State _____ Zip + 4 _____
Country _____ Telephone _____
(Required for credit card and institutional purchases)

Fax: _____ E-mail: _____
(Actual Purchase Order must accompany order)

Bill to (if different) _____ P.O. # _____
Name _____
Institution _____
Address _____ No. _____
City _____ State _____ Zip + 4 _____
Country _____ Telephone _____

Method of Payment

☐ VISA   ☐ MasterCard   ☐ DISCOVER

Check # _____
Account # _____ Exp. Date _____
Signature _____

Qty.	Book #	Title	Price
	0-7619-7765-1	**How The Brain Learns, Second Edition**	**$39.95**
	0-7619-7522-5	**Brain-Based Learning Video**	**$99.95**

(Attach a sheet of paper for ordering any other Corwin books.)

In CA and NY, add appl. Sales Tax	
In IL, add 6¼% Sales Tax	
In MA, add 5% Sales Tax	
In Canada, add 7% GST*	
Subtotal	
Shipping and Handling*	
Amount Due	